COLLECTOR'S GUIDE TO

TV TOYS
and
Memorabilia SECOND EDITION
1960s & 1970s

Greg Davis and Bill Morgan

COLLECTOR BOOKS
A Division of Schroeder Publishing Co., Inc.

The current values in this book should be used only as a guide. They are not intended to set prices, which vary from one section of the country to another. Auction prices as well as dealer prices vary greatly and are affected by condition as well as demand. Neither the authors nor the publisher assumes responsibility for any losses that might be incurred as a result of consulting this guide.

Searching For A Publisher?

We are always looking for knowledgeable people considered to be experts within their fields. If you feel that there is a real need for a book on your collectible subject and have a large comprehensive collection, contact Collector Books.

On the Cover

Clockwise: H.R. Pufnstuf lunch box, $150.00 – 175.00; Charlie's Angels pocketbook radio, $175.00 – 200.00; The Six Million Dollar Man shoes, $100.00 – 125.00; Bewitched comic book #1, $75.00 – 100.00; Welcome Back, Kotter cartoon set, $40.00 – 50.00; Starsky and Hutch Corgi Gran Torino, $200.00 – 250.00; The Flying Nun 11½" doll, $300.00 – 400.00; The Partridge Family David Cassidy 31" guitar, $250.00 – 300.00; That Girl board game, $200.00 – 250.00.

Cover design: Beth Summers
Book design: Karen Geary

COLLECTOR BOOKS
P.O. Box 3009
Paducah, KY 42002-3009

Copyright 1999 by Greg Davis and Bill Morgan

CONTENTS

FOREWORD

In the 1960s and 1970s, I wasn't just a child on television, I was also a child watching television. From 1966 to 1972, I played Tabitha on the classic TV series *Bewitched*. At the same time, in my imagination, I was singing "It's A Sunshine Day" with the Brady Bunch, driving Mr. French crazy along with Buffy and Jody, and saying goodnight to John-Boy, Mary Ellen, and the rest of the Waltons.

Television was such an important part of my childhood that I was delighted when I found the first edition of this book. It was like a trip into my past! There were photos of toys that I had, including Tabitha paper dolls and even *Bewitched* comic books, of course! There were also many toys that I wanted, like Mrs. Beasley, and toys that I never knew existed, like the *Love Boat* playset. I surely would have traded my Easy Bake Oven for a *Partridge Family* bus, and I never would have carried a Barbie doll lunch box if I'd known they made a *Brady Bunch* one.

A while back, I was able to stop by for a look at Bill and Greg's amazing collection. I felt like a kid in the best toy store in the world. Classic *TV Guides* bordered the ceiling and one wall was

ERIN MURPHY

covered with character costumes — "Look, Samantha! …Is that Farrah?" There were entire rooms devoted to shows like *Charlie's Angels* and *Beverly Hills, 90210*. Other rooms contained dolls and toys from every program I grew up watching. While admiring all the memorabilia, we reminisced about our favorite shows and exchanged trivia. I can't believe I remembered the theme song to *The New Zoo Review*. Four hours and a pizza later, I left with two new friends and a big smile on my face!

I keep their book in my living room, and as a novice collector I refer to it weekly. It has helped me to pass up overpriced, common items and helped me find some real bargains on extremely rare items. But mainly, I enjoy seeing the way my friends react to this book. Most of them shout out, "I had that," "I wanted that," "Wow! I didn't even know they made that!" And when they finally put the book down, they're always smiling!

I recently visited with Bill and Greg and was able to get a glimpse of all the terrific new photos they had taken for this revised edition. I'm sure you'll find this book not only valuable for collecting, but will also enjoy the trip back into the past just as much as I did.

Erin Murphy

PREFACE

Almost from the moment we completed the first edition of this book, we began gathering information for the second. Unlike other books that gloss over a wide range of television shows, leaving you wanting more, we've committed ourselves to developing the most comprehensive TV collectible guide available for the over 50 shows included inside. It can be very frustrating to blindly scour antique malls and flea markets, looking for something that may or may not have been made. As collectors, we know how much time and energy it takes to research the types of memorabilia related to our favorite shows. This book was designed to take the work out of your collecting excursions, leaving you with the fun part — searching for the items you know exist and must have!

We received hundreds of letters and e-mails from collectors all over the world after the first edition was released. It has been an incredible experience to correspond with and meet so many devoted collectors just like us. Several of the friends we've met have helped us track down and document the incredible pieces of memorabilia pictured in this new edition.

Some collectors have contacted us asking about memorabilia from other terrific shows, like *The Man from U.N.C.L.E.*, *The Munsters*, and *Sonny and Cher*. We'd love to include all shows from the '60s and '70s in this guide, but it's impossible. Not only are we limited in the amount of space in this book, we're limited on the size of our wallets as well. We own most of the memorabilia contained within these pages and have devoted our time and energy into making this guide as comprehensive as possible. We feel it's a more valuable resource to collectors this way. Who knows, maybe we'll strike it rich in the future and can afford to buy it all!

Not only have we received letters from collectors and met many new friends, we've been asked to contribute monthly columns to several collecting publications. Because of the additional research involved when writing about classic television memorabilia on a regular basis, we've kept our fingers on the pulse of collecting.

Since 1995, when we prepared our first guide, the field has been undergoing a major transformation. Memorabilia from the 1960s and 1970s is increasing in popularity as new collectors enter the market in search of their childhoods. Vintage artifacts are becoming increasingly scarce, pushing the value of television memorabilia higher and higher. We've taken this into consideration when estimating the worth of the items contained in this book. We also know that true monetary worth is subjective. It is based on the buyer's level of desire for an item. For instance, the price realized in an auction does not necessarily reflect the item's actual value. What a handful of collectors are willing to spend doesn't represent the majority. We've tried to create a guide that is based on the approximate value most collectors in the field would consider fair.

Although most of the new material covered in this book is from our own experience and research, there are still many people that have contributed to the revision. A very special thanks goes out to our friends and fellow collectors who have graciously shared their knowledge and collections with us. Those special people include: Ken Stovich, the "Charlie's Angels Super-Collector," who allowed us to photograph many items from his collection; Carl Kurtz, "Starsky & Hutch Guru," for helping us make this book an incredible Starsky and Hutch resource; Jeff Michael, "Flying Nun Archivist" and fan club president, whose devotion to his hobby has

been an inspiration to continue ours; Daniel Selby, "Osmond Aficionado," for helping us document items from his amazing Osmond collection; Nicolas Wall, "King of Bionics," and his friend Jane Paris, "Queen of Partridge Family," for being extremely helpful in researching items from the United Kingdom and photographing some rare pieces; Jim Sherrard, who was one of the first collectors to contact us and share his Bionic knowledge and photographs; Dave Kelleher for spending many hours on the phone sharing his Krofft knowledge and helping us uncover some "unknowns" and lay to rest a few rumors; Steven Van Antwerp, "A Very Special Brady Fan," whose vivid memory helped bring many of these shows back to life and inspired us to find the collectibles made for each one of them; and Nancy Stursa for giving Greg his first TV collectible that started it all, a *Three's Company* trading card pack.

There are also several others we'd like to thank who have contributed to making this book possible, including Casey Chamberlain, Daniel Morgan, and Kelsey Morgan for modeling the costumes; Bill Schroeder, Lisa Stroup, and the Collector Books' staff for believing in a revised edition; Leslie Sena, Steve Gidlow, Kevin Dickson, John Olvey, Jack Condon, Ron Lopez, Selina Zinn, and our good friend, who is as warm and endearing as we've known her to be on television, Erin Murphy.

PHOTO CREDITS

Most of the items in this guide are from our private collections and were photographed by us. The following pieces are the exception and we thank these collectors for use of the following photographs:

Susan Backer — *Little House on the Prairie* Tea Set.

Jeff and Kym Baker — *Beverly Hillbillies* Truck.

Thomas LaPan — *Wonder Woman* iron-on.

Dave McCullough — *Josie and the Pussycats* Give-a-Show Projector.

Jeff Michael — *Flying Nun* items including brunch bag with thermos, Bagatelle Game, fan club kit, Marble Maze Game, Numbered Pencil Coloring Set, and Weaving Loom Set.

Steven Miller — *Brady Bunch* trading card box.

Jim Sherrard — *Bionic Woman* small jigsaw puzzle, Sports Car, Lindsay Wagner Japanese book and fan club kit; *Six Million Dollar Man* movie cassette, Big Foot doll, Bionic stickers, Critical Assignment Legs, Maskatron doll, Mission Control Center, See-a-Show, T-shirt, and Video Center.

Nicolas Wall and Jane Paris — *Bionic Woman* bubble bath, Berwick costume, Super-size Jaime, slide projector set; *Bionic Woman* and *Charlie's Angels* Monty Gum card boxes; *Six Million Dollar Man* laser discs, playsuit by Dekker, Berwick costume, slippers, Turbo Moto, and 3-D viewer.

Scott Walker — *Pufnstuf* doll.

INTRODUCTION

Who would have ever thought that a single pack of *Three's Company* gum cards would have escalated into a collection of TV memorabilia consisting of over 8,000 items? Not us. But that is exactly what happened, and it seemed like it happened overnight.

Originally given to Greg as a funny addition to a birthday present from his mother, this single pack of stickers began what has become the most enjoyable hobby either one of us has ever had. We both grew up watching Jack, Chrissy, and Janet find their way in and out of weekly misunderstandings, but never knew we could buy trading stickers with color photos of the hilarious trio. Thumbing through the pack of stickers brought back fond memories of watching the show. It was such a thrill, we became anxious to see what the remaining set of stickers looked like.

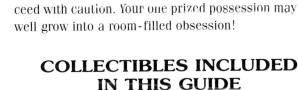

Rushing over to a local mall where the pack was purchased, we bought the remaining box and put together a complete set of 44 stickers and 16 puzzle pieces. It wasn't long before we discovered there were other classic TV trading cards in existence and soon found ourselves hunting card shows across the state looking for any sets we could get our hands on. Enlisting a few friends along the way, the mission to obtain every card from every set became so overwhelming at times, we often referred to the obsession as "card fever."

There are several antique and collectible guide writers who describe collecting as the act of hunting for items to complete a collection. They theorize that humans are hunters by instinct. The Webster's Dictionary describes collecting as accumulating objects in one place. We, however, have a different definition. Instead of completing a collection, we define it as "fulfilling an obsession." How else can we explain how rapidly our collection grew?

From TV trading cards, we turned our attention toward TV toys. Our desire to collect TV memorabilia comes as no surprise. After all, we grew up during the '60s and '70s watching television. It was the perfect babysitter; always available and free. We remember waking up on Saturday mornings to tune into the classics of our time, like *Josie and the Pussycats*, *H.R. Pufnstuf*, *Sigmund and the Sea Monsters*, and *The Krofft Supershow*. Then, at night, when our homework was done, we would sit down and watch *The Love Boat*, *Fantasy Island*, *Laverne and Shirley*, *Little House on the Prairie*, *The Brady Bunch*, and *The Partridge Family*. Reruns of television shows from the '60s made it possible for us to enjoy *Bewitched*, *Gilligan's Island*, *I Dream of Jeannie*, and *The Beverly Hillbillies*. Watching all these shows was comforting and dependable. We could always count on them to be there for our enjoyment.

Collecting TV memorabilia is like capturing those same feelings. It's a return to a time when everything seemed safer, and we could take refuge from the world in our television set.

So, whether collecting TV memorabilia is an instinctive act or simply a way to recapture your childhood, one thing is for certain. It is extremely contagious. If you're just beginning, proceed with caution. Your one prized possession may very well grow into a room-filled obsession!

COLLECTIBLES INCLUDED IN THIS GUIDE

In this guide, we have focused on items that were marketed during a television show's original run. Some of the items made include toys, dolls, books, games, posters, records, and school supplies. Most of these items will bear the name of the show with a picture of the cast or characters on the packaging. Although a lot of collectors include other items in their private collections, such as autographs, magazine articles, and photographs, it would be cumbersome to list, for example, all of the magazine covers on which Farrah Fawcett appeared. The purpose of this guide is to provide a comprehensive listing of items made for the show and not the related memorabilia.

The following items are a few that appear repeatedly in this guide, and to avoid being repetitive, a brief description is mentioned. In some cases, we include reasons for exclusion or inclusion.

BRITISH ANNUALS: The annuals included in this guide contain stories, illustrations, and activities published in the United Kingdom. Each annual year shown on the cover will bear a copyright of the prior year inside. The way we have listed the dates will correspond with the book's cover. If the date is shown, we list the cover date. If no date is shown, the copyright date from the inside is used.

DOLLS: A boxed doll can be a rare find. In some cases, the value is more then double a loose doll. To emphasize the rarity of these, we have placed a loose and boxed price for every doll in this book. A loose price includes all of the doll's original clothes and any accessories, but no packaging.

MAGAZINES: With the exception of *TV Guide*, the magazines included in this book are devoted entirely to the show or a single star thereof. The large number of magazines that celebrities have graced the cover of is so cumbersome, it would be nearly impossible to give comprehensive listings for them.

RECORDS: Some records included in this book do not bear the name of a television program. Most of these recordings were promoted by agents or pursued by merchandisers during the original run of the show and are inadvertently television memorabilia. Many of these were also released in different formats including reel-to-reel, 8-track tape, and cassette. The photo that appears on the album jacket will usually be the same on the other formats. We have not listed the other formats in this guide.

PAPER DOLLS: These can be found in a variety of conditions. Some may be cut or punched out from the original sheets and others remain untouched. If the dolls and clothes are complete and not torn or ripped, both cut and uncut sets can still be considered in excellent condition. The value, however, is twice as high for uncut sets than cut ones. A cut and uncut price for each set is listed.

TV GUIDES: Although *TV Guides* are quite collectible today, they were not marketed as official memorabilia and fall out of the scope of this guide. Due to their popularity with collectors, they are listed, but are not pictured, so we can maximize the space for harder-to-find memorabilia. The values listed are for those without mailing labels.

VIEW-MASTERS: Many of the View-Masters included in this guide were also released in the United Kingdom. Some of them were on cards, while others came in gift boxes that contain a viewer. We have only noted the releases known to us. An example of the United Kingdom variations can be seen with the *CHiPs* View-Master photos on page 78.

INTERNATIONAL ITEMS

Although we have included many foreign items in this guide, we are not claiming to be comprehensive on items made outside the United States. We have, however, included many new international items to this revision, especially those made for *Starsky and Hutch, The Bionic Woman, The Six Million Dollar Man, Charlie's Angels,* and *The Partridge Family.*

Most foreign toys contain unique artwork and original designs, sometimes making them more valuable and desirable to collectors than a United States version. On the other hand, some foreign companies merely purchase licensing rights from United States manufacturers and produce items almost identical to the United States versions. Because of the similarity, many of these items have not been listed. For example, most Topps trading cards were produced in Canada under the O-PEE-CHEE logo and bear no difference except for the manufacturer's name. Other foreign variations include HG Toys products made in Scotland by Thomas Salter Toys, Milton Bradley board games made in Canada by Somerville Industries Limited, Hasbro products made in Belgium by Raynal, and Kenner products by Denys Fisher in the United Kingdom. We've mentioned them when appropriate, but have not included every possible variation.

GRADING SCALE

GD (Good) = has many problems, tears, contents missing, etc.

VG (Very Good) = average, has some minor problems like creases, marks or wear, may be incomplete, but is still desirable to many collectors.

EX (Excellent) = above average and complete, may have some minor wear and use, but very desirable.

NM (Near Mint) = just about perfect with very minimal wear.

MT (Mint) = new, unused, store stock in its original condition.

Some other abbreviations often used by collectors and dealers to describe condition:

MOC = Mint on card.

MIB = Mint in box.

MIP = Mint in package.

SS = Still sealed, unopened.

C1 - C10 = Condition on a 1-10 scale, with 10 being the best.

PRICING

The values listed in this guide are for items found in excellent condition and based on opinions of collectors residing in the United States. If found in near mint or mint condition, it should be worth more. If found in good or very good condition, it should be worth less. For example, the value of incomplete puzzles and board games fall below what is considered excellent and therefore command a lower price. Values in this guide are also estimated for the packaging of the item pictured. For example, if a record player is shown with a box, the value should include the box, unless otherwise specified.

The values listed do not include realized auction prices. Although this may be a good indication of the popularity of an item, a high bid means the item was sold to the collector willing to pay more than anyone else. Auction prices do not reflect what most collectors would consider a fair price.

As any experienced collector knows, prices are influenced by several factors. These include condition, rarity, popularity, and geographical location. We feel one of the largest factors that can influence price is popularity. If there are several collectors focusing their hobby on one particular show, each may be willing to pay a premium to obtain an item to complete a collection. A collector may be willing to spend more, and a seller may be able to charge more for some items.

What we have tried to do is give overall collectible prices. We have averaged the factors of rarity, popularity, and geographical location.

INTERNET COLLECTING

You can't be in all places at once. Besides, who has the time it takes to spend hunting antique malls, flea markets, and garage sales every weekend? The best, and least expensive way, is staying home and looking for collectibles on the Internet. Think about it...no crowded aisles, 24-hour service, and delivery straight to your home. We don't think we have to sell you on the concept. Just try it, and you'll be amazed at how quickly your collection grows.

There are hundreds of search engines on the web that can help you find several sites that cater to your hobby. To narrow your search, try key words like "TV memorabilia," "TV collectibles," and "TV toys." A great place to start is at our web site, www.tvtoys.com. We have links to several collecting sites, making it convenient to browse around.

MAIL ORDER COLLECTING

If you're like the majority of TV memorabilia collectors, you have probably acquired much of your collection from sources close to home. Flea markets, antique malls, and thrift stores are excellent places to find those elusive pieces you've been looking for. But what happens when your local sources dry up? The dilemma can be overcome by extending your scope worldwide through mail order collecting.

It's a simple concept. You look through periodicals or search the Internet for sites advertising collectibles for sale, reserve the item, send payment, and voilà, you receive your TV treasure at your doorstep within a few weeks. But while mail order collecting is an easy and effective way to add items to your collection, there are several possible pitfalls you need to be aware of.

WHERE TO LOOK: There are several periodicals devoted to buying and selling TV memorabilia. Each can be found at newsstands and bookstores. For those of you who have access to a computer, the Internet can put you in touch with dealers around the globe at the click of a mouse.

TIMING: It is crucial that you make immediate contact with a seller if you spot an advertisement for an interesting item. Aggressive collectors always get the rarest items. For periodicals, find out when the next issue hits the stand or become a regular subscriber. Some publications even offer priority mailing for an additional fee.

CONDITION: Once you've found what you're looking for, make contact with the seller and ask for a complete description of the item in question. Most ads provide very little information about condition. For those that do, be warned — the seller's version of "mint" may be another person's "very good." Even experienced collectors like us have been victims of condition variance. Greg once purchased a box of Susan Dey paper dolls that were advertised as "mint" and verified with the seller that they were "like new." When the item was received, it was discovered that the doll clothing was cut out from the original sheets. When the seller was approached about condition, the response was that the contents were complete and in great shape, deserving a "mint" rating.

POSTAGE: Don't be surprised when the seller asks you to include additional money to cover shipping and handling. This is standard procedure. The additional cost depends on the size and weight of the item. For an average-sized item, such as a jigsaw puzzle or lunch box, expect to add about $6.00. Insurance and tracking fees are additional but are usually good investments, especially for valuable items.

SHIPPING CONTAINERS: To avoid getting a delicate item delivered in a flimsy envelope that's been folded and shoved into your mailbox, request that the item be packed in a sturdy box marked "fragile." We once ordered several vintage posters that were shipped in an inadequate cardboard mailer that got crushed in the middle, rendering the posters useless.

METHOD OF PAYMENT: Most sellers ask for a check or money order as the form of payment, but occasionally you'll find those that accept credit cards. Using a credit card is the quickest way to get your order. Sending a money order is the second preferred method because your order is usually shipped upon receipt of payment. The slowest method is to pay by check. It is customary for sellers to hold a check for 10 working days before sending out your order.

BOOTLEG MERCHANDISE: Uncovering unknown rarities is what makes the hunt so enjoyable and rewarding, but beware of bootleg merchandise. Some of these items include homemade buttons, rings, and celebrity photos pasted on cereal boxes that are being sold and traded as if authorized and legitimately manufactured. Some may be replicas, or worse yet, fakes! Your best weapon is education. Read up on your favorite shows and find out what was made and what the items look like. Read collecting magazines and price guides, and network with other collectors who share your passion for certain shows and types of collectibles. Ask if there is a copyright name and date on the item, and always inquire about a return policy. Most reputable dealers will accept returns but will not refund shipping costs.

Bill once participated in an auction for a Jimmy doll from the TV series *H.R. Pufnstuf.* The doll was advertised as original, and after verifying the description over the telephone prior to auction, it appeared he discovered a rare find. What he got was a fake. Someone had used a Jimmy hand puppet plastic head and sewed it onto a hand-made stuffed body. When the seller was contacted about the problem, Bill was told all sales were final.

We hope this book will help you avoid becoming a victim of bootleg merchandise. By being aware of these possible mail order mishaps, you will find that collecting by mail is a terrific way to increase the size of your TV memorabilia collection.

THE WORLD OF TV TOYS

We love hearing from other collectors and are always interested in learning about their collections. If you have any comments or know of other memorabilia not contained in this guide, please write to us at:

Bill Morgan and Greg Davis
P.O. Box 91-1491
Los Angeles, CA 90091-1239
or
e-mail: tvtoys@aol.com

You can also visit our all-TV web site "The World of TV Toys" at **www.tvtoys.com**

10 RULES OF COLLECTING

We reviewed these rules that appeared in our first edition and tried to determine if they needed to be updated. After reading them, we realized that they are just as appropriate now as they were a few years ago. If you have already read them in the first book, trust us, and read them again. It doesn't hurt to repeat these to yourself every so often. They can save you a lot of grief.

1. Always trust your instincts. If you see an item you want and can afford it, don't pass it up. It may never come around again.

2. Understand the phrase "out-of-print." If you really want it, buy it. Remember, money is still being printed, but *The Brady Bunch* game hasn't been manufactured since 1973.

3. Always ask what the price is. Most toy dealers and traders are willing to negotiate prices, even if the price is marked. You can even ask if a dealer gives discounts when visiting an antique mall.

4. Don't pass up a collectible just because it's not in mint condition. Mint items are scarce. Don't deny yourself the enjoyment of owning an item that you can upgrade later for one in better condition.

5. Have an inquiring mind. When searching for memorabilia, always ask sellers if they have any other items you're looking for. Just because you don't see it doesn't mean they don't have it. You can also give out "want lists" to identify items you're seeking.

6. Know where to look. Make sure to visit garage sales, antique malls, record stores, thrift shops, antique swap meets, and used bookstores. You can also browse through publications devoted to buying and selling memorabilia.

7. Enlist family and friends for help. You can't be in all places at once, so having others keep a lookout for items you want can be invaluable.

8. Make friends with other collectors. Building a network of co-collectors can help you locate items you're looking for. You can also trade with one another.

9. Be organized. Keep track of what you already have to avoid buying duplicates. This will also help you identify the items you are missing from your collection.

10. And, as always, *have fun!*

THE BEVERLY HILLBILLIES

SEPTEMBER 26, 1962 –
SEPTEMBER 7, 1971

274 EPISODES

PEAK POSITION:
#1 in the 1962–1964 seasons

—— CAST ——

Buddy Ebsen
Jed Clampett

Irene Ryan
Daisy "Granny" Moses

Donna Douglas
Elly May

Max Baer Jr.
Jethro Bodine

Raymond Bailey
Milburn Drysdale

Nancy Kulp
Jane Hathaway

BEVERLY HILLBILLIES CAR, Ideal, 1963. Two-foot long plastic car with five figures and accessories. Box features an illustration of the car and cast. $200.00–300.00 loose; $400.00–500.00 boxed.

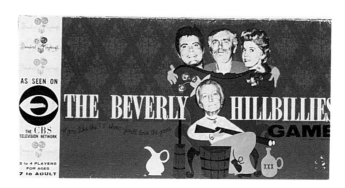

BOARD GAME, Standard Toykraft, 1963. $40.00 – 60.00.

Left:
BOOK, *The Saga of Wildcat Creek,* Whitman, 1966. $8.00–12.00.

Right:
BRITISH ANNUALS, World, 1964–1967. One for each year, except 1967 which had two annuals—one with Granny, Elly May, and Jethro on cover, the other Granny, Elly May, and cougar. 1964 annual pictured. $35.00–45.00 each.

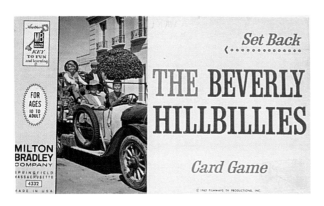

CARD GAME, Milton Bradley, 1963. $20.00–25.00.

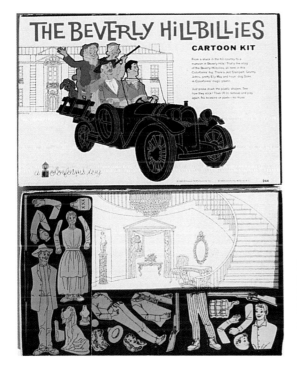

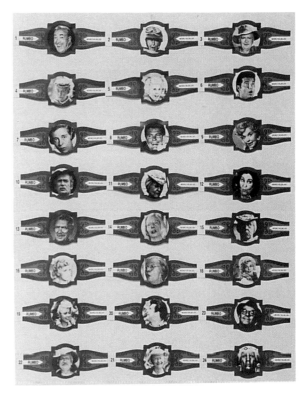

CIGAR BANDS, Rumbo, 1960s. European numbered set of 24. Each band measures 2½" in length. $75.00–100.00 set.

CARTOON KITS, Colorforms, 1963. Regular and deluxe. Regular set measures 12" x 8". Deluxe set measures 16" x 13". Deluxe set features an illustration of the cast in front of their home instead of their car. Regular set pictured. $60.00–80.00 regular; $100.00–125.00 deluxe.

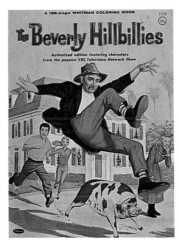

COLORING BOOK, Whitman, 1963. $25.00–35.00.

COLORING BOOK, Whitman, 1964. $25.00–35.00.

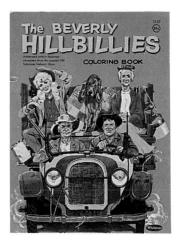

COLORING BOOK, Whitman, 1963. $25.00–35.00.

FRAME TRAY PUZZLES, Jaymar, 1963. Several different. $25.00–30.00 each.

COMIC BOOKS, Dell, 1963–1971. 21 issues; #1, 4, 5, 10, 12, 13, 14, 17, 20, 21 pictured. $75.00–125.00 for #1; $40.00–60.00 for #2; $30.00–40.00 each for #3–9; $15.00–25.00 each for #10–21.

JIGSAW PUZZLES, Jaymar, 1963. Several different. Puzzle #6572 pictured. $30.00–40.00 each.

LAPEL PINS, Nemo, 1962. 1" figural metal pins of cast characters on 3" x 3" card. Several different, including another with Jed and Duke. Elly May and Jethro pictured. $40.00–60.00 each.

DOLLS, Elly May Clampett, Unique, 1960s. 12" doll sold as a cereal premium mail-away. Two different versions. One has pants and the other a skirt. $50.00–75.00 each.

LUNCH BOX, Aladdin, 1963. Metal box with metal thermos. $125.00–150.00 lunch box; $50.00–75.00 thermos.

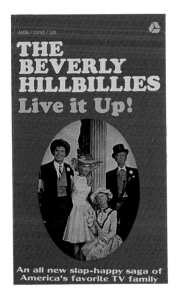

PAPERBACK BOOK, *The Beverly Hillbillies Live It Up,* Avon Books, 1965. $15.00–20.00.

PAPERBACK BOOK, *The Clampetts of Beverly Hills,* Avon Books, 1964. $15.00–20.00.

PAPERBACK BOOK, *The Beverly Hillbillies Book of Country Humor,* Dell Publishing Co., Inc., 1964. $20.00–25.00.

Left:
PAPER DOLL BOOKLET #1955, Whitman, 1964. $50.00–60.00 cut; $75.00–100.00 uncut.

Right:
PAPER DOLL BOOKLET #1819A, *Elly May,* Watkins Strathmore Co., 1963. $40.00–50.00 cut; $60.00–80.00 uncut.

Left:
RECORD/LP, "The Beverly Hillbillies," Harmony, 1968. Vocals by the entire cast and includes theme song. $40.00–60.00.

Right:
RECORD/LP, "Buddy Ebsen Says Howdy in Song and Story," Reprise, 1965. $25.00–35.00.

 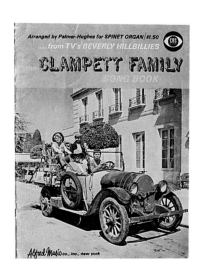

Left:
SHEET MUSIC, "Ballad of Jed Clampett," Carolintone Music Co., Inc., 1962. $30.00–40.00.

Right:
SONG BOOK, Alfred Music, 1963. $35.00–45.00.

TRADING CARDS, Topps, 1963. 66 photo cards in set. Backs include Hillbilly Gags. 1¢ or 5¢ wrappers. $350.00–500.00 set; $5.00–8.00 single cards; $50.00–75.00 1¢ wrapper; $125.00–150.00 5¢ wrapper; $400.00–500.00 display box.

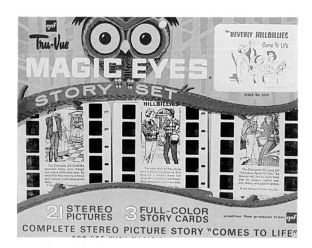

TRU-VUE MAGIC EYES STORY SET #5274, The Beverly Hillbillies Come to Life, GAF, 1963. 11" x 9" sleeve contains three rectangular story cards. $40.00–60.00.

VIEW-MASTER #B570, Sawyers, 1963. $35.00–45.00.

OTHER ITEMS NOT PICTURED

BOOK, *Granny's Hillbilly Cookbook,* Prentice Hall, 1966. 6" x 9" 261-page hardback book with jacket cover illustrating Granny wearing a chef's hat. $25.00–30.00.

CHARM BRACELET, 1960s. Metal chain with five plastic photo charms including Jed, Granny, Jethro, Elly May, and cast. $50.00–75.00.

COSTUME, Granny, Halco, 1971. $100.00–125.00.

COSTUME, Jed, Ben Cooper, 1963. $100.00–125.00.

CUT-OUT COLORING BOOK, *The Clampetts in Hollywood,* Golden Funtime Books, 1964. Illustrated cover similar to blue cover coloring book but with an orange background. $30.00–40.00.

HILLBILLY HAT, Tandy Leather Co., 1960s. Made of leather. $50.00–75.00.

HILLBILLY HAT, Arlington Hat Co., 1960s. Made of felt. $50.00–75.00.

MAGIC BUBBLE PIPE, Kellogg's Cereal, 1960s. Cereal premium. Plastic corn cob pipe creates bubbles with water. $50.00–75.00

MODEL KIT, Truck, MPC, 1960. Instructions include two methods of assembly. One is an older hillbilly style and the other is a mod style. $100.00–125.00.

MOVIE VIEWER, Acme Toy, 1964. Plastic mini-viewer with two strips of film on a blister photo card. $50.00–75.00.

PLASTIC PALETTE COLORING SET, Standard Toykraft, 1963. Illustration of cast on a 13" x 18" box. Has 10 pictures to color with crayons and eight paints. $75.00–100.00.

PUNCH OUT BOOK #1949, Whitman, 1964. 10" x 14" book with illustrated cast cover. $60.00–80.00.

RECORD/LP, "Granny of Beverly Hills," Nashwood, 1972. Vocals and comedy tracks by Irene Ryan. $40.00–60.00.

RECORD/45, "Mail Order Bride"/"Ballad of Jed Clampett," MGM, 1963. Vocals by Buddy Ebsen. Without picture sleeve. $10.00–15.00.

RECORD/45, "Howdy"/"Bonapart's Retreat," Reprise, 1965. Vocals by Buddy Ebsen. Without picture sleeve. $10.00–15.00.

RECORD/45, "Granny's Mini Skirt"/"Bring On the Show," Nashwood, 1972. Vocals by Irene Ryan. With picture sleeve. $30.00–40.00.

RECORD/45, "No Time at All"/"Time (To Believe in Each Other)," Motown, 1973. Vocals by Irene Ryan. Without picture sleeve. $10.00–15.00.

SLIDING SQUARES PUZZLE, Roalex, 1964. Hand-held plastic puzzle with illustration of cast on a 7" x 6" card. $50.00–75.00 on card.

TV GUIDES, 1962–1970. 11/10/62 Cast; 03/09/63 Ebsen & Douglas; 09/07/63 Ryan & Douglas; 02/27/65 Kulp, Ryan & Douglas; 03/12/66 Cast illustrated; 07/11/70 Cast illustrated. $15.00–25.00 each.

BEWITCHED

SEPTEMBER 17, 1964 –
JULY 1, 1972

252 EPISODES

PEAK POSITION:
#2 in the 1964–1965 season

—— CAST ——

Elizabeth Montgomery
Samantha Stephens/Serena

Dick York/Dick Sargent
Darrin Stephens

Agnes Moorehead
Endora

David White
Larry Tate

Irene Vernon/Kasey Rogers
Louise Tate

Erin/Diane Murphy
Tabitha

David/Greg Lawrence
Adam

Alice Pearce/Sandra Gould
Gladys Kravitz

George Tobias
Abner Kravitz

—— AUTHORS' NOTE ——
The spelling of "Tabatha" was changed during the fifth season to "Tabitha" with an "i." As a result, all of the memorabilia prior to then was labeled with the original spelling of "Tabatha."

ACTIVITY BOOK, Treasure Books, 1965. $25.00–30.00.

BOOK, *The Opposite Uncle.* Whitman, 1970. $15.00–20.00.

BOARD GAME, The Samantha and Endora Game, Game Gems, 1965. Box lid varies with either a black or pink bird. $150.00–175.00.

BRITISH ANNUALS, World Distributors Limited, 1967–1968. $50.00–75.00 each.

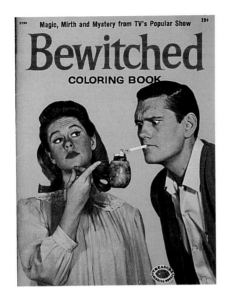

COLORING BOOK, Treasure Books, 1965. $100.00–125.00.

COMIC BOOKS #1–14, Dell, 1965–1969. #12 is a reprint of #1, and #14 is a reprint of #2. $75.00–100.00 #1; $40.00–60.00 #2; $20.00–40.00 #3–14.

CARD GAME, Stymie, Milton Bradley, 1965. $50.00–60.00.

Left:
COSTUME, Ben Cooper, 1965. Fabric outfit varies with plain or printed skirt. $150.00–175.00.

Right:
COSTUME, Ben Cooper, 1977. Vinyl outfit. $100.00–125.00.

DOLL, Samantha, Ideal, 1965. Original packaging includes 12" doll and broom in window display box. $500.00–600.00 loose with broom; $1,500.00–2,000.00 boxed.

DOLL, Tabatha, Ideal, 1966. 14" vinyl doll dressed in a 2-piece pajama outfit. Window box features photo of Samantha, Endora, and Darrin. Doll is marked "1965, Screen Gems Inc." on head and body. $200.00–300.00 loose; $1,000.00–1,500.00 boxed.

JIGSAW PUZZLES, Milton Bradley, 1964. Two different, including "Along for the Ride" and "Endora Pours." Puzzles include 12" x 14" color portrait insert of Samantha. $100.00–125.00 each.

PAPER DOLL BOX, Samantha, Magic Wand, 1965. $100.00–125.00 cut; $150.00–200.00 uncut.

PAPER DOLL BOX, Tabatha, Magic Wand, 1966. $75.00–100.00 cut; $125.00–150.00 uncut.

PAPERBACK BOOK, Bewitched, Young World Productions, 1967. European issue with no author credited. Color photos from the series inside. $50.00–60.00.

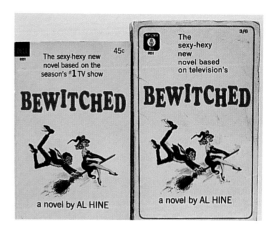

PAPERBACK BOOKS, Bewitched, Dell, 1965. Variations from different countries. United States and red-bordered British versions pictured. $30.00–40.00 each.

SHEET MUSIC, "Bewitched," Screen Gems-Columbia Music, Inc., 1964. $40.00–50.00.

STORYBOOK, Wonder Books, 1965. $25.00–30.00.

WRITING TABLETS, 1960s. Two 8" x 10" versions. 10¢ version pictured. 29¢ tablet features Montgomery, York, and Murphy on a gold background. $40.00–50.00 each.

OTHER ITEMS NOT PICTURED

BEWITCHED BROOM, Amsco, 1965. Three-foot long toy broom with plastic figural head of Samantha wearing a witch's hat. $300.00–400.00.

HI-CHAIR FEEDING SET, Amsco, 1965. 14" x 29" box contains a pink steel hi-chair, plate, eating utensils, and magic feeding bottle. $600.00–800.00.

MAGIC DOLL FEEDING BOTTLE, Amsco, 1965. Bottle features logo. Bottle packaged in a 5" x 8" window display box. $300.00–400.00.

MAGIC DOLL FEEDING BOTTLE SET, Amsco, 1965. 8" x 14" illustrated box contains vinyl bag, magic feeding bottle, and several other accessories. $600.00–800.00.

MAGIC COFFEE SET, Amsco, 1965. 14" x 18" window display box contains a toaster, stove burner, toy coffeepot with logo, and other accessories. $600.00–800.00.

TRADING CARDS, Topps, 1960s. Test issue of 28 unnumbered cards. Black and white photo cards with blank backs. No box or wrapper was made. $200.00–250.00 single cards.

TV GUIDES, 1964–1970. 01/28/64 Montgomery; 05/29/65 Montgomery and York; 06/18/66 Montgomery, Moorehead and Murphy illustrated; 05/13/67 Montgomery; 01/27/68 Montgomery; 03/22/69 Montgomery; 02/07/70 Montgomery and Sargent illustrated. $20.00–30.00 each.

THE BIONIC WOMAN

JANUARY 14, 1976 –
SEPTEMBER 2, 1978

57 EPISODES

PEAK POSITION:
#5 in the 1975–1976 season

—— CAST ——

Lindsay Wagner
Jaime Sommers

Richard Anderson
Oscar Goldman

Martin E. Brooks
Dr. Rudy Wells

Jennifer Darling
Peggy Callahan

ACTIVITY BOOKS, Grosset & Dunlap, 1976. Two different. $15.00–20.00 each.

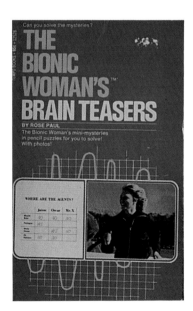

ACRYLIC PAINT BY NUMBER SETS, Craft Master, 1976. Four different titles, including "Bionic Hearing," "Fiery Rescue," "Leap from Death," and "A Time for Love." "Fiery Rescue" pictured. $30.00–40.00 each.

ACTIVITY BOOK, Brain Teasers, Tempo Books, 1976. $10.00–15.00.

BANK, Animals Plus Inc., 1976. 10" plastic figural. $30.00–40.00.

BIONIC ACTION CLUB KIT, Kenner, 1975. Contains a sticker, membership card, autographed photo, and a certificate. $50.00–75.00.

BIONIC BEAUTY SALON, Kenner, 1976. Playset for 12" doll. Box varies with photo of doll in jogging suit or blue jumpsuit. $40.00–60.00.

BIONIC TATTOOS AND STICKERS, Kenner, 1976. $10.00–15.00.

BIONIC EYEWEAR, Hudson, 1977. Fabric eyeglass case in box. $30.00–40.00.

BIONIC STICKERS, General Mills, 1977. Set of ten 2⅜" x 4⅛" stickers. Two stickers inside each Cheerios or Lucky Charms cereal boxes. A different set of eight was offered in 1976 and is pictured under *The Six Million Dollar Man*. $5.00–8.00 each sticker.

BOARD GAME, Parker Brothers, 1976. Parker Brothers United States version pictured. Denys Fisher made a similar United Kingdom version. $15.00–20.00 U.S. version; $25.00–30.00 U.K. version.

BOOK, *Lindsay Wagner,* 1976. 6" x 8" soft cover Japanese biography. $40.00–50.00.

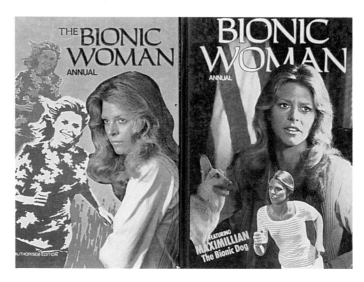

BRITISH ANNUALS, Brown Watson, 1977–78. $35.00–45.00 each.

BUBBLE BATH, Noveltime Products, 1977. Made in the United Kingdom. $50.00–75.00.

CARRIAGE HOUSE, Kenner, 1977. Playset for the 12" dolls. $200.00–250.00.

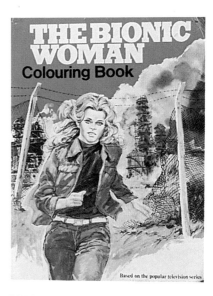

COLOURING BOOKS, Stafford Pemberton, 1977. Two different 9" x 12" books made in the United Kingdom. Book not pictured features an illustration of Jaime jumping from a helicopter. $40.00–50.00 each.

COLORING BOOKS, Treasure Books, 1976. Three different. $15.00–20.00 each.

COMIC BOOKS #1–5, Charlton, 1977–1978. $10.00–15.00 each.

COSTUME, Jaime, Berwick, 1976. British costume with no mask in 12" x 16" box. $60.00–80.00.

COSTUME, Jaime, Ben Cooper, 1975. $30.00–40.00.

CUP, TUMBLER, AND BOWL, Dawn, 1976. $15.00–20.00 cup or tumbler; $30.00–40.00 bowl.

Left:
DIP DOTS PAINTING DESIGN BOOK, Kenner, 1977. Box varies with blue or pink. $30.00–40.00.

Right:
DOLL, Fembot, Kenner, 1977. $75.00–100.00 loose; $175.00–200.00 boxed.

DOLLS, Jaime Sommers, Kenner, 1976. Three 12"
issues. Issue #1 dressed in a jogging suit; Issue #2
made in United States by Kenner with Jaime
dressed in a blue jumpsuit with mission purse and
made in the United Kingdom by Denys Fisher in a
solid box (not pictured); and Issue #3 includes
three fashions. Canadian versions were also made,
with French titles. $30.00–50.00 loose; $125.00–
150.00 boxed Issue #1; $150.00–175.00 boxed
U.S. Issue #2; $175.00–200.00 boxed U.K. Issue
#2; $200.00–250.00 boxed Issue #3.

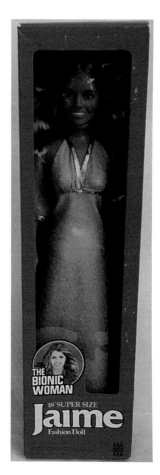

DOLL FASHIONS, Kenner, 1976. Kenner made two different types of fashions for 12" dolls in the United States. The Designer Collection consists of
seven different styles (Country Comfort, Gold Dust, Peach Dream, Casual
Day, Blue Mist, Floral Delight, and Silk 'n' Satin) and The Designer Budget
Fashions consist of nine styles (Lime Lite, Red Dazzle, Lunch Date, Tennis
Outfit, Elegant Lady, Party Pants, Fiesta, Classy Culottes, and Lilac Butter-
fly). Peach Dream and Red Dazzle pictured. Denys Fisher made similar versions in the United Kingdom. $25.00–30.00 each U.S. Designer Collection;
$20.00–25.00 each U.S. Designer Budget Fashion; $30.00–40.00 each U.K.
fashion.

FASHION DOLL, Jaime, Denys
Fisher, 1977. 18" doll released in
the United Kingdom only. Includes
gold gown and jewelry. $300.00–
400.00 loose; $600.00–800.00
boxed.

FAN CLUB KIT, Lindsay Wagner, 1978. Includes
membership card, color photos, 22" x 28" poster,
bookmarks, decal, and newsletter. $75.00–100.00.

GIVE-A-SHOW PROJECTOR, Kenner, 1977. $40.00–50.00.

JIGSAW PUZZLES, Whitman, 1976. Four different United Kingdom styles. $40.00–50.00 each.

IRON-ONS, 1970s. Several different. $20.00–25.00 each.

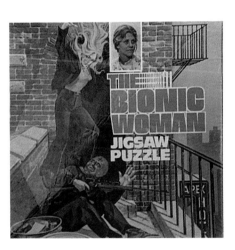

JIGSAW PUZZLES, APC, 1976. $25.00–30.00 each.

JIGSAW PUZZLES, APC, 1976. Three different canisters. $20.00–25.00 each.

LUNCH BOXES, Aladdin, 1977–1978. Two versions of the boxes and thermoses exist. Both boxes have identical fronts. One has Jaime opening car door on back (1977) and the other shows her running with the bionic dog (1978). Metal box with plastic thermos. $60.00–80.00 each box; $15.00–20.00 each thermos.

LUNCH BOX, Aladdin, 1970s. Plastic version made in Canada. $50.00–75.00.

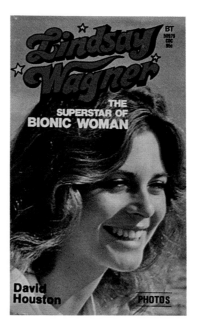

PAPERBACK BOOK, *Lindsay Wagner: Superstar of the Bionic Woman,* Belmont Tower Books, 1976. $20.00–25.00.

MODEL KIT, Bionic Repair, MPC, 1978. $40.00–50.00.

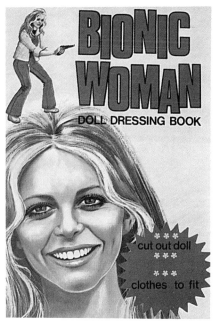

PAPERBACK BOOKS, 1970s. Top two are United States versions by Berkley Publishing Corporation, 1976–1977. Bottom two are United Kingdom versions by Star Books, 1977. $10.00–15.00 U.S.; $20.00–25.00 U.K.

PAPER DOLL, Children Books, 1978. Made in Italy. Also packaged with Steve Austin and pictured under *The Six Million Dollar Man.* $30.00–40.00.

PAPER DOLL BOOKLETS, Stafford Pemberton, 1978. Made in the United Kingdom. Two versions were made. One includes a story to read. $30.00–40.00 cut; $50.00–75.00 uncut.

PLAY-DOH ACTION PLAY SET, Kenner, 1977. Blue or pink box. $40.00–50.00.

POCKET SLIDING PUZZLE, APC, 1977. $35.00–45.00.

PLAYSUIT, Ben Cooper, 1975. Fabric costume with plastic mask. $40.00–50.00.

POSTER MAGAZINES, 1977. *Back From the Dead* by CLP and *Lindsay Wagner* by Pepperwell Ltd. Made in the United Kingdom. $40.00–50.00 each.

POSTERS, Pro Arts, Inc., 1976. 20" x 28" Jamie (spelled incorrectly), and 20" x 28" Sommers (not pictured). $50.00–75.00 each.

PRESS-OUT BOOK, World Distributors, 1977. Made in the United Kingdom. Contains cardboard pieces and pages to color. $50.00–75.00.

RECORD/LP, "Great Adventures," Wonderland, 1976. Narrated stories. $25.00–30.00.

SEE-A-SHOW VIEWER, Kenner, 1976. $25.00–35.00.

SHEET MUSIC, "The Bionic Woman," Leeds Music Corp., 1976. $25.00–30.00.

SHOWER AND DRESSING TABLE, Lili Ledy, 1975. Made in Mexico. Playset for the 12" dolls. $125.00–150.00.

SLIDE PROJECTOR SET, Chad Valley, 1977. Made in the United Kingdom. $50.00–75.00.

SPORTS CAR, Kenner, 1977. $125.00–150.00.

SLIPPERS, Universal, 1976. Children's slippers made in Great Britain. Pink or blue styles. $40.00–50.00.

STICKER FUN BOOKS, Stafford Pemberton, 1977–1978. Made in the United Kingdom. Yellow cover (1977) and blue cover (1978). $50.00–75.00 each.

STYLING BOUTIQUES, Kenner, 1977. Denys Fisher made a similar British version. $100.00–125.00 each.

TRADING CARDS, Monty Gum, 1976. Made in Holland. 81 cards in set. 2" x 1¾" in size. $175.00–200.00 set; $2.00–2.50 single cards; $15.00–20.00 wrapper; $100.00–125.00 display box.

TRADING CARDS, Donruss, 1976. 44 photo cards in set with puzzle backs. $45.00–55.00 set; $1.00–1.25 single cards; $5.00–8.00 wrapper; $40.00–50.00 display box.

WALLET, Faberge, 1976. Made in Canada. Blue or pink. $35.00–45.00.

WRISTWATCH, MZ Berger, 1970s. Working watch. $60.00–80.00.

OTHER ITEMS NOT PICTURED

A.M. WRIST RADIO, Illco, 1976. 3" round radio in yellow casing with a black leather band and logo. Comes in a window display box. $200.00–250.00.

BEACH TOWELS, 1970s. Two different illustrated styles. One pictures Jaime running and the other is a close-up. $40.00–60.00 each.

BIONIC BIKE, Kenner, 1970s. Child-size plastic bike with four wheels and packaged in a large photo cover box. $250.00–300.00.

BIONIC CYCLE, Kenner, 1977. $50.00–75.00.

BRUNCH BAG, Aladdin, 1970s. Dark blue vinyl bag with an illustrated close-up of Jaime. $125.00–150.00.

CLASSROOM, Kenner, 1977. Playset for the 12" dolls sold exclusively by Montgomery Ward. $400.00–500.00.

DOLL, Jaime Sommers, Lili Ledy, 1974. Sold in similar packaging as the first United States issue but made using a different mold. Jaime is smaller in height and has softer facial features than Kenner's version. $50.00–75.00 loose; $100.00–125.00 boxed.

DOLL FASHIONS, Les Vetements De Super Jaime, 1970s. European outfits similar to Kenner's United States' versions, including Silk 'n' Satin, Casual Day, and Country Comfort. $40.00–50.00 each.

DOME HOUSE, Kenner, 1975. Inflatable home for 12" dolls. $125.00–150.00.

FRAME TRAY PUZZLE, APC, 1976. Colorful illustration of Jaime tossing a criminal. $35.00–45.00.

GIRL'S COMB AND BRUSH SET, Faberge, 1976. Made in Canada. $40.00–60.00.

LASER DISC, *The Bionic Woman*, MCA, 1978. Full length feature in photo sleeve similar to those pictured under *The Six Million Dollar Man*. $40.00–50.00.

MOVIE CASSETTES, Kenner, 1977. Several different in numbered boxes sold separately for movie viewer. Some of the titles include "C'mon Jaime," "Run Jaime, Run," "The Bionic Woman to the Rescue," "Only Humans," and "Attempted Escape." $20.00–25.00 each.

MOVIE VIEWER, Kenner, 1977. Hand-held viewer for movie cassettes. $40.00–50.00.

PAINT YOUR OWN TV GREETING CARDS, Cartoonarama, 1978. Box cover has an illustration of Jaime. $50.00–75.00.

PAJAMAS, Rob Roy, 1970s. $35.00–45.00.

PAPERBACK BOOK, *La Femme Bionique: Super Jaime*, Ottawa, 1978. 5½" x 8" Canadian version of *Welcome Home, Jaime*. Includes 8 pages of black and white photos. $25.00–35.00.

PATCHES, 1970s. Made in the United Kingdom. Several different with illustrations of Jaime. $15.00–20.00 each.

POSTER, 1970s. Jaime illustration in felt. $50.00–75.00.

RAINCOAT, Universal, 1976. Illustration on yellow jacket. $50.00–75.00.

SPIRAL NOTEBOOK, 1970s. Colorful illustration of Jaime on cover. $30.00–40.00.

TOWER AND CYCLE, Kenner, 1977. Motorcycle with jumping action. $75.00–100.00.

TOOTHBRUSH, Kenner, 1970s. Battery operated on photo card. $100.00–125.00.

TV GUIDES, 1976–1978. 05/08/76 Wagner; 05/18/78 Wagner. $10.00–15.00 each.

THE BRADY BUNCH

SEPTEMBER 26, 1969 —
AUGUST 30, 1974

117 EPISODES

PEAK POSITION:
#31 in the 1971–1972 season

—— CAST ——

Robert Reed
Mike

Florence Henderson
Carol

Barry Williams
Greg

Maureen McCormick
Marcia

Chris Knight
Peter

Eve Plumb
Jan

Mike Lookinland
Bobby

Susan Olsen
Cindy

Ann B. Davis
Alice

THE BRADY KIDS

SEPTEMBER 16, 1972 –
AUGUST 31, 1974

22 EPISODES
of the animated cartoon.

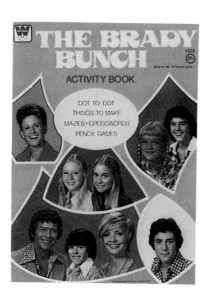

ACTIVITY BOOK #1252, Whitman, 1974. $30.00–40.00.

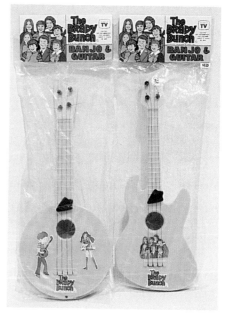

BANJO AND GUITAR, Larami, 1973, 5" x 14½". $60.00–80.00 each.

BOARD GAME, Whitman, 1973. $150.00–200.00.

BOYS TOYS, Larami, 1973. $75.00–100.00.

BRAIN TWISTERS, Larami, 1973. $40.00–50.00.

CHINESE & AMERICAN CHECKERS SET, Jay-Mar Products, 1973. Canadian toy on 6" x 11½" card. $30.00–40.00.

CHESS & CHECKERS, Larami, 1973. Two sets were made. Another set was packaged as just a chess set on a card. $40.00–50.00 each.

COLORING BOOKS, Whitman, 1972–1974. Four different including #1004 (1974), #1035 (1972), #1061 (1973) and #1657 (1974). $25.00–35.00 each.

CIGAR BANDS, R.J., 1970s. European set of 12. $75.00–100.00 set.

COMIC BOOKS #1-2, Dell, 1970. $50.00–60.00 each.

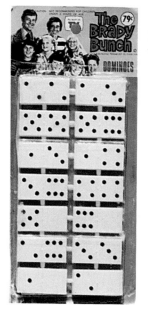

DOMINOES, Larami, 1973. $40.00–50.00.

COSTUME, Greg, Collegeville, 1969. Costume says "One of The Brady Bunch," but "Greg" is printed on box. $75.00–100.00.

FAN CLUB KIT, The Laufer Company, 1972. Offered through *Tiger Beat* and *Fave* magazines. Kit contains a personal message record, booklet with photos and bios, autographed portraits, stickers, birthday guide and fact sheet, membership card and wallet photos. $200.00–250.00.

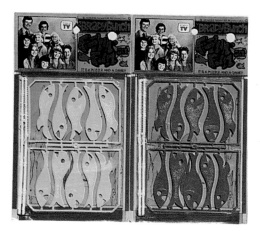

FISHIN' FUN SET, Larami, 1973. Made in purple or yellow. $30.00–40.00.

FRAME TRAY PUZZLE, Whitman, 1972. $50.00–75.00.

KITE FUN BOOK, Western Publishing Co., 1976. 5" x 7" booklet distributed by Pacific Gas & Electric, Southern California Edison and Florida Power & Light. Includes 16 pages of activities and comics that provide advice for safe kite flying. $35.00–45.00.

HAND TAMBOURINE, Larami, 1973. $40.00–50.00.

HEX-A-GAME, Larami, 1973. 5" x 8" $30.00–40.00.

LUNCH BOX, K.S.T., 1969. Metal box with metal thermos. $150.00–200.00 box; $50.00–75.00 thermos.

MAGIC SLATE, Whitman, 1973. $50.00–75.00.

OUTDOOR FUN SETS, Larami, 1973. Four different sets, including Gazebo, Swing Set, Carrousel, and Slide Set in 8" x 9" boxes. $40.00–50.00 each.

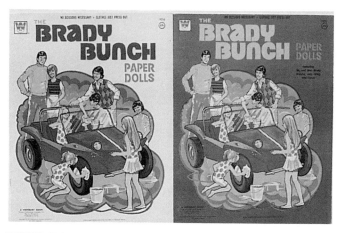

PAPER DOLL BOOKLETS #1976 and #1997, Whitman, 1973. Two different versions. White version has a pool inside; orange has no pool. $25.00–30.00 each cut; $40.00–50.00 each uncut.

PAPER DOLL BOXES, Whitman. #4784/7418, 1972 (left), #4320/7209, 1973 (center), and #4340/7420, 1974 (right). $40.00–50.00 each cut; $60.00–75.00 each uncut.

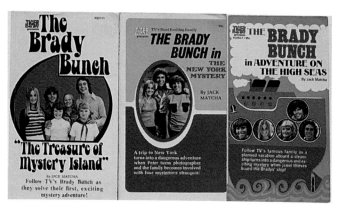

PAPERBACK BOOKS #1–5, Lancer, 1969–1970. $20.00–25.00 each #2 and 4; $10.00–15.00 each #1, 3, and 5.

PICK 'N' PLAY, Larami, 1973. $50.00–60.00.

PAPERBACK BOOKS, Tiger Beat, 1972–1973. *The Treasure of Mystery Island, The New York Mystery,* and *Adventure on the High Seas.* $8.00–12.00 each.

PISTOL PING PONG, Larami, 1973. $60.00–80.00.

RECORD/LP, "Meet the Brady Bunch," Paramount, 1972. $30.00–40.00.

RECORD/LP, "The Kids From the Brady Bunch," Paramount, 1972. $30.00–40.00.

RECORD/LP, "Merry Christmas from the Brady Bunch," Paramount, 1970. $75.00–100.00.

RECORD/LP, "Phonographic Album," Paramount, 1973. $30.00–40.00.

RECORD/LP, "Chris Knight & Maureen McCormick," Paramount, 1973. $100.00–150.00.

RECORDS/45s, Paramount, 1970–1973. "Frosty the Snowman"/"Silver Bells," (1970) and "Zuckerman's Famous Pig"/"Charlotte's Web," (1973) front and back pictured. Vocals by The Brady Bunch. $10.00–15.00 each without picture sleeve; $35.00–45.00 each with picture sleeve.

RECORD/45, "Love Doesn't Care Who's In It"/"Gum Drop," Capitol, 1974. Vocals by Mike Lookinland. $35.00–45.00.

RECORD/45, "Over and Over"/"Good For Each Other," Paramount, 1972. Vocals by Chris Knight. With a fold-open picture sleeve. $50.00–60.00.

RECORD/45, "Sweet Sweetheart"/"Sunny," Paramount, 1972. Vocals by Barry Williams. $40.00–50.00.

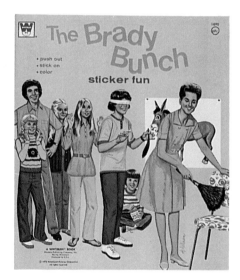

Left:
SHEET MUSIC, "(I'm a) Yo Yo Man," Martin Cooper Music, 1973. $40.00–50.00.

Right:
STICKER FUN BOOK, Whitman, 1973. $50.00–75.00.

SOUVENIR PHOTOS, Pitts Productions, 1973. 10" x 8" photo sold at The Brady Kids concerts. A black and white version was also offered. $20.00–25.00 each.

TALKING VIEW-MASTER #AVB568, Grand Canyon Adventure, GAF, 1971. $40.00–50.00.

TRADING CARDS, Topps, 1969. 88 cards in set with puzzle backs released in 1971. In 1970 a test set was issued with only the first 55 cards. Test cards are identical except for the copyright date and number of cards. No wrapper or box exists for the test cards. $800.00–900.00 set; $2,000–2,500 set, test cards; $10.00–15.00 single cards; $30.00–40.00 single test cards; $75.00–100.00 wrapper; $800.00–1,000.00 display box.

VIEW-MASTER #B568, Grand Canyon Adventure, GAF, 1971. $35.00–45.00.

OTHER ITEMS NOT PICTURED

BOOKLETS, *Chris Knight's Photo Album* and *The Secret of Chris Knight,* The Laufer Company, 1972. Sold as mail-away items through *Tiger Beat* and *Fave* magazines. $30.00–40.00 each.

COSTUME, Marcia, Collegeville, 1969. Box marked "Brady Bunch (Marcia)." $150.00–200.00.

DOLL, Kitty-Karry-All, Remco, 1969. Box has large photo of doll with a smaller cast photo that features Cindy holding the doll. Doll has blond pigtails and a dress with lots of pockets holding accessories. $150.00–175.00 loose; $400.00–500.00 boxed.

GOES SHOPPING, Larami, 1973. Plastic toy groceries in a window box with a photo of the three girls. $50.00–75.00.

JUMP ROPE, Larami, 1973. $50.00–75.00.

MOSAIC SET, Larami, 1973. Cast photo on 6½" x 11½" window display box containing a white pegboard with several color pegs used to create designs. $60.00–80.00.

PAPERBACK BOOK, "Every Girl Can Be Popular by Maureen McCormick," Tiger Beat, 1972. $30.00–40.00.

RECORD/45, "The Fortune Cookie Song"/"How Will It Be," RCA Records, 1971. Vocals by Eve Plumb. $20.00–30.00 without picture sleeve; $40.00–50.00 with picture sleeve.

RECORDS/45s, Paramount, 1972–1973. "Truckin' Back to You"/"Teeny Weeny Bit Too Long" (1973), "Little Bird"/"Just Singin' Alone" (1973) and "Harmonize"/"Love's in the Roses" (1974). Vocals by Maureen McCormick. All released without picture sleeves. $20.00–30.00 each.

RECORDS/45s, Paramount, 1972–1973. "We'll Always Be Friends"/"Time to Change" (1972); "I'd Love You to Want Me"/"Everything I Do" (1973); "Candy (Sugar Shoppe)"/"Drummer Man" (1972); "Time to Change"/"We Can Make the World a Whole Lot Brighter" (1972). All released without picture sleeves. $15.00–20.00 each.

SUPERMARKET, Larami, 1973. Plastic toy groceries in a cast photo window box. $50.00–75.00.

TOY TEA SET, Larami, 1973. Illustration of the Brady girls on card. $75.00–100.00.

TV GUIDE, 4/4/70 cast. $25.00–35.00.

THE BUGALOOS

SEPTEMBER 12, 1970 —
SEPTEMBER 2, 1972

17 EPISODES

— CAST —

Martha Raye
Benita Bizarre

Caroline Ellis
Joy

John Philpott
Courage

John McIndoe
I.Q.

Wayne Laryea
Harmony

Billy Barty
Sparky

Van Snowden
Tweeter

Joy Campbell
Woofer

Sharon Baird
Funky Rat

BOARD GAME, Milton Bradley, 1971. $50.00–60.00.

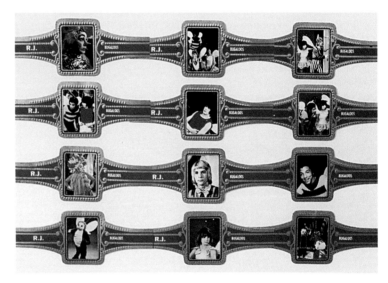

CIGAR BANDS, R.J., 1970s. European set of 12. $75.00–100.00 set.

Left:
COLORING BOOK #3967, Saalfield, 1971. $60.00–80.00.

Right:
LUNCH BOX, Aladdin, 1971. Metal box with plastic thermos. $100.00–125.00 box; $35.00–45.00 thermos.

COMIC BOOKS #1–4, Charlton, 1971–72. $20.00–30.00 each.

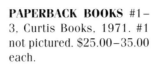

PAPERBACK BOOKS #1–3, Curtis Books, 1971. #1 not pictured. $25.00–35.00 each.

RECORD/LP, "The Bugaloos," Capitol Records, 1970. $50.00–60.00.

LUNCH BOX, Aladdin, 1971. Plastic version from Canada. $50.00–75.00.

RECORDS/45s, "The Senses of Our World"/"For a Friend," Capitol Records, 1971. Two different versions. One released in Japan with a picture sleeve and one in the United States without a picture sleeve. Japanese version pictured. $40.00–50.00 Japan; $10.00–15.00 United States.

OTHER ITEMS NOT PICTURED

BOOKLET, The Laufer Company, 1970s. Sold as a mail-away from *Tiger Beat* and *Fave* magazines. Contains text with black and white photos. $30.00–40.00.

COSTUMES, Ben Cooper, 1971. One style marked "Joy" has a sleeveless pink dress with a heart design. Another style has pant legs and an illustration of Courage, I.Q., and Harmony. $150.00–175.00 each.

CUT N' PASTE BOOK, Whitman, 1971. Illustrated cover similar to the coloring book. $75.00–100.00.

CHARLIE'S ANGELS

SEPTEMBER 22, 1976 —
AUGUST 19, 1981

115 EPISODES

PEAK POSITION:
#4 in the1977–1978 season

—— CAST ——

Kate Jackson
Sabrina Duncan

Jaclyn Smith
Kelly Garrett

Farrah Fawcett
Jill Munroe

Cheryl Ladd
Kris Munroe

Shelley Hack
Tiffany Welles

Tanya Roberts
Julie Rogers

David Doyle
John Bosley

John Forsythe
Charles Townsend

3-D VIEWER, Fleetwood, 1977. Plastic viewer made in three different colors, including yellow, blue and orange. $35.00–45.00.

A.M. WRIST RADIO, Illco, 1977. $250.00–300.00.

ANGELS' BEADS, Fleetwood, 1977. Sets vary with background photo of Sabrina, Kelly, Kris and Jill. Jewelry varies with show logo, title or the character names. $30.00–35.00 each.

ANGELS' COSMETICS, Fleetwood, 1977. $40.00–50.00.

ADVENTURE VAN, Hasbro, 1978. 16" plastic van for the 8½" dolls. $100.00–125.00.

BACKPACK, Travel Toys Inc., 1977. $125.00–150.00.

BEAUTY HAIR CARE SET, HG Toys, 1977. Jill or Kris version. $125.00–150.00

BEAUTY SETS, Fleetwood, 1977. Four different styles in yellow or white. $25.00–30.00 each.

BEAN BAG CHAIRS, Farrah, Zodiac Design, 1977. Small, medium, and large sizes, each made with three different photo variations. $300.00–400.00 each.

BEAUTY PRODUCTS, Farrah, Faberge, 1977. Several different products made in the United States. Canada made similar products with French titles. $15.00–20.00 each non-photo; $30.00–50.00 each photo.

BELT BUCKLES, Farrah, 1977. Two different styles, including a photo buckle and another shaped as a dripping faucet. $40.00–50.00 each.

BICYCLE, Huffy, 1970s. Obvious likeness of the show's logo on seat and "Angels" decals but does not include an official copyright. $75.00–100.00.

BOARD GAMES, Milton Bradley, 1977–1978. $20.00–30.00 each.

BOOK, *Cheryl Ladd,* 1981. 7" x 10" soft cover book from Japan. $40.00–50.00.

BOOK, *Drôles de Dames,* Ballantine Books, 1977. 5½" x 8" soft-cover book from Canada. $30.00–40.00.

BOOK, *Farrah Fawcett,* 1979. 6" x 8½" soft cover book from Japan. $40.00–50.00.

BOOK, *Farrah Fawcett Majors,* PAC Editions, 1978. 6½" x 9½" book from France. $30.00–40.00.

BOOK, *It Takes a Thief,* Stafford Pemberton, 1979. Made in the United Kingdom. Illustrated stories in a 7" x 8" hard cover book. $40.00–50.00.

BOOK, *Kate Jackson: A Special Kind of Angel,* EMC Corp., 1978. 8" x 9" hard cover book. $30.00–40.00.

BOOKLET, *Farrah, Kate and Jaclyn (An Unauthorized Biography),* 1976. Offered as a mail-away through teen magazines. $25.00–30.00.

BRITISH ANNUALS, Stafford Pemberton, 1978–1981. $25.00–35.00 each, 1978–80; $30.00–40.00, 1981.

BRUNCH BAG, Aladdin, 1977. Vinyl bag with plastic thermos. $100.00–125.00 bag; $15.00–20.00 thermos.

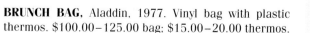

BUTTONS, Farrah, 1977. Several different styles. $15.00–20.00 each.

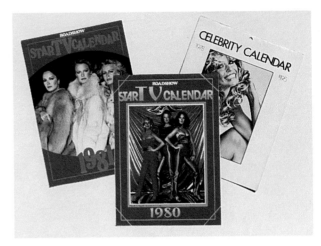

CALENDARS, 1978–1981. Several different. $30.00–40.00 each.

COIN PURSE, 1970s. 4" x 3½" silk purse. $100.00–125.00.

COLOURING BOOK, Stafford Pemberton, 1978. Made in the United Kingdom. $75.00–100.00.

COLORFORMS ADVENTURE SET, Colorforms, 1978. $40.00–50.00.

CORGI VANS, Mettoy, 1977. $30.00–40.00, 3"; $50.00–60.00, 5".

CUPS, MUGS, AND TUMBLERS, Farrah Fawcett, Thermo-Serv, 1977. Matching set for each of three styles. $20.00–30.00 each.

COSMETIC BEAUTY KIT, HG Toys, 1977. Jill or Kris version. $100.00–125.00.

CUPS, MUGS, AND TUMBLERS, Thermo-Serv, 1977. Matching set for Kris, Sabrina and Kelly. $50.00–75.00 each.

COSTUME, Farrah, Collegeville, 1977. $50.00–75.00.

COSTUME, Charlie's Angels, Collegeville, 1976. Box and costume marked "Charlie's Angels," but mask resembles Sabrina. Also made with a clear mask. $300.00–400.00.

DENIM JEANS, Azoulay, 1970s. $60.00–80.00.

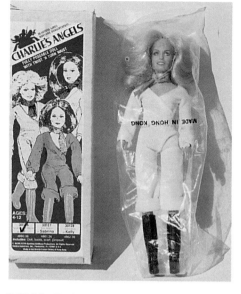

DOLLS, Kelly, Sabrina, Jill, and Kris, Hasbro, 1977. 8½" dolls. $20.00–25.00 each loose; $40.00–50.00 each carded.

DOLLS, Hasbro, 1977. 8½" dolls of Kelly, Sabrina, and Jill in boxes. Jill pictured. $20.00–25.00 each loose; $50.00–60.00 each boxed.

DOLLS, Cheryl Ladd and Kate Jackson, Mattel, 1978. 12" dolls. $35.00–45.00 each loose; $75.00–100.00 each boxed.

Left: **DOLL,** Farrah, Mego, 1980. 11½" doll. $25.00–35.00 loose; $75.00–100.00 boxed.
Right: **DOLL,** Farrah, OK Toys, 1970s. 11½" doll in plastic bag. Outfits vary with red, yellow or blue bathing suit or a white pantsuit. $30.00–40.00.

DOLLS, Farrah and Jaclyn Smith, Mego, 1977. 12¼" dolls. $35.00–45.00 Farrah loose; $45.00–55.00 Jaclyn loose; $75.00–100.00 Farrah boxed; $100.00–125.00 Jaclyn boxed.

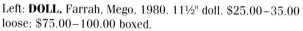

DOLL GIFT SETS, Hasbro, 1977. 8½" dolls in boxed sets with Jill or Kris versions. $175.00–200.00 each.

DOLL OUTFITS, Jill's Flying Skateboard Adventure/Kris' Flying Skateboard Adventure, Hasbro, 1977. Outfits for the 8½" dolls. Jill pictured. $40.00–50.00 Jill; $60.00–80.00 Kris.

DOLLS, Raynal, 1977. 8½" dolls made in Belgium $20.00–25.00 each loose; $75.00–100.00 each boxed.

DOLL OUTFITS AND ACTION GEAR, Raynal, 1977. Adventure sets made in Belgium for the 8½" dolls. $60.00–80.00 each.

DOLL OUTFITS AND ACTION GEAR, Hasbro, 1977. Adventure sets for the 8½" dolls. $40.00–50.00 each.

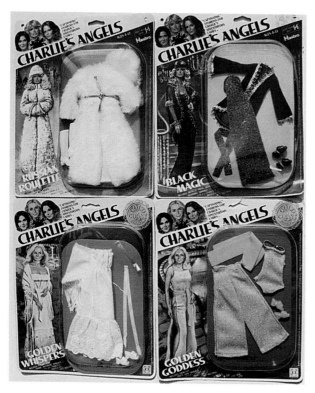

DOLL OUTFITS, Hasbro, 1977. Twelve different styles made by Hasbro in the United States for the 8½" dolls. Raynal made similar boxed outfits in Belgium. United States versions pictured. Russian Roulette and Black Magic also made for Kris doll. $30.00–40.00 each Hasbro outfit; $50.00–60.00 each Raynal outfit.

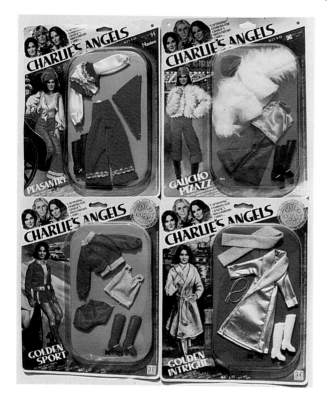

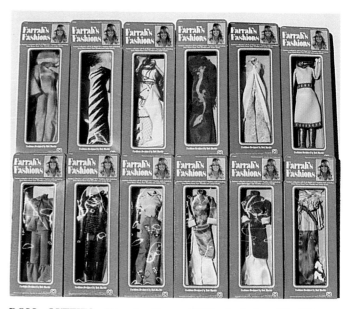

DOLL OUTFITS, Farrah, Mego, 1977. Includes 12 different boxed styles for the 12¼" doll. Top row (left to right): Pink Panther, Electric Feathers, Vagabond, Dragon Lady, Stepping Out, and Cherokee. Bottom row (left to right): Sun Kissed, Space Princess, Easy Living, Madame Chan (blue and red), and Peasant Lady. $50.00–60.00 each.

DOLL OUTFITS, Farrah, Mego, 1977. Includes four different carded styles for the 12¼" doll. Visions style made in pink and blue. $35.00–45.00 each.

DRESSER SETS, Fleetwood, 1977. Sets vary with photos of Sabrina, Kelly, Kris or Jill. Plastic comb, brush, and mirror came in different colors. $30.00–35.00 each.

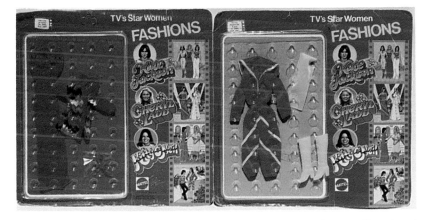

DOLL OUTFITS, TV's Star Women, Mattel, 1978. Outfits for the Cheryl and Kate 12" dolls. $25.00–35.00 each.

ELEGANT JEWELS, Fleetwood, 1977. $45.00–50.00.

FAN CLUB KIT, Charlie's Angels, 1977. Sabrina, Kelly and Kris featured in kit, which includes poster, iron-on, membership card, 35mm film strip and certificate. $175.00–200.00.

FAN CLUB KITS, Cheryl Ladd, FCCA, 1978–1979. 1979 kit pictured. $75.00–100.00 each.

FAN CLUB KIT, Farrah, FCCA, 1977. $100.00–125.00.

FAN CLUB KIT, Farrah, FCCA, 1980. $100.00–125.00.

FARRAH's GLAMOUR CENTERS, Mego, 1977. Regular or growing hair versions. $60.00–80.00 each.

FARRAH'S DRESSING ROOM PLAYSET, Mego, 1977. Playset for the 12¼" doll. $125.00–150.00.

FASHION DRESS-UP SET, HG Toys, 1978. $175.00–200.00.

FASHION TOTE, Hasbro, 1978. Carrying case for 8½" dolls and outfits. $35.00–45.00.

GOLDEN ALL-STAR BOOK #6420, Golden Press, 1977. Illustrated story-book. $20.00–25.00.

HAIR DRYER, Fleetwood, 1977. Jill or Kris versions. Jill version pictured. $35.00–45.00 each.

HIDE-A-WAY HOUSE PLAYSET, Hasbro, 1978. Playset for the 8½" dolls. Jill or Kris version. $150.00–175.00.

IRON-ONS, 1970s. Several different. $20.00–25.00 each.

JEWELRY SETS, Fleetwood, 1977. Different styles, including a heart-shaped pendant with a photo of Jill, Kelly, or Sabrina. $30.00–35.00 each.

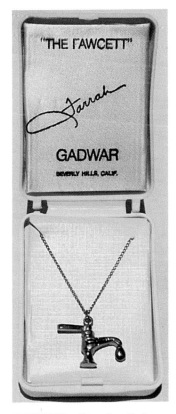

JEWELRY, Farrah, Gadwar, 1977. Several styles, including 14K gold-plated (shown), sterling silver, 14K gold with move-able handle, and 1½K diamond encrusted. Each has Farrah's engraved signature. $75.00–100.00 gold-plated.

IRON-ON TRANSFER PLUS FRAME-ABLE POSTER PRINTS, Photo-Lith International, 1970s. Matching iron-on and photo. Several different styles. $25.00–35.00 each.

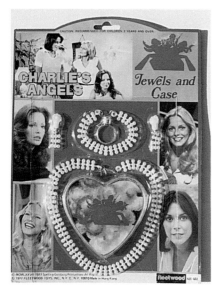

JEWELS AND CASE, Fleetwood, 1977. $35.00–45.00.

JIGSAW PUZZLE, HG Toys, 1977. 500-piece puzzle in a 9" x 11½" box. $30.00–40.00.

JIGSAW PUZZLE, HG Toys, 1976. 250-piece puzzle in a 7½" x 19" box. $40.00–50.00.

JIGSAW PUZZLES, HG Toys, 1976–1977. Six different United States versions by HG Toys, including #435-02 through #435-04 that feature Jill (1976), and #435-05 through #435-07 that feature Kris (1977). Kris versions contain the caption "The New Charlie's Angels." Frolic made Canadian versions with "The New" blocked out on packaging. $25.00–30.00 each.

JIGSAW PUZZLES, Farrah, APC, 1977. Three different 200-piece puzzles in 8½" x 11" boxes. $30.00–35.00 each.

JIGSAW PUZZLE, Farrah, APC, 1977. 405-piece puzzle in a 12½" x 16½" box. $35.00–40.00.

PENDANTS, Fleetwood, 1977. Several different. $40.00–50.00
Kris; $30.00–40.00 each for others.

PINBALL MACHINE,
Gottlieb & Co., 1978.
Full-size arcade game.
$800.00–1,000.00.

PILLOWS, Farrah, Zodiac Design, 1977.
Small, medium, and large sizes made with
three different photo variations. $100.00–
150.00 each.

PLAY MONEY, Farrah, 1970s. Several different. $15.00–20.00 each.

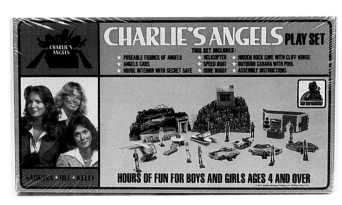

PLAY SET, Toy Factory, 1977. Includes cardboard punch-out characters, vehicles, helicopter, and buildings in an 18" x 10" box. $100.00–125.00.

POCKETBOOK RADIO, Illco Toys, 1977. Vinyl bag varies with or without photo sticker. $175.00–200.00.

POSTER ART KIT, HG Toys, 1977. Boxed version. $50.00–75.00.

POCKET FOLDERS, Stuart Hall, 1977. Several different. $30.00–40.00 each.

POSTER ART KITS, Board King/HG Toys, 1977. Board King made a board version with Kris, and HG Toys made a board version with Jill. $40.00–60.00 each.

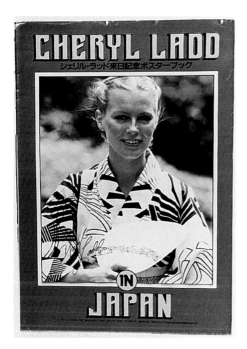

POSTER MAGAZINES #1-3, *Charlie's Angels Official Poster Monthly,* Paradise Press, 1977. $50.00–75.00 each.

POSTER MAGAZINE, *Cheryl Ladd in Japan,* 1970s. $35.00–45.00.

POSTER PUT-ONS, Bi-Rite Enterprises, Inc., 1977. Several different 8" x 10" styles to match various posters. $15.00–20.00 each.

POSTER PEN SET, Farrah Fawcett, Craft House, 1977. Includes a 16" x 22" poster on back. $75.00–100.00.

POSTER, Shelley Hack, Western Graphics Corporation, 1979. 21" x 32". $40.00–50.00.

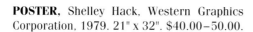

POSTERS, Charlie's Angels, 1976–1979. Several different cast posters. 23" x 35" Bi-Rite Enterprises, Inc., 1976 pictured. Others include: 23" x 35" Charlie's Angels '77–'78, Bi-Rite Enterprises, Inc., 1977; 23" x 35" Charlie's Angels '79, Bi-Rite Enterprises, Inc., 1979; 18" x 24" Charlie's Angels, 1970s. $30.00–50.00 each.

POSTERS, Jaclyn Smith, 1977–1979. Several different. 20" x 28" Jaclyn, Pro Arts Inc., 1979 pictured. Others include: 23" x 35" Kelly of Charlie's Angels, Bi-Rite Enterprises, Inc., 1977; 20" x 28" Ms. Smith, Pro Arts Inc., 1979; 20" x 28" Jaclyn Gold, Pro Arts Inc., 1979; 20" x 28" Jaclyn Pink, Pro Arts, Inc., 1979. $20.00–30.00 each Bi-Rite; $50.00–75.00 each Pro Arts.

POSTERS, Kate Jackson, 1977–1979. Several different. 20" x 28" Kate, Pro Arts Inc., 1979 pictured. Others include: 23" x 35" Sabrina of Charlie's Angels, Bi-Rite Enterprises, Inc., 1977; 20" x 28" Ms. Jackson, Pro Arts Inc., 1979; 28" x 40" Super Jackson, Pro Arts Inc., 1979. $75.00–100.00 Super Jackson; $50.00–75.00 each Pro Arts; $20.00–30.00 Bi-Rite.

POSTERS, Farrah, 1976–1979. Several different. 20" x 28" Mrs. Majors, Pro Arts Inc., 1977 pictured. Others include: 23" x 35" Farrah Fawcett-Majors as Jill of Charlie's Angels, Bi-Rite Enterprises, Inc., 1976; 20" x 28" Farrah, Pro Arts Inc., 1977; 20" x 28" Farrah Flower, Pro Arts Inc., 1977; 20" x 28" L.A. Farrah, Pro Arts Inc., 1977; 20" x 28" Farrah Paisley, Pro Arts Inc., 1977; 20" x 28" Farrah Blue, Pro Arts Inc., 1979; 28" x 40" Super Farrah, Pro Arts Inc., 1977. 24" x 72" Farrah Door Poster, Pro Arts Inc., $30.00–40.00; Farrah, L.A. Farrah, Farrah Flower, Farrah Fawcett-Majors as Jill, $60.00–80.00 each others.

POSTERS, Cheryl Ladd, 1977–1979. 20" x 28" Ms. Ladd, Pro Arts Inc., 1977 pictured. Others include: 23" x 35" Cheryl Ladd as Kris of Charlie's Angels, Bi-Rite Enterprises, Inc., 1977; 20" x 28" Cheryl Lace, Pro Arts Inc., 1978; 20" x 28" Cheryl Ladd, Pro Arts Inc., 1977; 20" x 28" Cheryl Black, Pro Arts Inc., 1979; 24" x 72" Giant Ladd, 1978. $50.00–75.00 Cheryl Black or Giant Ladd; $30.00–40.00 each others.

PRESS OUT BOOK, Stafford Pemberton, 1979. Made in the United Kingdom. $100.00–125.00.

PURSE, Farrah, Vanidades, 1970s. $40.00–50.00.

RAINY DAY SET, Travel Toys Inc., 1977. 12" x 18". $175.00–200.00.

RECORD/45, "You"/"Let Me Get To Know You," Nelson Barry Recordings, 1977. Vocals by J.P. Vigon with Farrah Fawcett on side A only. $40.00–50.00.

RECORDS/45s, Cheryl Ladd, Capitol/Warner Brothers, 1974–1982. Capitol issued "Think It Over"/"Here Is A Song" (1978) and "Missing You"/"Thunder In The Distance" (1979). $3.00–5.00 each without picture sleeves; $10.00–15.00 each with picture sleeves.
Other singles include: "Mama Don't Be Blue"/"The Family" with picture sleeve (Warner Brothers, 1974); "Country Love"/"He's Lookin' More Everyday Like The Man Who Broke My Heart" without picture sleeve (Capitol, 1976); "Skinny Dippin'"/"Good Good Lovin'" without picture sleeve (Capitol, 1978); "Skinny Dippin' (Disco Version)' 12" single with duplicate B side and no picture sleeve (Capitol, 1978); "You Make It Beautiful"/"Can't Say No To You" vocals with Frankie Valli, without picture sleeve (Capitol, 1982). $30.00–40.00 each with picture sleeve; $10.00–15.00 each others.

RECORDS/LPs, Cheryl Ladd, Capitol, 1978–1979. "Cheryl Ladd" (1978) and "Dance Forever" (1979). $15.00–20.00 each.

RECORDS/45s, Cheryl Ladd, Capitol, 1978–1981. Japanese imports with picture sleeves, including: "Think It Over"/"Here Is A Song" (1978); "Walking In The Rain"/"I'll Come Running" (1978); "Dance Forever"/ "Missing You" (1979); "Where Is Someone To Love Me"/"Just Like Old Time" (1980); "Walking In The Rain"/"I'll Come Running" reissued picture sleeve (1978); "Just Another Lover Tonight"/"Television" (1981); "Take A Chance"/"Victim of the Circumstance" (1981). $10.00– 15.00 each without picture sleeves; $25.00–30.00 each with picture sleeves.

RECORDS/LPs, Cheryl Ladd, Capitol, 1978–1983. Japanese imports: "The Best of Cheryl Ladd" (1983); "You Make It Beautiful" (1982), with four songs, two of which are with Frankie Valli; "Take A Chance" (1981) with poster and song lyric sheet. $40.00–50.00 each.

Other Japanese LPs include: "The Best of Cheryl Ladd" (1980); "Cheryl Ladd," same as United States' version (1978); "Dance Forever," same as United States' version (1979). $40.00–50.00 1980 LP; $25.00–30.00 each others.

RUGS, Farrah, Zodiac Design, 1977. Three different 18" x 24"" rugs. $100.00–125.00 each.

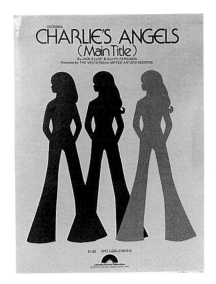

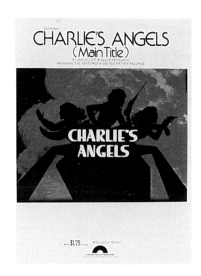

SHEET MUSIC, "Cheryl Ladd - Think It Over," Kengorus Music, 1978. $15.00–20 00.

SHEET MUSIC, "Charlie's Angels Theme," Columbia, 1977. Two different covers. $20.00–25.00 each.

Left:
SHEET MUSIC, "Farrah," Brut Productions, Inc. 1978. $40.00–50.00.

Right:
SHOULDER BAG, Fleetwood, 1977. $35.00–45.00.

SPIRAL NOTEBOOKS, Poster Books, 1977. Several different. $40.00–50.00 each.

SPIRAL NOTEBOOKS, Stuart Hall, 1977. Several different. $40.00–50.00 each.

T-SHIRTS, 1970s. Several different. $30.00–40.00 each.

Left:
SUNGLASSES, Fleetwood, 1977. Also made in yellow. $35.00–45.00.

Right:
TALK-TIME TELEPHONE, Fleetwood, 1977. Made in pink or blue. $35.00–45.00.

Left:
TARGET SET, Placo Toys, 1977. Jill or Kris version. $60.00–80.00.

Right:
TOY FASHION WATCH, GLJ Toy Co., 1977. $50.00–75.00.

TRADING CARDS, Monty Gum, 1979. 100-card set made in Holland. 2" x 1¾" in size. $300.00–400.00 set; $3.00–5.00 single cards; $20.00–25.00 wrapper; $300.00–400.00 display box.

TRADING CARDS SET #1, Topps, 1977. 55 cards and 11 stickers in set. Similar sets made in other countries with slightly higher values. $55.00–65.00 set; $1.25–1.50 single stickers; 75¢–$1.00 single cards; $5.00–8.00 wrapper; $20.00–25.00 box.

TRADING CARDS SET #2, Topps, 1977. 66 cards and 11 stickers in set. Similar sets made in other countries with slightly higher values. $55.00–65.00 set; $1.00–1.50 single stickers; 75¢–$1.00 single cards; $5.00–8.00 wrapper; $20.00–25.00 display box.

TRADING CARDS SET #3, Topps, 1977. 66 cards and 11 stickers in set. Similar sets made in other countries with slightly higher values. $45.00–55.00 set; $1.00–1.25 single stickers; 50¢–75¢ single cards; $3.00–5.00 wrapper; $15.00–20.00 display box.

TRADING CARDS SET #4, Topps, 1977. 66 cards and 11 stickers in set. Similar sets made in other countries with slightly higher values. $45.00–55.00 set; $1.00–1.25 single stickers; 50¢–75¢ single cards; $3.00–5.00 wrapper; $15.00–20.00 display box.

VENDING MACHINE JEWELRY DISPLAY, The Real Faucet, 1977. Plastic faucet keychains and necklaces. $40.00–50.00.

TRAVELERS, Fleetwood, 1977. $35.00–45.00.

WALLET, Travel Toy Inc., 1977. Blue or tan. $35.00–45.00.

OTHER ITEMS NOT PICTURED

CUBEMENSIONAL PUZZLE, Sharin Toy Co., 1977. Cardboard puzzle cube featuring Kris, Kelly, and Sabrina. $250.00–300.00.

FARRAH'S TRAVEL TRUNK, Mego, 1977. Made in Canada for the 12" doll. Photo of Farrah on packaging. $175.00–200.00.

RECORD/45, "Charlie's Angels Theme"/"Starsky and Hutch Theme," United Artists, 1977. Original theme for the TV series released without a picture sleeve. Instrumentals by the New Ventures. $15.00–20.00.

THREE-RING BINDERS, Stuart Hall, 1977. Different styles. $50.00–75.00 each.

TV GUIDES, 1976–1979. 09/25/76 Smith, Fawcett & Jackson; 05/21/77 Fawcett; 02/18/78 Smith, Ladd & Jackson; 08/26/78 Ladd; 12/29/79 Smith, Ladd & Hack. $20.00–25.00 each.

WALKIE-TALKIES, LJN Toys, 1976. Pair in window box with photos of Jill, Kelly, and Sabrina on packaging. $300.00–400.00.

WRISTWATCH, Farrah, 1970s. $100.00–125.00.

CHiPs

.45 MAGNUM TARGET SET, Larami, 1983. Back of card includes a full-color firing target. $30.00–40.00.

BOOK 'EM SET, Larami, 1983. Back of card includes a full-color firing target. $30.00–40.00.

SEPTEMBER 15, 1977 –
JULY 18, 1983

139 EPISODES

PEAK POSITION:
#19 in the 1979–1980 season

—— CAST ——

Erik Estrada
Officer Francis "Ponch" Poncherello

Larry Wilcox
Officer Jon Baker

Robert Pine
Sergeant Joe Getraer

Randi Oakes
Officer Bonnie Clark

Paul Linke
Officer Arthur Grossman

Tom Reilly
Officer Bobby "Hot Dog" Nelson

Tina Gayle
Officer Kathy Linahan

BOARD GAME, Ideal, 1981. $25.00–35.00.

BOARD GAME, Milton Bradley, 1977. $20.00–25.00.

BRITISH ANNUALS, World, 1980–1984. $20.00–25.00 each.

BULLHORN, Placo Toys, 1977. Plastic horn with header card. $25.00–35.00.

COLORING BOOK & ACCESSORIES SET, Play Press, 1983. 12" x 14" Italian coloring book packaged with Police Accessories Set (separated for photo). $50.00–60.00 set.

COLORFORMS, Colorforms, 1981. $20.00–25.00.

COSTUME, CHiPs officer, Ben Cooper, 1978. $30.00–40.00.

COLORING & ACTIVITY BOOKS, Waldman, 1983. Four different. $10.00–15.00 each.

DIE-CAST VEHICLES, Imperial, 1980. Several different. Helicopter and Rescue Ambulance not pictured. Five vehicles were also packaged in a window display box. $20.00–25.00 each; $75.00–100.00 boxed set.

DOLLS, Ponch, Jon, and Sarge, Mego, 1980. $20.00–25.00 each loose. $40.00–50.00 each carded.

EMERGENCY MEDICAL KIT, Empire, 1980. $30.00–40.00.

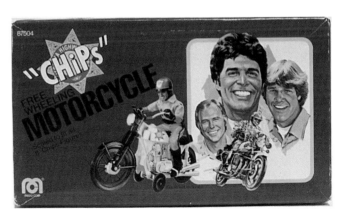

FREE WHEELING MOTORCYCLE, Mego, 1980. For the 8" dolls. $50.00–60.00.

FIGURES, Mego, 1977. Ponch, Sarge, Wheels Willy, Jimmy Squeaks, Jon, and Motorcycle. Jon and Motorcycle not pictured. $20.00–25.00 each.

HIGHWAY PATROL LAUNCHER & MOTOR-CYCLE, Mego, 1981. $35.00–45.00.

HIGHWAY PATROL CAR, Fleet-wood, 1978. $25.00–30.00.

JIGSAW PUZZLES, HG Toys, Inc., 1977. Three different, including Ponch, Jon, and #483-01 pictured. $20.00–25.00 each.

LUNCH BOX, Thermos, 1977. Plastic box with plastic thermos. $45.00–55.00 box; $15.00–20.00 thermos.

MOTORCYCLE HELMET SET, HG Toys, Inc., 1979. 15" x 6" x 16" $100.00–125.00.

MODEL KITS, Revell, 1980–1981. Several different, including Jon's Chevy 4x4 with T-shirt iron-on (1981), Kawasaki motorcycle (1980), Helicopter (1980), Ponch's Firebird with T-shirt iron-on (1980), and Z-28 Chase Car (1981). $30.00–45.00 each.

MOTORCYCLE POLICE ACTION SET, HG Toys, Inc., 1977. 12" x 2" x 15" $75.00–100.00.

MOTORCYCLE PATROL, Fleetwood, 1978. A similar package was issued in 1977 without a figure and labeled as "Motorcycle." $20.00–25.00.

POLICE ACCESSORIES SET, Fleetwood, 1978. $25.00–35.00.

Left:
POLICE ACCESSORIES SET, Paris Jouets, 1981. Made in France. $30.00–40.00.

Right:
POLICE BACK-UP COPTER, Fleetwood, 1977. $25.00–30.00.

POLICE SET, Buddy L, 1981. 15" x 4" x 10½" $100.00–125.00.

POSTER, Erik Estrada, 1970s. 18" x 24" $20.00–25.00.

POSTER, Dargis Associates, Inc., 1977. 23" x 35" $25.00–30.00.

POSTER, Erik Estrada, 1970s. 28" x 36" and a smaller size was also made. $25.00–30.00 large; $20.00–25.00 small.

Other posters include 25½" x 38" Estrada Giant, Fan Fares Inc., 1980; 17½" x 23" Estrada close-up, 1970s; 23" x 35" Estrada holding helmet, Dargis Associates, Inc., 1970s; 20" x 28" Randi Oakes, C/C Sales, 1980. $20.00–30.00 each.

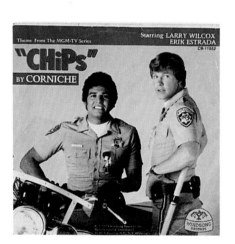

POSTER, Erik Estrada, Dargis Associates, Inc., 1979. 20" x 28" $20.00–25.00.

RECORD/45, Theme/"California Hustle," Windsong Records, 1979. Instrumentals by Corniche. $15.00–20.00.

RESCUE BRONCO, Fleetwood, 1979. $25.00–30.00.

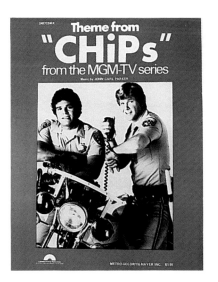

RESCUE COPTER, Fleetwood, 1979. $25.00–30.00.

SHEET MUSIC, "Theme from CHiPs," MGM Inc., 1979. $15.00–20.00.

SPIRAL NOTEBOOKS, Ponch, Stuart Hall, 1979. 6" x 9½" and 8½" x 11" sizes. $15.00–20.00 each.

Left:
RESCUE SQUAD POLICE BRON-CO, Buddy L, 1981. 5" x 3½" metal and plastic truck. $25.00–30.00.

Right:
SUNGLASSES, Fleetwood, 1977. $15.00–20.00.

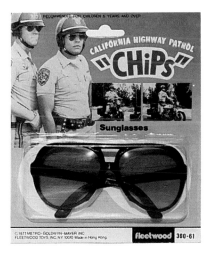

SUNGLASSES, WALLET, I.D. CARD & BADGE SETS, Fleetwood, 1978. Two variations. $20.00–25.00 each.

TARGET SET, Placo Toys, 1981. $60.00–80.00.

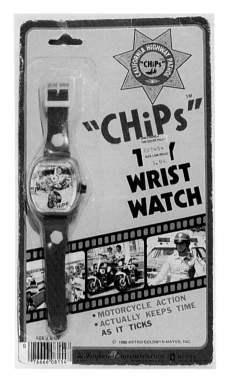

TRADING CARDS, Donruss, 1979. 60 numbered and 6 unnumbered stickers in set with puzzle backs. $40.00–50.00 set; 50¢–75¢ single stickers; $3.00–5.00 wrapper; $20.00–25.00 display box.

TOY WRISTWATCH, Imperial, 1980. Photo of Ponch and Jon on watch face. Moving motorcycle on hand. $40.00–50.00.

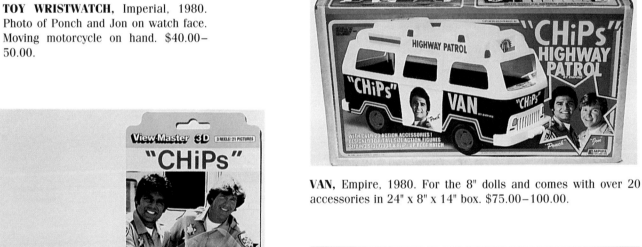

VAN, Empire, 1980. For the 8" dolls and comes with over 20 accessories in 24" x 8" x 14" box. $75.00–100.00.

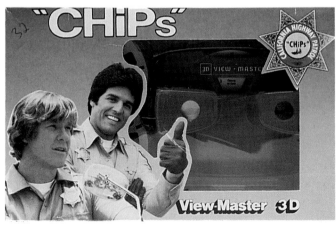

VIEW-MASTERS #L14 and #51, GAF, 1980. Envelope made in the United States and #51 was made in Belgium and packaged on a card for the United Kingdom. $15.00–20.00 U.S.; $25.00–30.00 U.K.

VIEW-MASTER #BL 014, View Master International, 1980. Made in Belgium for the United Kingdom. $35.00–40.00.

WALLET, Larami, 1979. Color of wallet varies. $25.00–30 00.

WALLET, Imperial, 1981. $20.00–25.00.

WIND N' WATCH SPEEDSTER, Buddy L, 1981. Packaging varies with a vertical or horizontal card $35.00–40.00.

OTHER ITEMS NOT PICTURED

BATTERY-OPERATED MOTORCYLE, 1970s. With figure attached. $50.00–60.00.

BICYCLE SIREN, 1970s. $30.00–35.00.

BINOCULARS, 1970s. Boxed. $30.00–40.00.

CAMERA, Fleetwood, 1978. Working 110 camera on card. $40.00–50.00.

COPTER, Empire, 1980. Two-foot plastic helicopter in box. $100.00–125.00.

FAN CLUB KIT, Erik Estrada, Fan Fares Inc., 1979. Called "The Smiling Circle," the fan club offered members seven photos, a welcome letter from Erik, biography profile, membership card and certificate, 18" x 24" exclusive color poster, and color folder to hold contents. $50.00–75.00.

FIGURES WITH VEHICLES, Mego, 1981. Packaged sets include Jon with motorcycle on card and Sarge with police car in a window display box. $50.00–75.00 each.

GUN HOLSTER & BADGE SET, Fleetwood, 1981. On illustrated card. $25.00–30.00.

HANDCUFFS, GUN, & BADGE SET, Fleetwood, 1977. On photo card. $30.00–35.00.

IRON-ONS, 1970s. Several different. $15.00–20.00 each.

MAGAZINE, *Erik's Personal Scrapbook,* Sterling, 1970s. *Teen Machine Magazine.* $15.00–20.00.

MOTORCYCLE, Empire, 1980. Similar to a "Big Wheel" riding toy with pedal action. $200.00–250.00.

MOTORCYCLE & BADGE SET, Fleetwood, 1977. Set on card. $30.00–35.00.

PAPERBACK BOOK, *The Erik Estrada Scrapbook,* Tempo Books, 1980. $10.00–15.00.

POLICE ACCESSORIES SET, Fleetwood, 1970s, Cap gun refills on card. $5.00–10.00.

POLICE SET WITH WATER JET, HG Toys, 1980. Boxed set. $50.00–75.00.

PUFFY STICKERS, Imperial, 1981. Six different. $10.00–15.00 each.

REMOTE CONTROL POLICE CAR, Pro Cision, 1982. 10" x 6" box picturing Ponch and Jon. $60.00–80.00.

REMOTE CONTROL MOTORCYCLE, Pro Cision, 1982. 16" x 9" photo box with bike and figures. $60.00–80.00.

SLEEPING BAG, 1977. $50.00–75.00.

SLOT CAR RACING SET, Ideal, 1981. Includes motorcycle and van slot cars in illustrated box. $75.00–100.00.

TARGET SET, 1978. Set comes with airflow power gun and safety flex darts. $60.00–80.00.

TV GUIDES, 1979–1982. 02/03/79 cast illustrated; 01/12/80 Estrada and Wilcox; 01/30/82 cast illustrated. $10.00–15.00 each.

DONNY & MARIE

JANUARY 23, 1976 –
JANUARY 19, 1979

73 EPISODES

PEAK POSITION:
Not in the top 25

—— CAST ——

Donny Osmond
Marie Osmond
Jimmy Osmond
and the Osmond Brothers

ADDRESS BOOK, AUTOGRAPH ALBUM, and DIARY, Continental Plastics Corp., 1977. $15.00–20.00 each.

BOARD GAME, Mattel, 1977. $25.00–35.00.

BATTERY POWERED TOOTHBRUSH, Pamco, 1977. With interchangeable scenes for the television set and toothbrushes for antennas. $50.00–75.00.

BOOKS, Osmond Publishing Co., 1979. *Disco Dancing with Donny & Marie* and *Close Dancing With Donny & Marie.* Other books include: *Donny & Marie: Breaking All the Rules,* EMC Corporation, 1977; *Donny & Marie,* Children's Press, 1978; *Donny & Marie,* Creative Education, 1980. $10.00–15.00 each.

BUTTONS, Pinning Co., 1976. 3" in diameter. Different styles. $5.00–8.00 each.

COLORFORMS DRESS-UP SET, Colorforms, 1977. Oversized 16" x 13" box. $35.00–45.00.

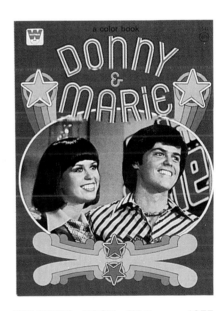

COLORING BOOK, Whitman, 1977. Paper dolls on back with clothes to color inside. $15.00–20.00.

CLOTHING LINE, Olive's Kids, Omnico, 1970s. Clothing line sponsored by Donny and Marie's mother, Olive Osmond. Each article has a tag attached with an illustration of the trio on the front and a "Thank you for your purchase" message on the back. $40.00–50.00 each tagged article.

CAMERA & PHOTO ALBUM SET, Gordy, 1976. $35.00–40.00.

COUNTRY AND ROCK RHYTHM SET & COUNTRY AND ROCK BAND, Gordy, 1976. $25.00–30.00 each.

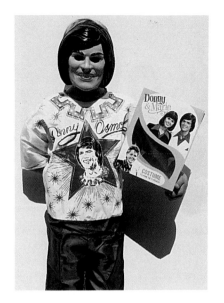

COSTUME, Donny, Collegeville, 1977. $30.00–40.00.

COSTUME, Marie, Collegeville, 1977. $30.00–40.00.

COSTUME, Jimmy, Collegeville, 1977. $30.00–40.00.

DOLLS, Donny and Marie, Mattel, 1976. 12" dolls sold separately or as a gift set. $15.00–20.00 each loose; $45.00–55.00 each boxed; $100.00–125.00 gift set.

Right:
DOLL, Marie, Mattel, 1976. 30" modeling doll with dress patterns inside. $50.00–60.00 loose; $100.00–125.00 boxed.

DOLL CASE, Mattel, 1978. $30.00–40.00.

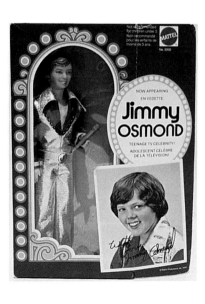

DOLL, Jimmy, Mattel, 1978. 10" doll. Canadian version pictured. $30.00–40.00 loose; $60.00–80.00 boxed.

DOLL OUTFITS, Mattel, 1976. Four different carded outfits for Donny and eight for Marie. Styles include Silver Shimmer, Starlight Night, Deepest Purple, and South o' the Border for both dolls. Marie exclusive styles include Soft Summer Night, Warm Wrap-Up, Satin 'n' Shine, and Fire on Ice. Starlight Night pictured. $20.00–25.00 each.

GOLDEN ALL-STAR BOOKS, Golden Press, 1977. $8.00–10.00 each.

DOLL OUTFITS, Mattel, 1977. Four different boxed styles for both Donny and Marie. Styles include Silver 'n' Shine, Country Hoedown, Glimmer O' Gold, and Peasant Sensation. Glimmer O' Gold pictured. $20.00–25.00 each.

GUITARS, Lapin, 1977. Two similar styles were made, including a 30" Country style and a 20" Rock style. Country style pictured. $60.00–80.00 each.

FRAME TRAY PUZZLES #B4542-1 and #B4542-2, Whitman, 1977. $10.00–15.00 each.

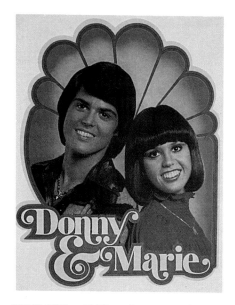

IRON-ONS, 1970s. Several different. $10.00–15.00 each.

JIGSAW PUZZLE, Whitman, 1976. Made in the United Kingdom. Box measures 8½" x 7". $30.00–40.00.

LITTLE GOLDEN BOOK, *Top Secret Project,* Golden Press, 1977. $8.00–10.00.

LUNCH BOX, Aladdin, 1976. Vinyl box and plastic thermos. $75.00–100.00 box; $10.00–15.00 thermos.

LUNCH BOX, Aladdin, 1977. Vinyl box and plastic thermos. $75.00–100.00 box; $10.00–15.00 thermos.

MAGAZINES, 1976–1977. Issue #1 of *Tiger Beat Presents Donny & Marie* by Laufer Publications, Inc. (1977), *Donny & Marie* Vol. 3, No. 2 by Laufer Publications, Inc. (1976) and *TV Superstar #3* by Sterling's Magazine (1977). Issues #2–4 of *Tiger Beat Presents Donny & Marie* not pictured. $15.00–20.00 each.

MAGIC SLATES, Whitman, 1977. Two different, including another version with a yellow background. $30.00–40.00 each.

MAIL-AWAY ITEMS, Osbro Productions, 1970s. Donny's purple socks and Sweet Dreams pillow case pictured. Several other items were offered exclusively through mail order, including: Donny and Marie message board; Donny's purple sock keychain; wall clock with black and white photo; paper kite with photo; 10" figural candles of Donny and Marie holding microphones; charm bracelet; posters; 2⅛" photo buttons; T-shirts; and Marie's heart necklace with roses. $30.00–50.00 each.

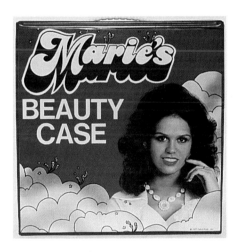

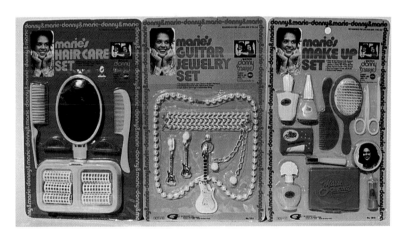

MARIE'S BEAUTY CASE, Osbro, 1977. 11" x 11" vinyl case. $30.00–35.00.

MARIE SETS, Gordy, 1976. Seven different sets. Hair Care Set, Guitar Jewelry Set, and Make-Up Set pictured. Others include a Hair Dryer Set, High Heel Shoes Set, Dresser Set, and Jewelry Set. $25.00–35.00 each.

MARIE'S BEAUTY PRODUCTS, 1976–1977. Several different products, including a Complexion Care Set and cologne by Luzier, Inc., 1977, and Your Face and Mine Set by Osbro Productions, Inc., 1976. $25.00–30.00 each.

MARIE'S MAKEUP CENTER, Mattel, 1976. $60.00–80.00.

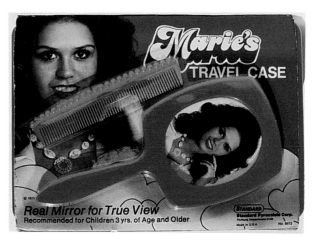

MARIE'S TRAVEL CASE, Standard Pyroxoloid Corp., 1977. $35.00–45.00.

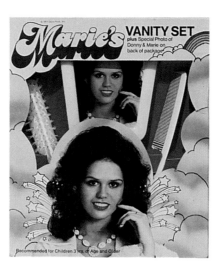

MARIE'S VANITY SET, Gordy, 1976. $30.00–40.00.

MARIE'S SHOULDER BAG, Gordy, 1976. $35.00–45.00.

MICROPHONE & SONG SHEETS, Gordy, 1976. $25.00–30.00.

MINI DRUM SET, JRI Inc., 1977. Play drum set in 22½" x 8½" box. $100.00–125.00.

NECKLACES, Osbro Productions, 1977. Several different. $20.00–25.00 each.

PAINT BY NUMBER SETS, Friends Industries Inc., 1977. Two different sets #801 and #802. Both boxes have the same photo with a different scene to paint inside. $30.00–40.00 each.

PAPER DOLL BOOKLET #1991, Whitman, 1977. $15.00–20.00.

PAPERBACK BOOKS, 1970s. Several different, including *The Real Donny & Marie*, Zebra Books, 1977, with T-shirt iron-on inside, *On Tour With Donny & Marie*, Tempo Books, 1977, and *Donny and Marie: The Dynamic Duo of Television*, Bonomo Publications, Inc., 1979. $5.00–10.00 each.

Left:
POCKET AM RADIO, LJN Toys, 1977. 3" x 5" $35.00–45.00.

Right:
PORTABLE RECORD PLAYERS, Peerless Vidtronic Corp., 1977. Two different styles to match record carrying cases. Yellow version not pictured. $40.00–50.00 each.

PORTABLE RECORD PLAYER & AM RADIO, LJN Toys, 1977. Comes with microphone to sing along. $50.00–75.00.

POSTERS, 1976–1979. Several different, including 23" x 35" Donny & Marie, #3575, Dargis Associates Inc., 1977 pictured. Others include: 23" x 35" Donny & Marie Collage, Dargis Associates Inc., 1976; 20" x 28" Donny & Marie, Pro Arts Inc., 1979; 28" x 40" Super Donny & Marie, Pro Arts Inc., 1979; 23" x 35" Donny & Marie #3424, Dargis Associates, Inc., 1977. $25.00–30.00 Super Donny & Marie; $20.00–25.00 each for others.

POSTER PEN SET, Craft House, 1977. 16" x 22" poster on back. $35.00–45.00.

RECORDS/LPs, Donny and Marie, Polydor, 1976. Only two albums were dedicated to the television show, including "Donny and Marie" and "New Season." $10.00–15.00 each.

RECORD CASES, Peerless Vidtronic Corp., 1977. Sizes for LPs and 45s. $30.00–40.00 LPs; $25.00–30.00 45s.

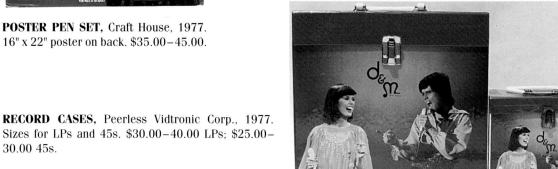

RECORD CASES, Peerless Vidtronic Corp., 1977. Sizes for LPs and 45s. $30.00–40.00 LPs; $25.00–30.00 45s.

RECORD/45, "Deep Purple"/"Take Me Back Again," MGM Records, 1975. Released in Belgium. $15.00–20.00.

Left:
SHEET MUSIC, "May Tomorrow Be a Perfect Day," Osmusic, 1977. Several others made including one for "Deep Purple." $8.00–10.00 each.

Right:
STICKER BOOK #2188, Whitman, 1977. $15.00–20.00.

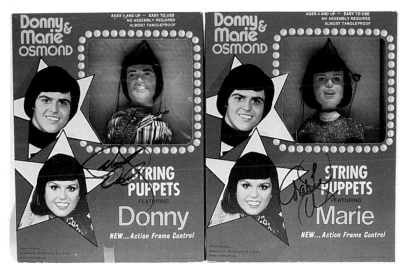

STRING PUPPETS, Donny and Marie, Osbro Productions Inc., 1978. Both puppets also sold as a gift set in one box. $50.00–75.00 each; $100.00–150.00 gift set.

TELEVISION STAGE SET, Mattel, 1976. Playset for 12" dolls. Includes flexible record. $60.00–80.00.

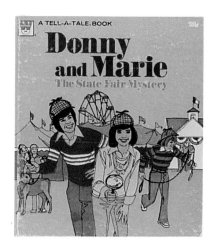

TELL-A-TALE BOOK, *The State Fair Mystery,* Whitman, 1977. $5.00–8.00.

VAN, Lapin, 1978. 18½" x 11" for play with dolls. $60.00–80.00.

WALLET & MONEY SET, Gordy, 1976. $20.00–25.00.

WIRELESS MICROPHONE, LJN, 1977. Packaging varies. $50.00–75.00.

OTHER ITEMS NOT PICTURED

BRUNCH BAG, Aladdin, 1976. Oval-shaped vinyl bag with plastic thermos. Illustration matches that of the vinyl box of the same year. $100.00–125.00 box; $10.00–15.00 thermos.

BRUNCH BAG, Aladdin, 1977. Oval-shaped vinyl bag with plastic thermos. Illustration matches that of the vinyl box of the same year. $100.00–125.00 box; $10.00–15.00 thermos.

COLOR YOUR OWN MUGS SET, Craft House, 1977. $35.00–45.00.

DISCO AMPLIFIER COMBOS, Vanity Fair, 1977. Two different sets. Both have an amplifier with photo of Donny and Marie and a microphone attachment. Another has a separate unit for guitar attachment. $60.00–80.00 each.

DOLL OUTFITS, Mattel, 1977. Six unnamed outfits, and two "Fashion-Pak" sets containing three outfits, were sold exclusively by Montgomery Ward mail order. They were shipped in white boxes with a black and white photo label on box top. $20.00–25.00 single boxed outfits. $40.00–50.00 fashion packs.

FAN CLUB KIT, Osbro Productions Inc., 1977. Includes an 8" x 10" black and white photo, photo stickers, bi-monthly newsletters, fan club merchandise offers, and a bumper sticker. $50.00–75.00.

KAZOO, Lapin, 1977. Plastic toy on photo card. $35.00–45.00.

KEYS AND WATCH, Gordy, 1976. On photo card. $25.00–30.00.

MAGIC SET, Gordy, 1976. Plastic pieces on photo card. $25.00–30.00.

PATTERNS, Butterick, 1977. Several different Personality Doll Wardrobe patterns were made for the Marie doll. Package contains photo of Marie and doll pictured with several outfits. $15.00–20.00 each.

PATTERNS, Butterick, 1977. Several other patterns were packaged for women and also pictured Marie at top of package. $3.00–5.00 each.

PORTABLE SING ALONG AM RADIO, LJN Toys, 1977. Plastic white radio with photo and a microphone attached to the side. $75.00–100.00.

READING PROGRAM, 1978. Includes a cassette or LP of hits. $20.00–25.00.

RECORD PLAYER WITH CASSETTE DECK, Vanity Fair, 1976. 17" x 4" x 10" with a color photo of Donny and Marie on the battery compartment. Comes with a tinted dust cover. $75.00–100.00.

TAMBOURINE, Lapin, 1977. 6" round with same decal as guitars. $30.00–40.00.

TRAVEL SETS, 1977. Comb and brush in photo box. One for both Donny and Marie. $35.00–45.00 each.

TV GUIDES, 1976–1977. 08/07/76 Donny & Marie; 10/08/77 Donny & Marie illustrated. $8.00–10.00 each.

EIGHT IS ENOUGH

MARCH 15, 1977 –
AUGUST 29, 1981

112 EPISODES

PEAK POSITION:
#12 in the 1978–1979 season

—— CAST ——

Dick Van Patten
Tom Bradford

Diana Hyland
Joan Bradford

Betty Buckley
Sandra "Abby" Bradford

Grant Goodeve
David

Lani O'Grady
Mary

Laurie Walters
Joanie

Susan Richardson
Susan

Dianne Kay
Nancy

Willie Aames
Tommy

Connie Needham
Elizabeth

Adam Rich
Nicholas

KITE FUN BOOK, Western Publishing Co., 1979. 5" x 7" booklet distributed by Pacific Gas & Electric, Southern California Edison, and Florida Power & Light. Includes 16 pages of activities and comics that provide advice for safe kite flying. $25.00–35.00.

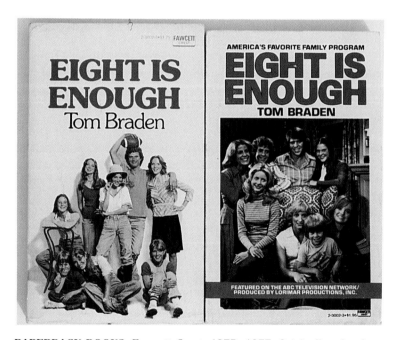

PAPERBACK BOOKS, Fawcett Crest, 1975–1977. Originally a hardcover book in 1975, the story was released as a paperback in 1976 and replaced with a cast cover in 1977. Hardcover book not pictured. $10.00–15.00 hardcover; $5.00–8.00 illustrated cover; $10.00–15.00 cast cover.

JIGSAW PUZZLE, APC, 1970.
$25.00–30.00.

SHEET MUSIC, Cherry Lane Music Co.,
Inc., 1977. $20.00–25.00.

VIEW-MASTER #K76, GAF, 1980. $20.00–
25.00.

OTHER ITEMS NOT PICTURED

FAN CLUB KIT, Willie Aames, Fan Club Images, 1979. Available through mail order. Contains a photo of Willie in a "photo-kissing" frame, 5" x 7" signed color photo, two 8" x 10" black and white autographed photos, four color wallet-size photos, biography profile, 17" x 22" color poster, membership card and scroll, and color folder to hold contents. $40.00–60.00.

POSTERS, 1970s. Several different, including: 23" x 35" cast collage, Dargis Associates, Inc.; 23" x 29" Willie Aames as Tommy, Marathon Graphics, LTD., 1978; 22" x 28" Willie with open shirt, Fan Club Images, 1979. $20.00–25.00 each.

T-SHIRT, Willie Aames, Fan Club Images, 1979. Available as a mail-away from the fan club. $20.00–25.00.

TV GUIDE, 12/16/78 cast. $10.00–15.00.

FAMILY

MARCH 9, 1976–
JUNE 25, 1980

94 EPISODES

PEAK POSITION:
Not in the top 25

—— CAST ——

James Broderick
Douglas Lawrence

Sada Thompson
Kate Lawrence

Meredith Baxter Birney
Nancy Maitland

Gary Frank
Willie

Kristy McNichol
Buddy

Quinn Cummings
Annie

BOOKS, 1979. Several different containing bios, photos, and chapters about the TV show. Books include hard and soft cover *Kristy and Jimmy McNichol,* Tempo Books, 1979; *Kristy and Jimmy: TV's Talented McNichols,* Tempo Books, 1979; and *Kristy McNichol,* Xerox Corporation, 1979. $5.00–10.00 each.

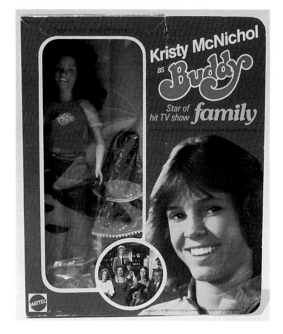

DOLL, Kristy McNichol as Buddy, Mattel, 1978. $25.00–35.00 loose; $50.00–75.00 boxed.

DOLL, Kristy McNichol, Mego, 1978. $25.00–35.00 loose; $50.00–75.00 boxed.

PAPERBACK BOOKS #1–3, Ballantine, 1976–1977. $5.00–10.00 each.

JIGSAW PUZZLE, Kristy McNichol, APC, 1979. $20.00–25.00.

RECORDS/LPs and 45s, RCA, 1978. Several different recordings with Kristy and her brother, Jimmy. Records include a full-length album "Kristy and Jimmy McNichol," with poster and fan club insert, and singles "He's So Fine"/"He's A Dancer" and "Page by Page"/"Girl, You Really Got Me Goin'." $10.00–15.00 each.

OTHER ITEMS NOT PICTURED

FAN CLUB KIT, Kristy McNichol, FCCA, 1979. Kit contains membership card and scroll, 8" x 10" color photo, two 4" x 5" photos, biography profile, color postcard, 16" x 20" color poster, six color wallet photos, 2 color bookmarks, 5" x 7" color photo, and color folio to hold contents. $50.00–75.00.

IRON-ON, Kristy McNichol, FCCA, 1979. Same photo as Ms. Kristy Pro Arts poster. $10.00–15.00.

POSTERS, 1977–1979. Several different, including: 23" x 29" Kristy as Buddy collage, Dargis Associates, Inc., 1977; 23" X 29" Kristy McNichol as Buddy, Dargis Associates, Inc., 1978; 20" x 28" Kristy McNichol, Pro Arts Inc., 1979; and 20" x 28" Ms. Kristy, Pro Arts, Inc., 1979. A few others were also made that include her brother Jimmy. $25.00–30.00 each.

SPIRAL NOTEBOOK, Kristy McNichol, Poster Books, 1979. Kristy folding arms in red jacket pictured on front. $15.00–20.00.

TV GUIDES, 1978–1980. 01/21/78 cast; 03/15/80 cast. $5.00–10.00 each.

FAMILY AFFAIR

SEPTEMBER 12, 1966 –
SEPTEMBER 9, 1971

138 EPISODES

PEAK POSITION:
#5 in the 1967–1970 seasons

—— CAST ——

Brian Keith
Bill Davis

Sebastian Cabot
Mr. French

Anissa Jones
Buffy

Johnny Whitaker
Jody

Kathy Garver
Cissy

BOARD GAME, Remco, 1968. $100.00–125.00.

BOARD GAME, Where's Mrs. Beasley?, Whitman, 1971. $40.00–50.00.

BOOK, *Buffy Finds a Star,* Whitman, 1970. $10.00–15.00.

BUFFY BEAUTY BOUTIQUE CASES, Amsco, 1969–1971. Three different that include a vinyl case with cardboard photo sleeve and beauty products attached. Pink case (1969), yellow case with pink daisies (1970), and yellow case with close-up of Buffy (1971). $125.00–150.00 each with sleeve; $35.00–45.00 each loose.

BUFFY FASHION WIG, Amsco, 1971. Brown or blond styles. $100.00–125.00.

BUFFY MAKE-UP & HAIRSTYLING SET, Amsco, 1971. $60.00–80.00.

CARTOON KIT, Colorforms, 1970. $40.00–50.00.

BUFFY WIG CASE, Amsco, 1971. Vinyl case with cardboard photo sleeve. $60.00–80.00 with sleeve.

COLORING BOOKS, Whitman, 1968–1969. Four different, including photo cover (1968), *Color by Number* (1969), *Buffy and Jody* (1969), and orange cover (1968). $20.00–30.00 each.

CLOTHING LINE, 1960s. Both Johnny Whitaker and Anissa Jones had a clothing line. Anissa's line featured a photo tag and came with replacement buttons. Back and front of Buffy's tag pictured. $150.00–175.00 each tagged article; $30.00–40.00 each tag.

COLORING BOOKS, *Mrs. Beasley,* Whitman, 1970–1975. Four different, including #1110 (1970), *Coloring Book with Doll and Cut-Out Clothes* (1972), *Color and Read* (1972), and #1648 (1975). $20.00–30.00 each.

COMIC BOOKS #1–4, Gold Key, 1970. #1 includes a Buffy pull-out poster. $40.00–50.00 #1 with poster; $20.00–25.00 #2–4.

COOKBOOK, *Buffy's Cookbook,* Berkley, 1971. Offered in stores and as a mail-away through Kellogg's cereal. Cereal box features a photo of the book and order form. Book includes a recipe for "Marshmallow Treats." $15.00–20.00 cookbook; $40.00–50.00 cereal box.

COSTUMES, Buffy and Mrs. Beasley, Ben Cooper, 1970. Buffy costume pictured. $75.00–100.00 each.

DOLL, Mrs. Beasley, Mattel, 1967. 20" talking doll. $150.00–200.00 loose with glasses; $500.00–600.00 boxed.

DOLLS, Buffy and Mrs. Beasley, Mattel, 1967. 6" Buffy with 3" Mrs. Beasley. $75.00–100.00 loose set; $150.00–175.00 boxed set.

DOLLS, Buffy and Mrs. Beasley, Mattel, 1968. 10" talking Buffy with 4" Mrs. Beasley. $100.00–125.00 loose set. $200.00–225.00 boxed set.

FRAME TRAY PUZZLE #4558, Whitman, 1971. $30.00–40.00.

FUN BOX, Whitman, 1970. Contains a coloring book, drawing paper, construction paper, magic slate, sewing cards, yarn, and a box of crayons. $50.00–60.00.

JEWELRY, 1970s. Several different, including a necklace, tie clip, and cuff links. Jody cuff links pictured. $50.00–75.00 each boxed set.

Left:
JIGSAW PUZZLE #4426, Whitman, 1970. $35.00−45.00.

Right:
JIGSAW PUZZLE #4609, Whitman, 1970. $35.00−45.00.

LUNCH BOX, K.S.T., 1969. Metal box with metal thermos. $100.00−125.00 box; $40.00−60.00 thermos.

ORGAN AND SONG BOOK, Audion Organs, 1971. Electric 12-chord, child-size organ contains a "Family Affair" sticker and includes a songbook with cast photos. A promotional 21" x 44" cast poster and die-cut mobile was also available. $200.00−300.00 organ; $35.00−45.00 songbook.

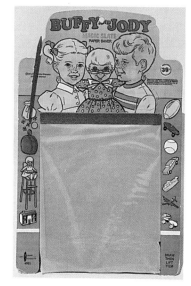

MAGIC SLATE, Buffy and Jody, Watkins Strathmore Co., 1970. $35.00−45.00.

PAPER DOLL BOOKLETS, Buffy, Whitman, 1968−1969. Two different, including Buffy with Mrs. Beasley (1968) and Buffy (1969). $20.00−25.00 each cut; $35.00−45.00 each uncut.

PAPER DOLL BOOKLETS, Mrs. Beasley, Whitman, 1970–1972. Two different, including orange cover (1972) and green cover (1970). $10.00–15.00 each cut; $25.00–35.00 each uncut.

PAPER DOLL BOXES, Whitman, 1970–1974. Three different, including Buffy and Jody (1970), Family Affair (1970), and Mrs. Beasley (1974). $20.00–25.00 each cut; $40.00–50.00 each uncut.

RAG DOLLS, Mrs. Beasley, Mattel, 1968. 10" doll in red or blue dress. $15.00–20.00 each.

RECORD/45, "Lem, The Orphan Reindeer"/"Opus Lem," Aquarian Records, 1960s. Vocals by Kathy Garver. Picture sleeve includes information for the Kathy Garver Fan Club. $30.00–40.00.

RECORD/45, "Every Little Boy Can Be President"/"The Garden Song," United Artists, 1968. Vocals by Johnny Whitaker. $35.00–45.00.

RAG DOLL, Mrs. Beasley, Mattel, 1973. 14" doll. $35.00–45.00 loose; $50.00–75.00 boxed.

SHEET MUSIC, "Every Little Boy Can Be President," Sam Fox Publishing Company, Inc, 1968. $25.00 – 35.00.

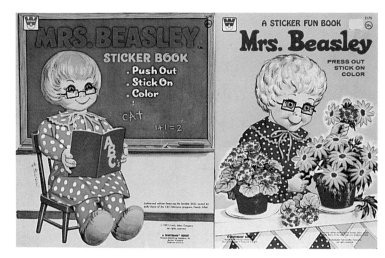

STICKER BOOKS, Whitman. 1972 – 1975. #1679 (1972) and #2170 (1975). $30.00 – 40.00 each.

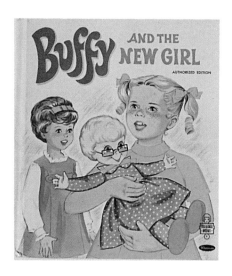

TELL-A-TALE BOOK, "Buffy and the New Girl," Whitman, 1969. $10.00 – 15.00.

TINY-TETHERED TABLE TENNIS SETS, Atech Enterprises, Inc., 1969. Sets vary with box sizes 24" x 16½" and 32" x 24." Larger box pictured. $125.00 – 150.00 each.

TOY TEA SET, Chilton Toys, 1960s. 46-piece set with "Buffy" plates. $60.00 – 80.00 set.

TRACE AND COLOR BOOKS, Whitman, 1969. Two different versions, including one with a color photo in the center. $25.00–35.00 each.

VIEW-MASTER #B571, GAF, 1969. $30.00–40.00.

WRITING TABLET, 1960s. Kathy Garver's name is printed on upper left corner, but blacked out prior to distribution. $35.00–45.00.

OTHER ITEMS NOT PICTURED

ALARM CLOCK, 1960s. Clock face features the names of Buffy and Jody. $100.00–150.00.

BUFFY SHOES, Acrobat, 1960s. Two-toned brown leather shoes with gold buckles. Inside sole reads "Made for Buffy by Acrobat." Buffy's photo on side of box. $100.00–150.00.

TV GUIDES, 1967–1969. 04/22/67 Jones, Cabot & Keith; 12/16/67 Sebastian Cabot; 09/07/68 Cast; 05/31/69 Jones, Cabot & Whitaker. $20.00–25.00 each.

WRISTWATCHES, Watch-It-Watch, Sheffield Watch Corp, 1969. Yellow window box features photo of Buffy and Jody. Front of watch with the names of Buffy and Jody. The back of watch is clear so you can "watch" the gears move. Boy or girl versions made as well as different color bands. $100.00–150.00 each.

FANTASY ISLAND

JANUARY 28, 1978–
AUGUST 18, 1984

154 EPISODES

PEAK POSITION
#17 in the 1977–1978 season

—— Cast ——

Ricardo Montalban
Mr. Roarke

Herve Villechaize
Tattoo

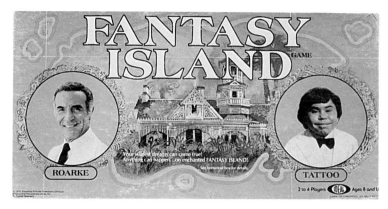

BOARD GAME, Ideal, 1978. $25.00–35.00.

COSTUME, Tattoo, Ben Cooper, 1978. $40.00–50.00.

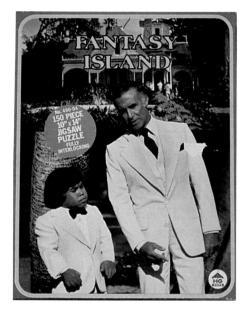

JIGSAW PUZZLE, HG Toys, 1977. $20.00–25.00.

PAPERBACK BOOKS #1–2, Ballantine Books, 1978–1979. $8.00–12.00 each.

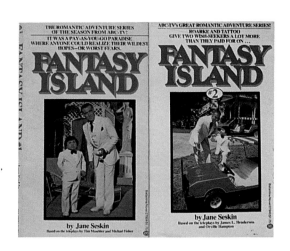

PAPERBACK BOOK, *Fantasy Island,* Weekly Reader, 1981. $8.00–12.00.

POSTER ART SET, Craft Master, 1978. $40.00–50.00.

RECORD/45, "Why"/"When a Child is Born," Epic, 1980. Vocals by Herve Villechaize with Children of the World. $15.00–20.00.

SHEET MUSIC, "Theme from Fantasy Island," Golden Torch Music Corp., 1979. $20.00–25.00.

OTHER ITEMS NOT PICTURED

IRON-ONS, 1970s. Several different. $10.00–15.00 each.

POSTERS, Pro Arts Inc., 1979. Two different, including 20" x 28" Tattoo and 20" x 28" Roarke. $20.00–25.00 each.

TV GUIDES, 1978–1980. 07/01/78 cast illustrated; 03/24/79 Montalban illustrated; 03/01/80 cast illustrated. $10.00–15.00 each.

FLIPPER

SEPTEMBER 19, 1964 –
MAY 14, 1967

88 EPISODES

PEAK POSITION:
#25 in the 1964–1965 season

—— CAST ——

Brian Kelly
Porter Ricks

Luke Halpin
Sandy

Tommy Norden
Bud

ACTIVITY BOX, Whitman, 1966. 9" x 12" box includes pictures to color, pages of color pieces to punch out and attach to pictures, glue, and crayons. $40.00–50.00.

BOOK, *The Mystery of the Black Schooner,* Whitman, 1966. $10.00–15.00.

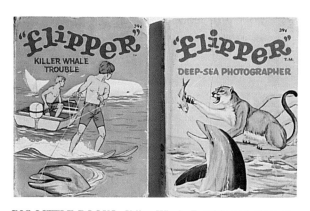

BIG LITTLE BOOKS, *Killer Whale Trouble* and *Deep Sea Photographer,* Whitman, 1967. $10.00–15.00 each.

BOARD GAME, Flipper Flips, Mattel, 1966. $50.00–75.00.

COLORING BOOKS, Whitman, 1960s. Several different. $15.00–20.00 each.

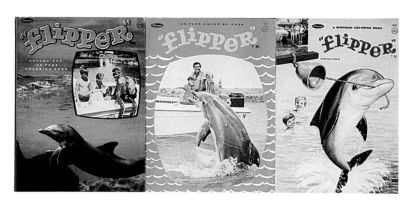

COMIC BOOKS #1–3, Gold Key, 1966–1967. $20.00–30.00 each.

CIGAR BANDS, Spanera, 1960s. European set of 24. $50.00–75.00 set.

FRAME TRAY PUZZLES, Whitman, 1965–1966. $20.00–25.00 each.

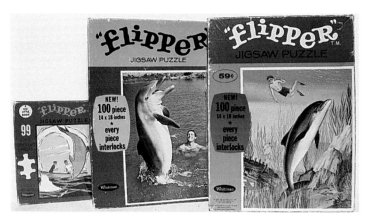

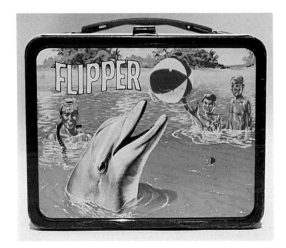

JIGSAW PUZZLES, Whitman, 1965–1968. Several different boxed versions. $20.00–30.00 each.

LUNCH BOX, K.S.T., 1966. Metal box with metal thermos. $100.00–125.00 box; $40.00–50.00 thermos.

FLIPPER

Left:
MAGIC SLATES, Whitman/Lowe, 1960s. Whitman 1967 version pictured. Lowe magic slate made in 1963. $25.00–35.00 each.

Right:
PAINTLESS PAINT BOOK, Whitman, 1964. $20.00–25.00.

PLASTIC STICK-ONS, Standard Toykraft, 1965. $40.00–50.00.

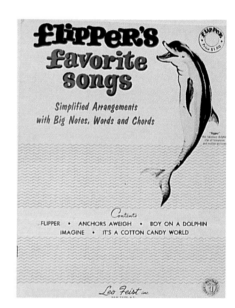

SONG BOOK, Leo Feist, Inc., 1965. $15.00–20.00.

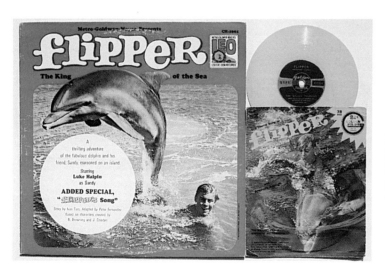

RECORDS, 1960s. "Flipper, the King of the Sea," MGM Records and "Flipper the Fabulous Dolphin," Golden Records. Single pictured was released as a 78 rpm on yellow vinyl. It was also released as a 45 rpm on black vinyl. $25.00–30.00 each.

SPOUTING DOLPHIN, Bandai, 1968. Battery-operated 8" plastic dolphin swims and spouts water. $60.00–80.00.

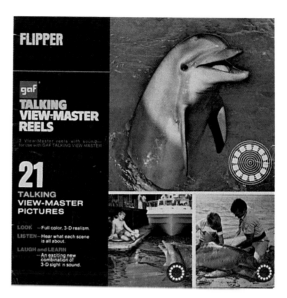

TALKING VIEW-MASTER #AVB45, GAF, 1966. $25.00–30.00.

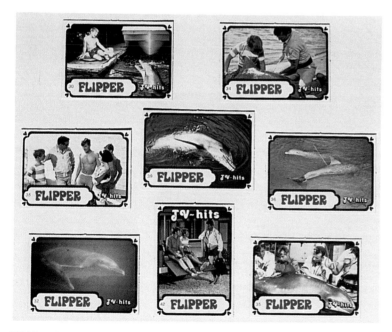

TRADING CARDS, Monty Gum, 1970s. Single cards from the "TV Hits" set. Wrapper and box pictured under *Kung Fu* section, page 173. $1.00–1.25 single cards.

VIEW-MASTER #B485, Sawyer, 1966. $20.00–25.00.

OTHER ITEMS NOT PICTURED

BANK, 1960s. 17½" plastic figural. $50.00–75.00.

BATHTUB PUMP, Louis A. Boettiger Co. Inc., 1969. An 8" figural bath toy of Flipper on an illustrated card. Squirts water when fin is pumped. $50.00–75.00.

BOARD GAME, 1960s. Made in Japan. Cast illustration on box cover. $75.00–100.00.

BRITISH ANNUAL, 1966. $25.00–35.00.

CARD GAME, Hinkosha, 1960s. Made in Japan. 5" x 7" illustrated box. $50.00–75.00.

COLOR BY NUMBER SET, Hasbro, 1966. $50.00–60.00.

COSTUME, Flipper, Collegeville, 1964. $75.00–100.00.

FLIPPER PLUSH TOY, Knickerbocker, 1976. 17" stuffed dolphin toy with sailor hat and "Flipper" written on side. A musical version was also made. $25.00–30.00 non-musical. $40.00–50.00 musical.

FLIPPER'S MAGIC FISH, Topps, 1960s. 10 different fish in set. Came in paper wrappers. $150.00–200.00 set; $15.00–20.00 single fish; $30.00–40.00 wrapper.

FRAME TRAY PUZZLE SET, Whitman, 1966. Set of 4 in 9" x 11" box. $40.00–50.00.

MODEL KIT, Revell, 1965. Flipper jumps out of water with Sandy holding a fish. $60.00–80.00.

MUSICAL UKULELE, Mattel, 1968. Instrument with illustration of Flipper. $75.00–100.00.

MUSIC BOX, Mattel, 1966. Metal box with crank. Flipper pops out like a jack-in-the-box. $125.00–150.00.

PAINT BY NUMBERS SET, 1960s. Boxed set. $50.00–75.00.

PINBACK BUTTONS, 1964. Different styles, including Bud, Flipper, and Bud & Flipper. $10.00–15.00 each.

PUNCHO, Coleco, 1966. Blow-up punching bag shaped like a dolphin with "Flipper" written across bottom. $50.00–75.00.

RIDING TOY, Irwin, 1965. Plastic figural Flipper with red wheels and handles for riding. $125.00–150.00.

RUB-ONS #2746, Hasbro, 1960s. $30.00–40.00.

SHEET MUSIC, MGM, 1963. Theme with photo or illustrated cover. $15.00–20.00 each.

SQUIRT GUN FIGURAL, 1960s. Water toy on card. $40.00–50.00.

STARDUST TOUCH OF VELVET BY NUMBERS, Hasbro, 1960s. Two pictures to color in a 15" x 11" box. $50.00–75.00.

STICKER BOOK, Whitman, 1966. Illustration of Flipper and photo of Bud on cover. $25.00–30.00.

STITCH-A-STORY, Hasbro, 1966. Illustrations of Flipper in plastic frames. $40.00–60.00.

TRADING CARDS, Topps, 1966. Test set of 30. No wrapper or box exist. Photo cards with puzzle backs. $1,500.00–1,700.00 set; $40.00–50.00 single cards.

TRU-VUE MAGIC EYES STORY SET, GAF, 1964. 11" x 9" sleeve contains three rectangular story cards. $30.00–40.00.

TV GUIDES, 1965–1966. 06/05/65 Flipper and Kelly; 07/09/66 Flipper and Kelly. $10.00–15.00 each.

WALLET, 1960s. Vinyl wallet with photo. $35.00–45.00.

WRISTWATCH, ITF-MGM, 1960s. Glow-in-the-dark illustration of Flipper on watch face. $125.00–150.00.

THE FLYING NUN

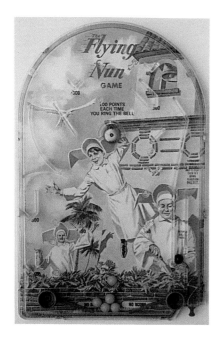

BAGATELLE GAME, Hasbro, 1967. 10½" x 16". $75.00–100.00.

SEPTEMBER 7, 1967–
SEPTEMBER 18, 1970

82 EPISODES

PEAK POSITION:
#34 in the 1967–1968 season

—— CAST ——

Sally Field
Sister Bertrille

Marge Redmond
Sister Jacqueline

Madeleine Sherwood
Reverend Mother Pluseato

Alejandro Rey
Carlos Ramirez

Shelley Morrison
Sister Sixto

Linda Dangcil
Sister Ana

BOARD GAME, Milton Bradley, 1968. $50.00–60.00.

BRUNCH BAG, Aladdin, 1968. Vinyl bag with plastic thermos. $200.00–225.00 bag; $35.00–45.00 thermos.

CHALKBOARD, Hasbro, 1967. 24" x 16" $60.00–80.00.

COLORING BOOKS, Saalfield, 1968. Two different. U.S. version #4572 and Spanish version #1518 with title "La Novicia Voladora." Both have same photo cover. $30.00–40.00 each.

COSTUME, Ben Cooper, 1967. $100.00–125.00.

COMIC BOOKS #1–4, Dell, 1967. $25.00–30.00 #1; $15.00–20.00 #2–4.

Left: **DOLL,** Sister Bertrille, Hasbro, 1967. 4" doll. $50.00–60.00 loose. $125.00–150.00 boxed.

Right: **DOLL,** Sister Bertrille, Hasbro, 1967. 11½" doll. $125.00–150.00 loose; $300.00–400.00 boxed.

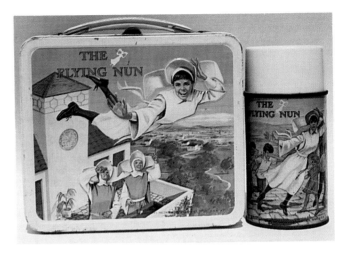

LUNCH BOX, Aladdin, 1968. Metal box with metal thermos. $150.00–175.00 box; $50.00–75.00 thermos.

FAN CLUB KIT, Sally's Friends. 1967. Club membership recognizes Sally Field in her role as "Gidget" and "The Flying Nun." Kit includes membership card, book cover, bio, black and white photos, and writing pen. Folder pictured. $100.00–125.00.

MARBLE MAZE GAME, Hasbro, 1967. 12" x 12". $100.00–125.00.

FLYING TOY, Ray Plastic, Inc., 1970. $60.00–80.00.

NUMBERED PENCIL COLORING SET, Hasbro, 1967. 11" x 10". $75.00–100.00.

PAPER DOLL BOOKLETS, Saalfield/Artcraft, 1968–1969. #1317 (Saalfield, 1969), #5121 (Artcraft, 1968), and #5134 (Saalfield, 1969). #5134 was also issued as #5124 with the Artcraft logo on cover, and #5121 was also issued as #5131 by Saalfield. $25.00–35.00 each cut; $50.00–75.00 each uncut.

OIL PAINTING BY NUMBERS, Hasbro, 1967. 10" x 11". $75.00–100.00.

PAPER DOLL BOX, Saalfield, 1969. $35.00–45.00 cut; $75.00–$100.00 uncut.

PAPERBACK BOOKS #1–5, Ace Books, 1968–1970. $10.00–15.00 each.

Left:
RECORD/LP, "Sally Field, Star of The Flying Nun," Colgems, 1967. Vocals by Sally Field. $35.00–45.00.

Right:
RECORD/45, "Felicidad"/"Find Yourself a Rainbow," Colgems, 1967. Vocals by Sally Field. $20.00–25.00.

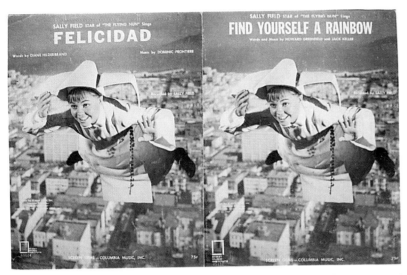

SHEET MUSIC, Columbia Music, Inc., 1967. Two different. $25.00–30.00 each.

SONGBOOK, Columbia Music, Inc., 1967. Includes several black and white photos and bio of Sally Field. $50.00–60.00.

TRADING CARDS, Donruss, 1968. 66 cards in set with puzzle backs. $200.00–250.00 set; $3.00–4.00 single cards; $10.00–15.00 wrapper; $40.00–50.00 display box.

STITCH-A-STORY, Hasbro, 1967. 8½" x 8½". $75.00–100.00.

VIEW-MASTER #B495, GAF, 1967. $40.00–50.00.

WEAVING LOOM SET, Hasbro, 1967. 12" x 12". $100.00–125.00.

OTHER ITEMS NOT PICTURED

DOLL, Sister Bertrille, Hasbro, 1967. 18" doll. $250.00–300.00 loose; $500.00–600.00 boxed.

LUNCH BOX, Aladdin, 1968. Square vinyl box with plastic thermos. Same illustration as the vinyl brunch bag. $225.00–250.00 bag; $35.00–45.00 thermos.

RECORDS/45s, "Months of the Year"/"Gonna Build a Mountain," and "You're a Grand Old Flag"/"Golden Days," Colgems, 1967. Without picture sleeves. Vocals by Sally Field. $10.00–15.00 each.

TV GUIDES, 1968–1969. 09/30/67 Field; 03/16/68 Field & Rey; 05/03/69 Field & Sherwood. $15.00–20.00 each.

GIDGET

BOARD GAME, Standard Toykraft, 1965. $75.00–100.00.

CARD GAME, Fortune Teller Game, Milton Bradley, 1966. $40.00–50.00.

SEPTEMBER 15, 1965–
SEPTEMBER 1, 1966

32 EPISODES

PEAK POSITION:
Not in the top 25

—— CAST ——

Sally Field
Frances "Gidget" Lawrence

Don Porter
Russell Lawrence

Betty Connor
Anne Cooper

Peter Deuel
John Cooper

Lynette Winter
Larue

COMIC BOOKS #1–2, Dell, 1966.
$30.00–40.00 each.

PAPER DOLLS, Standard Toykraft, 1965. $50.00–75.00 cut; $125.00–150.00 uncut.

SHEET MUSIC, "(Wait 'Til You See) My Gidget," Screen Gems, 1965. Three additional photos on back. $25.00–35.00.

OTHER ITEMS NOT PICTURED

RECORD/45, "(Wait 'Til You See) My Gidget"/"Our World," MGM, 1965. Theme from the television show. Vocals by Johnny Tillotson. Without picture sleeve. $10.00–15.00.

TV GUIDE, 05/28/66 Field. $20.00–25.00.

GILLIGAN'S ISLAND

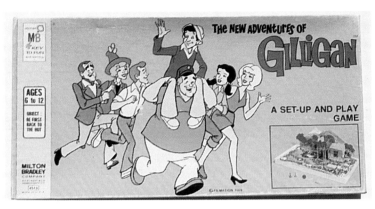

BOARD GAME, *The New Adventures of Gilligan,* Milton Bradley, 1974. $40.00–50.00.

BOOK, *Gilligan's Island,* Whitman, 1966. $30.00–40.00.

COLORING BOOK, Whitman, 1965. $75.00–100.00.

DIP DOTS PAINTING DESIGN BOOK, *The New Adventures of Gilligan,* Kenner, 1975. Box set based on the cartoon series. Includes a 20-page booklet, watercolor paints and brush. Booklet pictured. $100.00–125.00 boxed set.

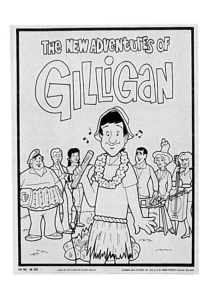

SEPTEMBER 26, 1964– SEPTEMBER 3, 1967

98 EPISODES

PEAK POSITION: #19 in the 1964–1965 season

—— CAST ——

Bob Denver
Gilligan

Alan Hale, Jr.
Jonas "Skipper" Grumby

Jim Backus
Thurston Howell III

Natalie Schafer
Mrs. "Lovey" Howell

Tina Louise
Ginger Grant

Russell Johnson
Professor Roy Hinkley

Dawn Wells
Mary Ann Summers

THE NEW ADVENTURES OF GILLIGAN

SEPTEMBER 7, 1974– SEPTEMBER 4, 1977

24 EPISODES of the animated cartoon.

FIGURES, Gilligan, Skipper, and Mary Ann, Playskool, 1977. 3½" soft rubber figures from the cartoon series. $25.00–35.00 set.

GILLIGAN'S FLOATING ISLAND, Playskool Inc., 1977. 14" x 10½" boxed playset from the cartoon series. $125.00–150.00.

TRADING CARDS, Topps, 1965. 55 cards in set. Backs of cards have photos that create a mini-movie when fanned. $600.00–800.00 set; $10.00–15.00 single cards; $75.00–100.00 wrapper; $800.00–1,000.00 display box.

WRITING TABLET, 1960s. $30.00–40.00.

OTHER ITEMS NOT PICTURED

BOARD GAME, Game Gems, 1965. Cover photo of Mr. Howell, Gilligan, and the Skipper with illustrated bodies in boat. $400.00–500.00.

TV GUIDES, 1965–1966. 05/08/65 Louise and Denver; 06/11/66 Hale, Louise, and Denver. $25.00–35.00 each.

GOOD TIMES

DOLL, Talking J.J., Shindana Toys, 1975. 23" cloth doll with 9 different sayings. $40.00–50.00 loose; $75.00–100.00 boxed.

DOLL, J.J., Shindana Toys, 1975. 15" cloth doll with vinyl head. $25.00–35.00 loose; $45.00–55.00 boxed.

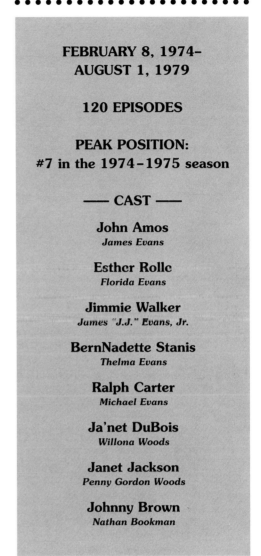

FEBRUARY 8, 1974–AUGUST 1, 1979

120 EPISODES

PEAK POSITION:
#7 in the 1974–1975 season

—— CAST ——

John Amos
James Evans

Esther Rolle
Florida Evans

Jimmie Walker
James "J.J." Evans, Jr.

BernNadette Stanis
Thelma Evans

Ralph Carter
Michael Evans

Ja'net DuBois
Willona Woods

Janet Jackson
Penny Gordon Woods

Johnny Brown
Nathan Bookman

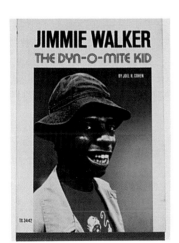

PAPERBACK BOOK, *Jimmie Walker: The Dyn-O-Mite Kid,* Scholastic, 1976. 5½" x 8½". $8.00–10.00.

RECORD/LP, "Dyn-O-Mite," Buddah Records, 1975. Spoken comedy by Jimmie Walker. $15.00–20.00.

RECORD/LP, "Young and In Love," Mercury, 1976. Vocals by Ralph Carter. $8.00–12.00.

TRADING CARDS, Topps, 1975. 55 cards and 21 stickers in set. 44 cards have puzzle backs and 11 have behind the scenes trivia. $60.00–80.00 set with stickers; 75¢–$1.00 single cards; $1.00–1.25 single stickers; $3.00–5.00 wrapper; $30.00–40.00 display box.

SOCKS, Expression Wear Inc., 1975. $15.00–20.00.

OTHER ITEMS NOT PICTURED

IRON-ON, J.J. "Dyn-O-Mite," 1970s, $10.00–15.00.

RECORDS/45s, Mercury, 1975–1976. "When You're Young and In Love," "Extra, Extra Read All About It," "Number One In My Heart"/"Headin' Back To Love Again." Vocals by Ralph Carter. Without picture sleeves. $3.00–5.00 each.

TV GUIDES, 1974. 06/29/74 Rolle and Amos; 12/14/74 cast. $8.00–10.00 each.

GREEN ACRES

ANTIQUE FORDSON TRACTOR, ERTL, 1969. 7" x 4" x 4½" box. $125.00–150.00.

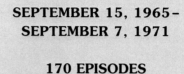

SEPTEMBER 15, 1965–
SEPTEMBER 7, 1971

170 EPISODES

PEAK POSITION:
#6 in the 1966–1967 season

—— CAST ——

Eddie Albert
Oliver Douglas

Eva Gabor
Lisa Douglas

Pat Buttram
Eustace Haney

Tom Lester
Eb Dawson

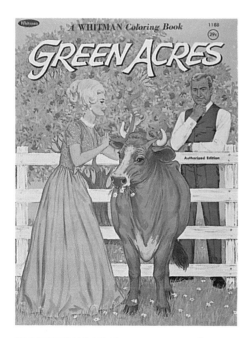

COLORING BOOK, Whitman, 1967. $40.00–50.00.

PAPER DOLL BOX, Whitman, 1968. $30.00–40.00 cut; $50.00–60.00 uncut.

PAPER DOLL BOOKLET, Whitman, 1967. $30.00–40.00 cut; $60.00–75.00 uncut.

RECORDS/LP, "The Eddie Albert Album," Columbia, 1967. Contains the theme song performed by Eddie Albert only. $15.00–20.00.

OTHER ITEMS NOT PICTURED

BOARD GAME, Standard Toykraft, 1965. Photo cover of Lisa and Oliver. $100.00–125.00.

RECORD/45, "Green Acres"/"Turn Around," Columbia, 1965. Theme from the television show. Vocals by Eddie Albert. Without picture sleeve. $10.00–15.00.

TV GUIDES, 1966–1970. 01/08/66 Gabor and Albert; 09/03/66 Gabor; 09/02/67 Gabor and Albert; 09/06/69 Gabor and Albert; 08/29/70 Albert. $10.00–15.00 each.

WRITING TABLET, 1960s. Cover photo of Lisa and Oliver. $25.00–35.00.

H.R. PUFNSTUF

AUTHORS' NOTE: *A 98-minute motion picture, Pufnstuf, was released August 19, 1970 that was based on the TV series. The movie spawned several items that were exclusive to the movie and some that were a crossover of both the movie and the TV show. An example of this is the board game that bears the title of the TV show but includes "Boss Witch," one of the movie characters, on the game's spinner. There was also a Krofft theme park that opened for one season during the summer of 1976, in Atlanta, Georgia. The image of H.R. Pufnstuf dominated memorabilia sold at the park, but some items featured other Krofft characters. All of the items from the movie and theme park are considered part of the H.R. Pufnstuf collection and are included in this section.*

BELT BUCKLE, Sid and Marty Krofft, 1976. 1¾" x 2" metal buckle from the Krofft theme park with incorrect spelling "HR Puff N Stuff." $75.00–100.00.

BOARD GAME, Milton Bradley, 1971. $60.00–80.00.

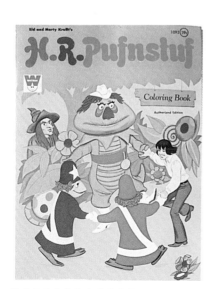

COLORING BOOK, Whitman, 1970. $50.00–75.00.

SEPTEMBER 6, 1969–
SEPTEMBER 4, 1971

17 EPISODES

—— CAST ——

Jack Wild
Jimmy

Billie Hayes
Witchiepoo

Roberto Gamonet
Pufnstuf (suit)

Lennie Weinrib
Pufnstuf (voice)

Walker Edmiston
Freddy the Flute (voice)

Joy Campbell
Orson

Angela Rossitto
Seymour

Johnny Silver
Ludicrous Lion

Johnny Silver
Dr. Blinky

Joy Campbell
Cling (red)

Angela Rossitto
Clang (green)

ADDITIONAL MOVIE CAST

Martha Raye
Boss Witch

Mama Cass
Witch Hazel

COMIC BOOKS #1–8, Gold Key/Whitman, 1970–1971. Some covers feature scenes from the movie. $75.00–100.00 #1; $30.00–40.00 #2–8.

COSTUMES, Witchiepoo and H.R. Pufnstuf, Collegeville, 1971. Witchiepoo was made in a variety of styles and packaging. While all are similar in design, some costumes are packaged in boxes while others are hung on cards. Outfits are made from fabric or vinyl, and one includes synthetic hair attached to the mask. Only one fabric costume of H.R. Pufnstuf was made; his image is silk-screened on the chest. $75.00–100.00 each Witchiepoo; $150.00–200.00 H.R. Pufnstuf.

Left:
DOLL, Pufnstuf, My-Toy, 1970. 22" stuffed doll. $800.00–1,000.00 loose; $1,200.00–1,500.00 boxed.

Right:
DOLL, Witchiepoo, My-Toy, 1970. 19" stuffed doll. $400.00–600.00 loose; $800.00–1,000.00 boxed.

DOLLS, Cling and Clang, My-Toy, 1970. 14" stuffed dolls. Other dolls not pictured include Orson, Seymour, Ludicrous Lion, Judy, Dr. Blinky, and Shirley. $600.00–800.00 each loose. $1,000.00–1,200.00 each boxed.

FRAME TRAY PUZZLES, Whitman, 1970. $40.00–50.00 each.

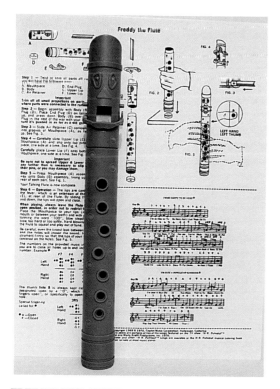

FREDDY THE FLUTE, RB Toy Development Co., 1970. Available only as a mail-away item from Kellogg's. Plastic flute with movable mouth, instructions and song sheet. The two songs included are "Happy to Be Here" and "Bundle of Sunshine." $500.00–600.00.

FUN RINGS, Sid and Marty Krofft Productions Inc., 1970. Seven different 1¼" rings available as a Kellogg's cereal premium only. Each ring was made in blue, red, purple, and green plastic with either silver or gold embossing. The combined variation set totals 56. Ring designs include Cling & Clang, Jimmy & Freddy, Ludicrous Lion, Orson, Pufnstuf, Seymore, and Witchiepoo. $75.00–100.00 each.

JIGSAW PUZZLE, Whitman, 1970. A 20" round puzzle in a 10" x 10" box. $50.00–60.00.

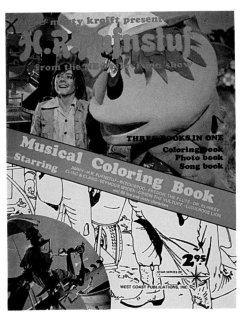

LOBBY CARDS AND PRINTS, Universal Pictures, 1970. Set of eight cards and eight prints. Each features a scene from the motion picture. Lobby cards measure 11" x 14" while the prints are 8" x 10" of the same photos. $30.00–40.00 each card; $20.00–25.00 each print.

MUSICAL COLORING BOOK, West Coast Publications, Inc., 1970. Inside includes the score to 12 songs from the TV show, along with eight different full-page color photos of the cast. Each photo is placed next to a line art drawing of the same scene for coloring. $100.00–125.00.

LUNCH BOX, Aladdin, 1971. Metal box with plastic thermos. $150.00–175.00 box; $50.00–60.00 thermos.

PENNANTS, Sid and Marty Krofft Productions Inc., 1970. Eight different 8½" plastic pennants available as a Kellogg's cereal premium only. Pennants came in pairs that required scissors to separate. $50.00–75.00 each pair.

PATCHES, Sid and Marty Krofft Productions Inc., 1969. Eight different 1¾" x 2" patches available as a Kellogg's cereal premium only. Each patch has an adhesive backing that contains character bios. $20.00–25.00 each.

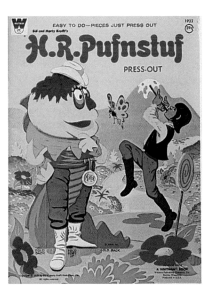

POSTERS, Royal Screen Craft, 1970. Four different 21" x 31½" blacklight posters, including "Different" (pictured), "Zap the World" (pictured), "Jimmy and Freddy Flute," and "It's the Only Way to Fly." $100.00–125.00 each.

PRESS-OUT BOOK, Whitman, 1970. 8½" x 12" book includes stand-ups of show characters, props, and backdrops. $125.00–150.00.

POSTERS, Universal Pictures, 1970. Used in promotion of the motion picture and made in different sizes. All contain the same photo and artwork. 22" x 28" size, known as a "half sheet," is pictured. $50.00–75.00 each.

Left:
PUPPETS, Sid and Marty Krofft Productions Inc., 1970. Five different felt hand puppets available as a mail-away from Kellogg's only. Puppets include Cling, Clang, Ludicrous Lion, Pufnstuf and Witchiepoo. Pufnstuf pictured. $100.00–150.00 each.

Right:
PUPPETS, Remco, 1970. Eight different vinyl hand puppets. Seymore not pictured. $125.00–175.00 each loose; $400.00–500.00 each boxed.

RECORD/45, "H.R. Pufnstuf," Capitol Records, 1969. Fold-open sleeve contains photos of cast and song lyrics. Original soundtrack offered as a Kellogg's mail-away only. $75.00–100.00.

RECORD/45, "Pufnstuf," Mr. Pickwick, 1970s. Contains the song "Pufnstuf" from the motion picture and three other unrelated tracks. Vocals not credited. $40.00–50.00.

RECORD/LP, "Pufnstuf," Capitol, 1970. Original soundtrack from the motion picture. $60.00–80.00.

RECORDS/LPs, Jack Wild, 1970–1972. Three different pictured, including: "The Jack Wild Album," Capitol (1970); "Everything's Coming Up Roses," Buddah (1971) and "A Beautiful World," Buddah (1972). Others from Japan include "Everything's Coming Up Roses," and "Punch & Judy" released as an alternate title of "A Beautiful World." $25.00–35.00 each U.S.; $40.00–50.00 each Japan.

RECORDS/45s, Jack Wild, 1970–1972. United States' single, "Some Beautiful"/"Picture of You," Capitol (1970) and Japanese single "Punch & Judy"/"A Beautiful World," Buddah (1972) pictured. Other Japanese singles with picture sleeves include "Everything's Coming Up Roses"/"Hello! Jack," Buddah (1972), and "Cotton Candy"/"Apeman," Buddah (1971). $20.00–30.00 each U.S.; $25.00–35.00 each Japan.

REMEMBRANCE CHARM BRACELET, Krofft International, 1975. From the theme park. $125.00–175.00.

TELL-A-TALE BOOK, Whitman, 1970. $20.00–30.00.

SONGBOOK, "Songs from Pufnstuf," Hawaii Music Company, 1970. Six songs from the movie soundtrack with no pictures inside. $50.00–75.00.

UMBRELLA, Sid and Marty Krofft Productions Inc., 1976. From the theme park. Tag contains the caption, "Your rainy day Krofft friends," with an illustration of Pufnstuf. Sigmund, Honk, Cling & Clang, and the Lost Saucer are illustrated with Pufnstuf on two of the eight panels. Color of the umbrella varies with black, red, or blue. $125.00–150.00.

OTHER ITEMS NOT PICTURED

BOOKLETS, *Jack Wild's Wild Life* and *Jack Wild's Private Photo Album,* The Laufer Company, 1971. Both were offered as mail-away items from *Tiger Beat* and *Fave* magazines. $40.00–50.00 each.

CANVAS TOTE BAG, Sid and Marty Krofft Productions Inc., 1976. From the theme park. 13" x 14" canvas bag with illustration of Pufnstuf on front and "The World of Sid and Marty Krofft" written on the back. $125.00–150.00.

CLOTH DOLLS, H.R. Pufnstuf, Sid and Marty Krofft Productions Inc., 1973. Stuffed doll shaped like H.R. Pufnstuf. Size of doll varies from approximately 12" to 18" in height. $200.00–250.00 small; $300.00–400.00 large.

COMIC BOOK, March of Comics #360, Western Publishing Company, 1971. Cast pictured on 5" x 7" cover with 16 pages. $40.00–60.00.

PLAYING CARDS, Krofft, 1976. Several styles including a 3" round deck with character illustrations on back, mini deck with Krofft logo, and a generic set in a vinyl case with Pufnstuf on the front and Krofft characters on the back. Case includes pencil and paper. $75.00–100.00 round; $50.00–75.00 mini; $100.00–125.00 deck with case.

RECORD/45, "Pufnstuf"/"Nonsense," Decca, 1970. Vocals by The Pufnstuf. Side A is an alternate version from the soundtrack while side B is exclusive to the single. Released without a picture sleeve. $25.00–30.00.

STICKER FUN BOOKS, Whitman, 1970. Two different. One has Pufnstuf mask on back. $125.00–150.00 each.

WALLET, Sid and Marty Krofft Productions Inc., 1976. Plastic wallet from the theme park. Illustration of Pufnstuf on the front and other characters on the back. $100.00–125.00.

SOUVENIR MUGS, CUPS & DISHES, Sid and Marty Krofft, 1976. Several sizes, styles, and artwork from the theme park. Other items were made including salt and pepper shakers. Ceramic mug pictured. $50.00–75.00 each.

HAPPY DAYS

JANUARY 15, 1974 –
JULY 19, 1984

256 EPISODES

PEAK POSITION:
#1 in the 1976–77 season

—— CAST ——

Henry Winkler
Arthur "Fonzie" Fonzarelli

Ron Howard
Richie Cunningham

Tom Bosley
Howard Cunningham

Marion Ross
Marion Cunningham

Erin Moran
Joanie Cunningham

Anson Williams
Warren "Potsie" Weber

Donny Most
Ralph Malph

FONZ AND
THE HAPPY DAYS GANG

NOVEMBER 8, 1980 –
SEPTEMBER 18, 1982

13 EPISODES
of the animated cartoon.

—— AUTHOR'S NOTE ——

On September 25, 1982, the series was incorporated into THE MORK & MINDY/LAVERNE & SHIRLEY/FONZ HOUR and ran until September 3, 1983.

ACRYLIC PAINT BY NUMBER SETS, Craftmaster, 1976. Four different U.S. and Canadian versions, including Aaaay...the Fonz (pictured), Juke Box Saturday Night, I'm Cool, and Mean Machine. $20.00–30.00 each.

ACTIVITY AND COLORING BOOK, Grosset & Dunlap, 1976. $10.00–15.00 each.

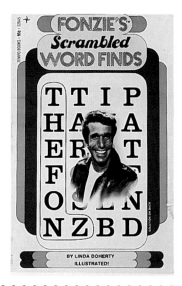

ACTIVITY BOOKS, Tempo Books, 1976. Several different 5" x 8" paperback books, including *Fonzie's Scrambled Word Finds.* $10.00–15.00 each.

BAGATELLE GAME, Imperial, 1982. 5½" x 10" game from the cartoon series. $10.00–15.00.

BEACH TOWEL, Fonzie, Franco Mfg. Co., 1970s. 32" x 55". $35.00–45.00.

BELT, *The Fonz and the Happy Days Gang,* Paramount, 1981. $10.00–15.00.

BELT BUCKLES, Fonzie, Paramount Pictures Corp., 1976. Two styles with brass finish. Other shows Fonzie holding thumbs up. $15.00–20.00 each.

BEDROOM ACCESSORIES, Burlington, 1970s. Several pieces, including bedspread, sheets, pillow cases, draperies, and valance. Sheet pattern pictured. $50.00–60.00 bedspread; $20.00–25.00 others.

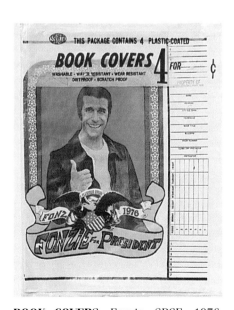

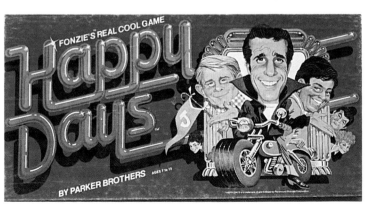

BOARD GAME, Parker Brothers, 1976. $10.00–15.00.

BOOK COVERS, Fonzie, SPCE, 1976. Four different in package. $15.00–20.00.

BOOKS, 1976–1978. Several different 8½" x 11" books pictured, including *The Official Fonzie Scrapbook*, Grosset & Dunlap (1976) hard and soft cover editions; and *The Other Side of Henry Winkler*, Warner Books, Inc. (1976). Others include *The Fonz & Henry Winkler*, Castle Books, (1978) hard cover, and *Henry Winkler: Born Actor*, EMC Corporation (1978). $10.00–15.00 each.

BRITISH ANNUALS, Stafford Pemberton, 1979–1981. $20.00–25.00 each.

BUBB-A-LOONS, Imperial, 1981. From the cartoon series. $15.00–20.00.

BUMPER STICKERS, The Pinning Co., 1976. 12" x 4" and 4" x4" styles. $8.00–10.00 each.

BUTTONS, Fonzie, 1970s. Several different sizes and styles. $5.00–8.00 each.

CALENDAR, Ballantine Books, 1976. 1977 calendar with color photos. $25.00–30.00.

CANDY BOXES, Phoenix, 1976. Eight numbered boxes in set. $10.00–15.00 each box.

CLOTH DOLL, Fonzie, Samet and Wells, Inc., 1976. 16". $25.00–30.00.

CARD GAME, The Fonz, Hanging Out at Arnold's, Milton Bradley, 1976. $15.00–20.00.

COLORFORMS, The Fonz, Colorforms, 1976. $15.00–20.00.

CLOTHING LINE, Rob Roy, 1976. Various styles of clothing. Fonzie for President T-shirt pictured. $20.00–25.00 each.

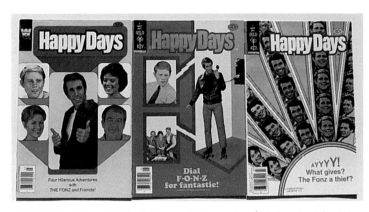

COMIC BOOKS #1-6, Gold Key 1979-1980. $10.00-15.00 each.

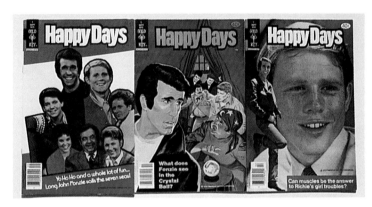

COLORING AND ACTIVITY BOOKS, Waldman, 1983. Four different. $10.00-15.00 each.

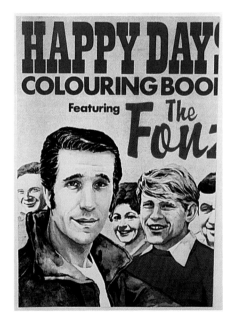

COLOURING BOOK, Stafford Pemberton, 1978. $25.00-35.00.

COSTUME, The Fonz, Ben Cooper, 1976. $30.00-35.00.

CUP, The Fonz, Paramount, 1977. From Burger King restaurants. $10.00-15.00.

CUPS, MUGS, and TUMBLERS, Fonzie, Dawn, 1976. Mug styles not pictured. $10.00-15.00 each.

FLIP-A-KNOT TOY, National Marketing, 1977. Photo of Richie and Joanie on back. $10.00–15.00.

FONZ VIEWER, Larami, 1981. From the cartoon series. $20.00–25.00.

DOLLS, Mego, 1976. 8" dolls of Fonzie, Richie, Potsic, and Ralph. Fonzie sold on card and in boxes. $25.00–35.00 loose; $60.00–80.00 Fonzie carded; $50.00–60.00 others carded; $50.00–75.00 Fonzie boxed.

FONZIE GARAGE PLAYSET, Mego, 1977. Playset for the 8" dolls. $150.00–200.00.

FONZIE MOTORCYCLE, Mego, 1978. For 8" dolls. $50.00–75.00.

GLASSES, Libbey Glass Co., 1977. Six different in set. Two different series. Glasses from series #1 were sold in stores and given out by Pizza Hut as a premium. Premiums will have the Pizza Hut logo on the back. Series #2 contains different designs with a record illustration on the back. $15.00–20.00 each Series 1; $25.00–35.00 each Series 2.

IRON-ONS, 1970s. Several different styles. $10.00–15.00 each.

GREETING CARDS, Metropolitan Greetings Inc., 1976. Several different assortments. $15.00–20.00 each box.

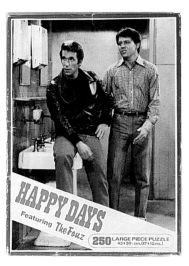

JIGSAW PUZZLE, Fonzie, HG Toys, 1976. In canister. $25.00–30.00.

JIGSAW PUZZLES, Stafford Pemberton, 1977. Several different made in the United Kingdom. $30.00–40.00 each.

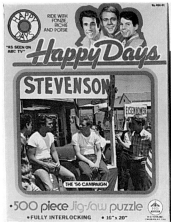

GUITARS, Lapin, 1976. 20" black plastic guitar in an 8" x 22" box with four cut-out color photos on back. Larger version also made. $125.00–150.00 each.

JIGSAW PUZZLE, The Fonz, HG Toys, 1976. Giant 250 pieces. $30.00–40.00.

JIGSAW PUZZLES, HG Toys, 1974. Two different. $25.00–30.00 each.

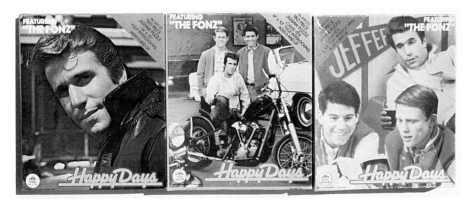

JIGSAW PUZZLES, HG Toys, 1976. Three different. $10.00–15.00 each.

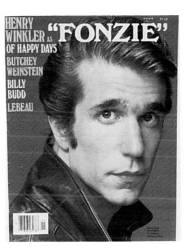

KITE FUN BOOK, Western Publishing Co., 1978. 5" x 7" booklet distributed by Pacific Gas & Electric, Southern California Edison, and Florida Power & Light. Includes 16 pages of activities and comics that provide advice for safe kite flying. $15.00–20.00.

MAGAZINES, Sterling's Magazine, 1976. Several different devoted to Fonzie and the *Happy Days* cast, including *Henry Winkler Magazine* (pictured) and *TV Superstar No.1 - Henry 'Fonzie' Winkler and His Pals.* $15.00–20.00 each.

KNEE-HI NYLONS, Pretty Legs Mills, Inc., 1976. $15.00–20.00.

LUNCH BOX, Thermos, 1977. Plastic version from Canada, including thermos. $40.00–50.00.

LUNCH BOXES, Thermos, 1977–1978. Two different versions, including Fonzie, Richie, and Potsie on front (1977) and Fonzie only on front (1978). Metal box with plastic thermos. $50.00–75.00 each box; $10.00–15.00 each thermos.

MIRACLE BUBBLE SHOOTER, *The Fonz and the Happy Days Gang,* Imperial, 1981. $15.00–20.00.

MODEL KITS, 1976–1982. Several different pictured, including The Fonz and his Bike, MPC (1976) with figure, '54 Chevy, Revell (1982), '41 Willys, Revell (1982), and '57 Chevy Nomad, Revell (1982). Other model kits include: T' Bucket, Revell (1982); '29 Model A Pickup, Revell (1982), '31 Model A Delivery, Revell (1982); Fonzie's Dream Rod, MPC (1976); Draggin' Wagon, Palmer (1974); Rock N' Roll Rod, Palmer (1974); and Burger Buggy, Palmer (1974). $50.00–75.00 MPC and Palmer versions; $25.00–35.00 Revell.

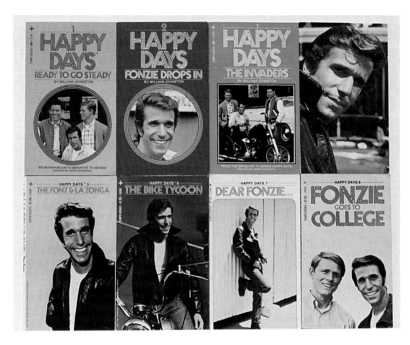

NECKLACES, Fonzie, 1970s. Several different, including "Fonzie for President" with a mirror back (pictured). Others include a circular image in metal, thumbprint pressed in metal, figural leather jacket, and figural motorcycle. $15.00–20.00 each.

PAPERBACK BOOKS #1–8, Tempo Books, 1974–1977. #2 made with two different covers. Also packaged in a display box numbered 1–6 (1976). $30.00–40.00 boxed set; $5.00–8.00 each #1–6; $10.00–15.00 each #7–8.

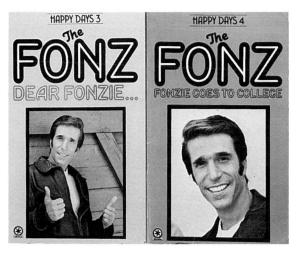

PAPERBACK BOOKS, Universal, 1977. Several different made in the United Kingdom based on the United States versions. #3 and #4 pictured. $10.00–15.00 each.

PAPER DOLL BOX, Fonzie, Toy Factory, 1976. $15.00–20.00 cut; $25.00–35.00 uncut.

PHOTO ALBUM, Gordy, 1983. $15.00–20.00.

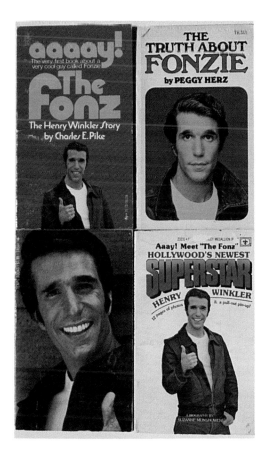

PAPERBACK BOOKS, Fonzie, 1976–1977. 1976 books include *The Fonz: The Henry Winkler Story,* Pocket Books; *The Truth About Fonzie,* Scholastic Books; *The Official Fonzie Scrapbook,* Tempo; *Hollywood's Newest Superstar,* Berkley; *Henry Winkler and Fonzie,* Zebra Books, 1977, with T-shirt iron-on (not pictured). $8.00–10.00 each.

PATCHES, 1970s. Several different. $8.00–10.00 each.

PILLOWS, Fonzie, Zodiac Design, 1970s. Sizes vary. $30.00–40.00 each.

PINS, *The Fonz and the Happy Days Gang,* Gordy, 1981. Several different. $10.00–12.00 each.

PLAY SET, Toy Factory, 1976. $30.00–40.00.

PINBALL MACHINE, Coleco, 1976. Originally sold in a photo box. Complete game includes metal legs. $175.00–200.00 boxed.

POSTER MAGAZINES, Sportscene Publishers LTD., 1977. Made in the United Kingdom. Several different. $20.00–25.00 each.

POSTERS, 1976–1981. Several different, including 20" x 28" Erin Moran, Pro Arts Inc., 1981 (pictured). Others include 11" x 17" Happy Days, Dargis Associates, Inc., 1976; 23" x 35" The Fonz!, Dargis Associates, Inc., 1976; 20" x 28" Scott Baio, Pro Arts Inc., 1979; 23" x 35" Scott Bio as Chachi, Marathon Graphics, LTD., 1978; 23" x 35" and 12" x 18" Fonz for President, The Pinning Co., 1976; 23" x 29" The Fonz blacklight poster, 1970s, and The Nifty Fifties Fonzie blacklight felt poster, I. Papermaster, 1976. $20.00–25.00 each blacklight; $15.00–20.00 others.

PUFFY STICKERS, *The Fonz and the Happy Days Gang,* Imperial, 1981. Six different styles. Styles B, C, E, and F pictured. $8.00–10.00 each.

RECORD PLAYER, Vanity Fair, 1976. $50.00–75.00.

RECORDS/LPs, London Records, 1976. "Fonzie, Fonzie, He's Our Man," vocals by the Heyettes (pictured) and "The Fonz Party," vocals by the Fonzettes. $10.00–15.00 each.

RECORD/LP, "Fonzie Favorites," Ahed, 1976. Compilation of '50s hits. Also includes original TV theme and Fonzie phrases. $15.00–20.00.

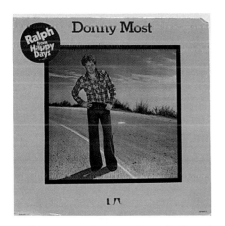

RECORD/LP, "Donny Most," United Artists, 1976. $10.00–15.00.

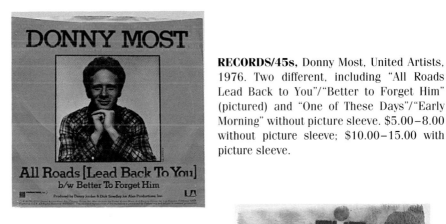

RECORDS/45s, Donny Most, United Artists, 1976. Two different, including "All Roads Lead Back to You"/"Better to Forget Him" (pictured) and "One of These Days"/"Early Morning" without picture sleeve. $5.00–8.00 without picture sleeve; $10.00–15.00 with picture sleeve.

RUB-DOWN TRANSFER GAMES, *The Fonz and the Happy Days Gang,* APC, 1981. Several different. $5.00–10.00 each.

RUGS, Zodiac Design, Fonzie, 1976. Several different styles. $35.00–45.00 each.

RECORD/45, "Deeply"/"I Want To Believe In This One," Chelsea, 1977. Vocals by Anson Williams. $10.00–15.00.

143

SODA CANS, R.C. Cola, 1978. 35 cans in set of Nehi came in four different flavors — orange, red soda, grape, and strawberry. #2 pictured. $8.00–10.00 each.

TALKING VIEW-MASTER #AVB586, The Not Making of a President, GAF, 1974. $20.00–25.00.

THERMOS, The Fonz, King Seeley, 1976. $30.00–40.00.

TRADING CARD SET #1, Topps, 1976. First series has 44 blue-bordered cards and 11 yellow-bordered stickers in set. Cards have puzzle and trivia backs. $40.00–50.00 set; 75¢–$1.00 single cards; $1.00–1.25 single stickers; $3.00–5.00 wrapper; $15.00–20.00 display box.

TRADING CARD SET #2, Topps, 1976. Second series has 44 red-bordered cards and 11 red-bordered stickers in set. Cards have puzzle and trivia backs. $40.00–50.00 set; 75¢–$1.00 single cards; $1.00–$1.25 single stickers; $3.00–5.00 wrapper; $15.00–20.00 display box.

TRANSISTOR FIGURAL RADIO, Fonzie, Sutton Associates, 1974 $50.00 75.00.

WALKMAN RADIO, Larami, 1981. From the cartoon series. $20.00–25.00.

WALLET, Gordy, 1983. $25.00–30.00.

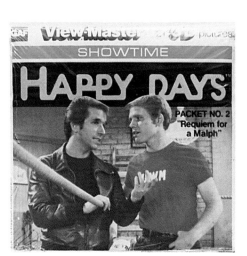

VIEW-MASTERS, GAF. Left: #B586, The Not Making of a President, 1974. Right: #J13, Requiem for a Malph, 1978. $15.00–20.00 each.

WRISTWATCH, Fonzie, Time Trends, 1976. Comes in a photo box. $75.00–100.00.

OTHER ITEMS NOT PICTURED

ACRYLIC PAINT BY NUMBERS, Hasbro, 1981. From the cartoon series. Contains six acrylic paints and two 8" x 10" pictures to paint. $25.00–30.00.

BEAN BAG CHAIR, Fonzie, 1970s. Red and white panels with an illustration of Fonzie holding thumbs up. $125.00–150.00.

CHALK STATUE, Fonzie, 1976. $15.00–20.00.

COMB, Ace, 1976. Photo of Fonzie on package. $15.00–20.00.

COSTUME VEST AND MASK, Ben Cooper, 1970s. Packaged in an illustrated plastic bag. Same mask as boxed costume but with a vest outfit. $35.00–45.00.

FONZ WALLET, Larami, 1981. From the cartoon series. $15.00–20.00.

FONZIE BUBBLE BATH, 1977. Photo of the Fonz on bottle and box. $40.00 – 50.00

FONZIE HAT, PPC, 1976. Colorful illustrations on an all-fabric hat. $20.00 – 30.00.

FONZIE'S JALOPY, Mego, 1978. Snap-together hot rod for 8" dolls. Box contains illustration of cast in car. $60.00–80.00.

FONZIE'S LEATHER JACKET, Ben Cooper, 1970s. "The Fonz" is written on the inside lining. $60.00–80.00.

GUITAR 'N MIKE SET, Gordy, 1983. Plastic toys on 6" x 12" photo card. Guitar has a photo of Joanie and Chachi. $25.00–30.00.

HI-BOUNCE BALL, Imperial, 1981. Illustration of Fonzie inside ball on card. From the cartoon series. $15.00–20.00.

JUKEBOX RADIO, 1970s. 6" tall orange and red radio shaped like a jukebox with a color photo of Fonzie. $25.00–30.00.

MEMO BOARD, 1970s. Photo of the Fonz with "Fonzie" quotes on a brick background. Wipe-off board with pen. $30.00–40.00.

MIRROR, Fonzie, 1970s. Made in the United Kingdom. $40.00–50.00.

MOD MOBILE, The Fonz, 1976. 11" x 14" figural portrait of the Fonz on heavy black cardboard. $15.00–20.00.

POCKET FLIX CASSETTE, Ideal, 1978. Cassette on photo card for the Pocket Flix Viewer. $10.00–15.00.

RECORDS/45s, 1970s. Several different, including theme song "Happy Days"/"Cruisin' with the Fonz," Pratt and McLain, 1976, without picture sleeve. Foreign singles were also made, including "Happy Days"/"Rock Around the Clock," Warner Italy Records, 1978, with cast picture sleeve. $8.00–10.00 each U.S.; $15.00–20.00 others.

SLEEPING BAG, 1970s. $40.00–60.00.

SPIRAL NOTEBOOKS, Randim Marketing Inc., 1977. Several different from Canada. $15.00–20.00 each.

STICKER ALBUM, Panini, 1979. Italian sticker book. 324 stickers available in sets to place in book. $30.00–40.00 album; $10.00–15.00 each sticker pack.

TRICYCLE, 1970s. Child's pink bike with the Fonz decals and a seat featuring a heart with the caption "I Love the Fonz," and "Sit On It." $40.00–50.00.

TV GUIDES, 1974–1984. 06/15/74 Howard and O'Dare; 01/10/76 Howard and Winkler; 01/07/78 cast; 12/15/79 Winkler; 04/17/82 Winkler, Baio, and Moran; 04/23/83 Winkler and Purl; 04/28/84 cast of 1974–1984. $8.00–10.00 each.

THE HARDY BOYS & NANCY DREW MYSTERIES

ACTIVITY BOOKS, Hardy Boys, Tempo Books, 1977. Six different 5" x 8" paperback books. $10.00–15.00 each.

ACTIVITY BOOKS, Nancy Drew, Tempo Books, 1977. Six different 5" x 8" paperback books. $15.00–20.00 each.

BOARD GAME, The Hardy Boys Mystery Game, Parker Brothers, 1978. $15.00–20.00.

JANUARY 30, 1977–
AUGUST 26, 1979

45 EPISODES

PEAK POSITION:
Not in the top 25

—— CAST ——

Parker Stevenson
Frank Hardy

Shaun Cassidy
Joe Hardy

Edmund Gilbert
Fenton Hardy

**Pamela Sue Martin/
Janet Louise Johnson**
Nancy Drew

William Schallert
Carson Drew

—— AUTHORS' NOTE ——

Originally aired as separate shows, alternating biweekly in the same time slot, then merged as one show early in 1978. In the Fall of 1978, The Hardy Boys finished the series run without Nancy Drew. There were 45 episodes made up of 27 Hardy Boys, 10 Nancy Drew, and 8 combined.

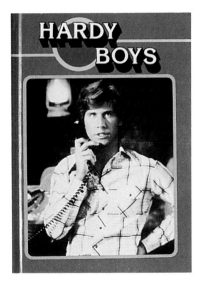

BOOK, *The Hardy Boys,* Creative Education, 1979. $10.00–15.00.

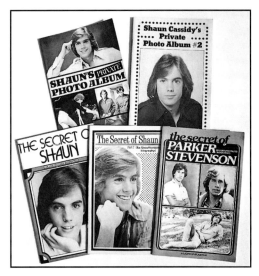

BOOKLETS, Laufer Publications, 1977–1979. Several different offered as mail-away items from *Tiger Beat* and *Fave* magazines. $10.00–15.00 each.

BRITISH ANNUALS, Hardy Boys/ Nancy Drew, Grandreams, 1977– 1980. 1980 annual pictured. $25.00–30.00 each.

BUTTON, Shaun Cassidy as Joe Hardy, Fun Time, 1978. 3". $5.00–8.00.

BOOKS, Grosset & Dunlap, 1978. Several different based on both series. Stories and photos from actual episodes. $20.00–25.00 each.

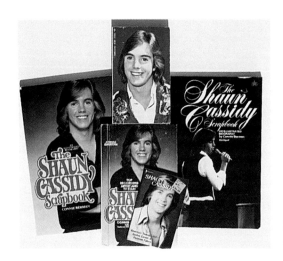

CLOTHING LINE, 1970s. Several different styles, including shirts, pants, and jacket. $35.00–45.00 each article.

BOOKS, Shaun Cassidy, 1970s. Several different books with soft and hard covers. $5.00–15.00 each.

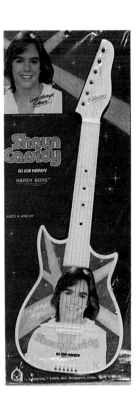

COSTUMES, Joe Hardy, Frank Hardy, or Nancy Drew, Collegeville, 1978. Shaun Cassidy as Joe Hardy pictured. $60.00–80.00 Nancy Drew; $40.00–50.00 each others..

DISCO AMPLIFIER, Shaun Cassidy as Joe Hardy, Vanity Fair, 1977. $40.00–50.00.

Right:
GUITARS, Shaun Cassidy as Joe Hardy, Carnival Toys, Inc., 1978. 20" and 31" versions with similar packaging. 31" version pictured. $60.00–80.00 20". $80.00–100.00 31".

DOLLS, Joe and Frank Hardy, Kenner, 1978. $30.00–40.00 each loose; $60.00–80.00 each boxed.

IRON-ONS, 1970s. Several different. $10.00–15.00 each.

FAN CLUB KIT, Nancy Drew, FCCA, 1978. Kit contains membership card and scroll, 8" x 10" color photo, two 4" x 5" photos, biography profile, color postcard, 16" x 20" color poster, six color wallet photos, two color bookmarks, 5" x 7" color photo, and color folio to hold contents. $60.00–80.00.

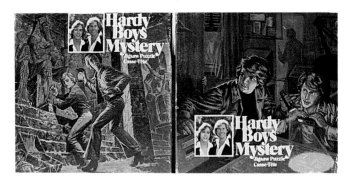

JIGSAW PUZZLES, Hardy Boys, APC, 1978. Several different. $15.00–20.00 each.

LUNCH BOX, K.S.T., Hardy Boys, 1977. Metal box with plastic thermos. $50.00–60.00 box; $10.00–15.00 thermos.

JIGSAW PUZZLES, Hardy Boys and Shaun Cassidy, APC, 1978. Several different. $20.00–25.00 each.

MIRRORS, Shaun Cassidy, 1970s. Two different 8" x 10" styles. $35.00–45.00 each.

MAGAZINES, *The Official Hardy Boys Magazine,* 1979. Several different 6" x 8" magazines produced in the United Kingdom. $30.00–40.00 each.

MODEL KIT, Revell, 1978. $30.00–40.00.

PAINT YOUR OWN TV GREETING CARDS, Cartoonarama, 1978. $50.00–75.00.

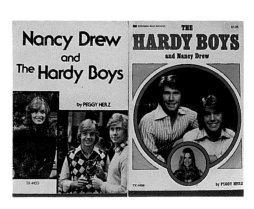

PAPERBACK BOOKS, *Nancy Drew and The Hardy Boys* and *The Hardy Boys and Nancy Drew,* Scholastic, 1977. $8.00–10.00.

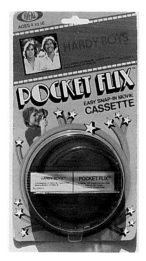

POCKET FLIX CASSETTE, Ideal, 1978. Cassette for pocket flix viewer. $15.00–20.00.

PORTABLE AM RADIO, Shaun Cassidy as Joe Hardy, Vanity Fair, 1977. 8½" x 6" plastic AM radio and P.A. system. Microphone not pictured. $35.00–45.00.

POSTER PUT-ONS, Bi-Rite, 1977. Three different styles. $10.00–15.00 each.

Left:
POSTER, Pamela Sue Martin as Nancy Drew, Pro Arts Inc., 1977, 20" x 28". $25.00–30.00.

Right:
POSTERS, Pro Arts Inc., 1977. 28" x 40" Super Hardy Boys pictured. Others include: 27" x 77" Shaun life-size; 20" x 28" Shaun jacket; 20" x 28" Shaun Cassidy; 28" x 40" Super Cassidy; 20" x 28" Parker; 20" x 28" Parker Blue; 20" x 28" Sleuths; and 24" x 72" Giant Shaun Cassidy door poster. $25.00–30.00 each 20" x 28"; $35.00–45.00 others.

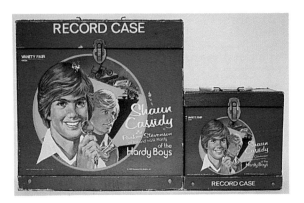

RECORD CASES, Vanity Fair, 1978. Sizes for LPs and 45s. $30.00–40.00 LP; $25.00–30.00 45.

RECORD PLAYER, Vanity Fair, 1978. Electric or battery-operated versions. $60.00–80.00.

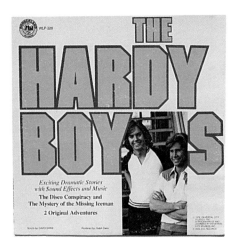

RECORD/LP, "The Hardy Boys Mysteries," Wonderland Records, 1978. Narrated adventure stories. $20.00–25.00.

RECORDS/LPs, Shaun Cassidy, Warner Brothers, 1977–1980. Six different, including: "Shaun Cassidy," (1977); "Born Late," (1977); "Under Wraps," (1978); "That's Rock 'N' Roll/Shaun Cassidy Live," (1979); "Room Service," (1979); and "Wasp," (1980). $10.00–12.00 each.

RECORDS/45s, Shaun Cassidy, Warner Brothers, 1977–1980. Several different, including: "Do You Believe In Magic?"/"Teen Dream," (1977); "Midnight Sun"/"She's Right," (1978); "That's Rock 'N' Roll"/"I Wanna Be With You," (1977); United Kingdom picture disc "Hard Love"/"Right Before Your Skies," (1978), also released as United Kingdom 12" picture disc (not pictured). $8.00–10.00 each United States with picture sleeve; $15.00–20.00 each United Kingdom.

Other singles include: "Da Doo Ron Ron"/"Holiday," (1977); "Strange Sensation"/"Hey Deanie," (1977); "Rebel Rebel"/"Our Night," (1978); "Our Night"/"Right Before Your Skies," (1978); "Are You Afraid of Me?"/"You're Usin' Me," (1979); "A Star Beyond Time"/"Heaven In Your Eyes," (1980); "Rebel Rebel"/"Cool Fire," (1980); and "Cool Fire"/"So Sad About Us," (1980). $8.00–10.00 each with picture sleeve; $3.00–5.00 each without picture sleeve.

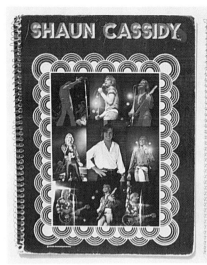 

SPIRAL NOTEBOOKS, Shaun Cassidy, Stuart Hall, 1977. $10.00–15.00 each.

SHEET MUSIC, Shaun Cassidy, Warner Brothers Publications, Inc., 1970s. Several different. $0.00–10.00 each.

OTHER ITEMS NOT PICTURED

FAN CLUB KITS, The Hardy Boys or Shaun Cassidy, FCCA, 1977. Two separate kits, each containing a membership card and scroll, 8" x 10" color photo, two 4" x 5" photos, biography profile, color postcard, 16" x 20" color poster, six color wallet photos, two color bookmarks, 5" x 7" color photo, and color folio to hold contents. $60.00–80.00 each.

JEWELRY, Shaun Cassidy as Joe Hardy, Universal, 1978. Several different items including a lapel pin and charm bracelet. $35.00–45.00 each.

JIGSAW PUZZLES, Nancy Drew, APC, 1970s. Several different styles in boxes and canisters. $30.00–40.00 each.

LUNCH BOX, Nancy Drew, K.S.T., 1977. Metal box with plastic thermos. $60.00–80.00 box; $15.00–20.00 thermos.

MAGAZINES, Shaun Cassidy, 1970s. Several different dedicated entirely to Cassidy, including *Tiger Beat Presents Shaun Cassidy* by the Laufer Company, 1978. $15.00–20.00 each.

MAGAZINES, The Hardy Boys, 1970s. Several different dedicated entirely to the show, including *Teen Beat's Super Special Shaun and Parker* by Ideal Publishing, 1979. $20.00–25.00 each.

PENNANTS, Shaun Cassidy as Joe Hardy, Fun Time, 1978. Two different full color versions, including a mini-pennant attached to a 14" pencil and a 9" x 21" banner on yellow felt. $15.00–20.00 each.

PILLOWCASE, Shaun Cassidy, 1970. Close-up photo of Shaun. $25.00 – 35.00.

POSTER PEN SET, Hardy Boys, Craft House, 1977. Includes seven pens and 16" x 22" poster on back. $40.00–50.00.

SPIRAL NOTEBOOKS, Poster Books, 1977. Several different to match the Pro Arts' posters. $15.00–20.00 each.

TV GUIDE, 11/05/77. Cassidy and Stevenson. $8.00–10.00.

WRISTWATCH, 1970s. Working watch. $50.00–75.00.

STAND-UP, Shaun Cassidy as Joe Hardy, Sun Unlimited, Inc., 1978. 12" die-cut figure of Shaun. $15.00–20.00.

I DREAM OF JEANNIE

BOARD GAME, Milton Bradley, 1965. $75.00–100.00.

SEPTEMBER 18, 1965–
SEPTEMBER 8, 1970

139 EPISODES

PEAK POSITION:
#26 in the 1968–1969 season

—— CAST ——

Barbara Eden
Jeannie

Larry Hagman
Major Anthony Nelson

Bill Daily
Major Roger Healey

Hayden Rorke
Dr. Alfred Bellows

Emmaline Henry
Amanda Bellows

Barton MacLane
General Martin Peterson

JEANNIE

SEPTEMBER 8, 1973–
SEPTEMBER 30, 1975

16 EPISODES
of the animated cartoon.

BOTTLE, Jim Beam, 1964. This bottle type was decorated for use as Jeannie's bottle on the show. $60.00–80.00.

BOOK, *Bezaubernde Jeannie,* Fernseh-Buch, 1971. 5" x 7½" hard cover book from Germany with text, and black and white illustrations inside. $60.00–80.00.

COMIC BOOKS #1–2, Dell, 1966. $80.00–100.00 #1; $60.00–80.00 #2.

COSTUME, Jeannie, Ben Cooper, 1973. Based on the cartoon series. $50.00–60.00.

COSTUME, Jeannie, Ben Cooper, 1974. Based on the cartoon series. $40.00–50.00.

DOLL, Jeannie, Libby Majorette Doll Corp., 1966. 20" doll. Box has photo of Barbara Eden on sides and bottom. Doll varies with a pink or green outfit. $300.00–400.00 loose; $600.00–800.00 boxed.

DREAMY FASHIONS, Remco, 1977. 36 different outfits for the 6" doll. Fashions came in boxes and on cards. $20.00–25.00 each.

DOLL, Jeannie, Remco, 1977. 6" doll. $30.00–40.00 loose; $60.00–80.00 boxed.

DREAM BOTTLE PLAYSET, Remco, 1976. Based on the cartoon series. 16" x 17½" boxed playset includes an exclusive 6½" doll in a pink outfit. $150.00–200.00.

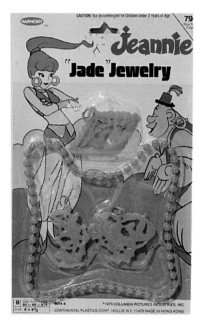

JADE JEWELRY, Harmony, 1975. $25.00–30.00.

PAPERBACK BOOK, Pocket Books, 1966, 5¼" x 8". $50.00–75.00.

PARTY SUPPLIES, Contempo, 1973. Cups, napkins, tablecloth, 7" and 9" plates, and invitations. Based on the cartoon series. $20.00–25.00 each.

PLAYSUIT, Ben Cooper, 1974. Fabric dress-up set, including pants, vest, hat, veil, belt, and earrings. $50.00–60.00.

RECORD/LP, "Miss Barbara Eden, Star of I Dream of Jeannie," Dot Records, 1967. $100.00–125.00.

REUSABLE WRITING SLATE, Rand McNally, 1975. From the cartoon series. $40.00–50.00.

OTHER ITEMS NOT PICTURED

COLORING BOOK, 1970s. Illustration of the cartoon cast on cover. $100.00–125.00.

DOLL OUTFIT, Libby Majorette Doll Corp., 1966. Large boxed accessory for the 20" Libby doll. $200.00–250.00.

COSTUME, Jeannie, Ben Cooper, 1965. $125.00–150.00.

KNITTING AND EMBROIDERY KIT, Harmony, 1975. Illustration of cartoon Jeannie on card. $30.00–35.00.

MAGIC LOCKET, Harmony, 1975. Four-way vision mirror and chain on 5½" x 7" card with illustration of cartoon Jeannie. $40.00–50.00.

RECORD/45, "I Wouldn't Be a Fool"/"Bend It!," Dot Records, 1967. Vocals by Barbara Eden. With picture sleeve. $50.00–75.00.

RECORDS/45s, Barbara Eden, Dot Records, 1967. "Rebel"/"Heartaches;" "I'm a Fool to Care"/"Pledge of Love." Vocals by Barbara Eden. Without picture sleeves. $20.00–25.00 each.

TV GUIDES, 1966–1969. 02/05/66 Eden and Hagman; 09/24/66 Eden; 07/06/68 Eden; 11/22/69 Eden and Hagman. $25.00–35.00 each.

JOSIE AND THE PUSSYCATS

**SEPTEMBER 12, 1970–
SEPTEMBER 2, 1972**

16 EPISODES

**JOSIE & THE PUSSYCATS IN
OUTER SPACE**

**SEPTEMBER 9, 1972–
SEPTEMBER 4, 1976**

16 EPISODES

— CARTOON VOICES —

Janet Waldo
Josie

Jackie Joseph
Melody

Barbara Pariot
Valerie

Jerry Dexter
Alan

Casey Kasem
Alexander Cabot

Sherry Alberoni
Alexandra Cabot

Don Messick
Sebastian

— SINGING VOICES —
(First 16 episodes only)

Cathy Dougher
Josie

Patrice Holloway
Valerie

Cheryl Ladd
Melody

ACTIVITY BOOK, Crossword Puzzles, Tempo Books, 1976. 5" x 8" paperback book. $20.00–25.00.

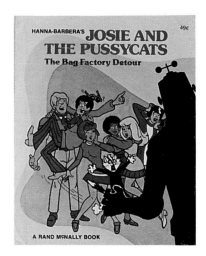

BOOK, *The Bag Factory Detour,* Rand McNally, 1971. Came in both hardback and softback versions. $10.00–15.00.

CLIP 'N' CASH, Larami, 1970s. $30.00–40.00.

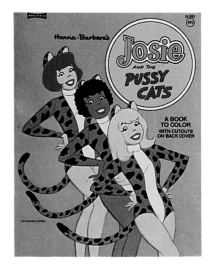

COLORING BOOK, Rand McNally, 1975. $40.00–50.00.

COMIC BOOKS, #45–106, Radio Comics, 1970–1982. #s 1–44 are without the Pussycats and predate the TV show. #48, 73, and 78 pictured. #55–74 are Giant issues with 52 pages. $5.00–10.00 each.

COMIC-STIKS, Deco Manufacturing Co., 1972. Set of five character stickers on card. $40.00–50.00.

GLASS, Hanna-Barbera, 1977. From the Pepsi Collector Series. $30.00–40.00.

JIGSAW PUZZLES, Hope, 1972. Several different canisters made in the United Kingdom, including green and purple versions. $40.00–50.00 each.

COSTUMES, Josie, Ben Cooper, 1971. Two different versions, all fabric (pictured); vinyl top and solid colored legs, 1972. $125.00–150.00 each.

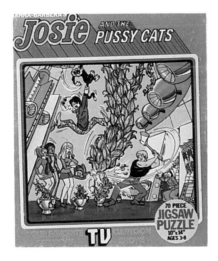

JIGSAW PUZZLE, HG Toys, 1976. $30.00–40.00.

CUPS, Radio Comics, 1976. Plastic cups from 7-11 convenience stores. Josie not pictured. $25.00–30.00 each.

PROJECTOR SETS, Kenner, 1971–1973. 13" x 3" x 9" box with 16 color slide strips pictured. Includes slides from other cartoon series along with *Josie and the Pussycats.* Similar sets were sold in 1972 as Screen-A-Show cassette projector and in 1973, as Cassette Movie Projector. $60.00–80.00 each.

MARVY MARKERS, Uchida of America Corp., 1974. Picture to color on the back. $40.00–50.00.

JOSIE AND THE PUSSYCATS

PATCHES, Hanna-Barbera, 1973. Several different came as premiums from Wonder Bread. $15.00–20.00 each.

MUG, Radio Comics, 1971. Came as a premium with Safeguard Soap pack. $10.00–15.00.

PAPER DOLL BOOKLET #1982, Whitman, 1971. $30.00–40.00 cut; $60.00–80.00 uncut.

PENCIL TOPPERS, Hanna-Barbera, 1971. Came as premiums from Honeycomb Cereal. Several different colors and characters. $25.00–30.00 each.

PENDANT JEWELRY SETS, Larami, 1972–1973. Two different. Another version issued in 1973 includes a pink set of earrings and pendant, along with a green set. $25.00–30.00 each.

RECORDS/45s, Capitol/Kellogg's, 1970. Four different available only as Kellogg's mail-away premiums. Each was numbered and sent in an illustrated mailer. #1 "Letter to Mama"/"Inside Outside Upside Down," #2 "Josie (TV theme)"/"With Every Beat of My Heart," #3 "Voodoo"/"If That Isn't Love," #4 "I Wanna Make You Happy"/"It's Gotta Be Him." $30.00–40.00 each without mailer; $60.00–80.00 each with mailer.

PENDANTS, Larami, 1973. $20.00–25.00.

160

RECORD/LP, "Josie and the Pussycats," Capitol, 1970. $200.00–225.00.

SPOONS, Hanna-Barbera, 1970. Came as premiums from Honeycomb Cereal. Several characters and colors including Sebastian (not pictured), $25.00–30.00 each.

SLICK TICKER PLAY WATCH, Larami, 1973. $50.00–75.00.

Left:
SQUEAKER TOYS, Lambert-Kay, 1972. 3½" Sebastian and Bleep. Sebastian pictured. $40.00–50.00 each.

Right:
TV CARTOON TATTOOS, Topps, 1971. Hanna-Barbera cartoon tattoos, including *Josie and the Pussycats.* 16 sheets in a set. $100.00–125.00 set; $6.00–8.00 single sheets; $8.00–10.00 wrapper; $40.00–60.00 display box.

OTHER ITEMS NOT PICTURED

VANITY SET, Larami, 1973. $25.00–35.00.

BANK, 1970s. Ceramic Bleep figural made in Mexico. $35.00–45.00.

CHALKBOARD, 1970s. $50.00–75.00.

FASHION JEWELRY SET, Larami, 1973. Includes earrings, ring, bracelet, and a silver purse on card. $40.00–50.00.

FRAME TRAY PUZZLES, Whitman, 1971. Set of 4 in box. $125.00–150.00.

GUITAR, Larami, 1973. Small plastic toy guitar on card. $50.00–75.00.

HARMONICA, Larami, 1973. Plastic toy on card. $50.00–75.00.

MAGIC SLATE, Whitman, 1971. $50.00–75.00.

PUFFY STICKER, Josie, H.B.P. Inc., 1979. Sold loose in a box with seven other Hanna-Barbera characters. $5.00–8.00.

RECORDS/45s, Capitol, 1970. Two different singles from the LP, including "Every Beat of My Heart"/"It's All Right with Me" and "Stop, Look and Listen"/ "Say Yeah!" without picture sleeves. $25.00–35.00 each.

UNDEROOS UNDERWEAR, 1970s. $35.00–45.00.

WATCH, Bradley, 1971. Working watch with three interchangeable bands. $200.00–250.00.

JULIA

**SEPTEMBER 17, 1968–
MAY 25, 1971**

86 EPISODES

PEAK POSITION:
#7 in the 1968–1969 season

—— CAST ——

Diahann Carroll
Julia Baker

Lloyd Noylan
Dr. Morton Chegley

Marc Copage
Corey Baker

Lurene Tuttle
Hannah Yarby

Michael Link
Earl J. Waggedorn

Betty Beaird
Marie Waggedorn

Hank Brandt
Len Waggedorn

Fred Williamson
Steve Bruce

COLORFORMS DRESS-UP KIT,
Colorforms, 1969. $30.00–40.00.

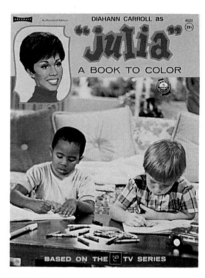

COLORING BOOK #4662, Saalfield,
1969. $20.00–25.00.

COLORING BOOK #9523, Saalfield, 1968. Blue or red cover.
$20.00–25.00.

PAPER DOLL BOOKLET #5140, Saalfield,
1971. $15.00–20.00 cut; $30.00–35.00
uncut.

COSTUME, Ben Cooper, 1960s.
$40.00–50.00.

OTHER ITEMS NOT PICTURED

PAPER DOLL BOX #6055, Saalfield, 1969. $20.00–25.00 cut; $35.00 45.00 uncut.

TELL-A-TALE BOOK, *Corey Baker of Julia*, Whitman, 1970. $8.00–10.00.

PAPER DOLL BOX #6055, Saalfield, 1969. $20.00–25.00 cut; $35.00–45.00 uncut.

VIEW-MASTER #B572, GAF, 1969. $25.00–35.00.

ACTIVITY BOX, Things To Do With Corey and Earl, Artcraft, 1960s. $40.00–50.00.

COLORING BOOK, Saalfield, 1969. Photo cover of Julia with her arms around Corey. $20.00–25.00.

DOLL, Julia, Mattel, 1968. Non-talking 11½" doll in nurse's outfit and straight hair. She has a "twist and turn" waist and bendable legs. $175.00–200.00.

DOLL, Julia, Mattel, 1968. Talking 11½" doll with brown hair, dressed in a gold and silver metallic jumpsuit. $200.00–225.00.

DOLL OUTFITS, Julia, Mattel, 1969. Four different outfits, including "Candlelight Capers" outfit in window box with photo of Julia. $40.00–50.00 each.

DOLL SET, Julia Simply Wow Set, Mattel, 1969. Boxed set containing one of the boxed dolls and an additional outfit. The outfit is a white and blue dress and is only available with the set. Sold as an exclusive catalog item. $600.00–800.00 boxed set.

HOSPITAL SET, Transogram, 1970. Plastic accessories in photo box. $75.00–100.00.

LUNCH BOX, K.S.T., 1969. Metal box with metal thermos. $60.00–80.00 box; $30.00–40.00 thermos.

PAPER DOLL BOOKLET #1335/4458/ 4435, Saalfield, 1968. Illustration of Julia and Corey on white background. Booklets vary with all three numbers listed. $15.00–20.00 cut; $30.00–35.00 uncut.

PAPER DOLL BOOKLET #4472, Artcraft, 1969. $15.00–20.00 cut; $30.00–35.00 uncut.

PAPER DOLL BOX #6055, Saalfield, 1969. Yellow box with illustration of Julia and children. $20.00–25.00 cut; $35.00–45.00 uncut.

PAPER DOLL BOX #6055, Saalfield, 1968. White box with illustrated photos inside squares on cover. $20.00–25.00 cut; $35.00–45.00 uncut.

TRADING CARDS, Topps, 1960s. 33 cards in test issue. No wrapper or box exist. $1,300.00–1,600.00 set; $40.00–50.00 single cards.

TV GUIDES, 1968–1970. 12/14/68 Carroll; 06/28/69 Carroll and Copage; 03/14/70 Carroll; 12/26/70 Carroll and Williamson. $8.00–10.00 each.

THE KROFFT SUPERSHOW

90-minute show eventually cut to one hour, including segments of the following:

—— CAST ——

KAPTAIN KOOL & THE KONGS
Various short segments between episodes

Michael Lembeck
Kaptain Kool

Debra Clinger
Superchick

Mickey McMeel
Turkey

Louise DuArt
Nashville

Bert Sommer
Flatbush

BIGFOOT AND WILDBOY

20 episodes

Ray Young
Bigfoot

Joseph Butcher
Wildboy

Yvonne Regalado
Cindy

Moika Ramirez
Suzie

DR. SHRINKER
16 episodes

Jay Robinson
Dr. Shrinker

Teddy Eccles
Brad

Jeff McKay
Geordie

Susan Lawrence
B.J.

Billy Barty
Hugo

ELECTRA WOMAN & DYNA GIRL
8 (two-part) episodes

Deidre Hall
Laurie/Electra Woman

Judy Strangis
Judy/Dyna Girl

Norman Alden
Frank Heflin

THE LOST SAUCER
16 episodes

Ruth Buzzi
Fi

Jim Nabors
Fum

Jarrod Johnson
Jerry

Alice Playten
Alice

Larry Larson
Dorse

MAGIC MONGO
15 episodes

Lenie Weinrib
Magic Mongo

Helaine Lembeck
Lorraine

Robin Dearden
Christy

Paul Hinckley
Donald

WONDERBUG
16 episodes

John Anthony Bailey
C.C.

David Levy
Barry

Carol Anne Seflinger
Susan

Frank Welker
Wonderbug (voice)

CHALKBOARD, Board King, 1977. 18" x 12" chalkboard made in different colors, including green and orange. Original packaging includes chalk, eraser and a round photo sticker attached to the board's left corner. Sticker varies with either a photo of *Electra Woman and Dyna Girl,* or *Kaptain Kool and the Kongs.* $50.00–75.00.

THE KROFFT SUPERSHOW

COMIC BOOKS #1–6, Whitman/Gold Key, 1976. $10.00–15.00 each.

LUNCH BOX, Aladdin, 1976. Metal box and plastic thermos. $75.00–100.00 box; $25.00–30.00 thermos.

RECORD/LP, "Stories from the Krofft T.V. Supershow," Peter Pan, 1978. $20.00–25.00.

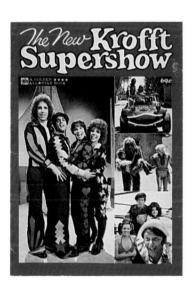

Left:
GOLDEN ALL-STAR BOOK, The New Krofft Supershow, Golden Press, 1978. $15.00–20.00.

Right:
IRON-ON TRANSFERS, Golden Press, 1977. 8" x 11" booklet with six iron-ons that include Kaptain Kool, Electra Woman, Bigfoot and Wildboy, Schlep, Wonderbug and Magic Mongo. $25.00–30.00.

OTHER ITEMS NOT PICTURED

CURTAINS AND BEDSHEET SET, Sid and Marty Krofft Productions Inc., 1978. $75.00–100.00 set.

KAPTAIN KOOL & THE KONGS

FRAME TRAY PUZZLE, Whitman, 1978. $10.00–15.00.

JIGSAW PUZZLES, HG Toys, 1977. Two different, including #445-11 pictured and another featuring Flatbush from the first season. $25.00–35.00 each.

GUITARS, Emenee, 1977. Two different plastic guitars, including a 34" and 27" version. $100.00–125.00 34"; $75.00–100.00 27".

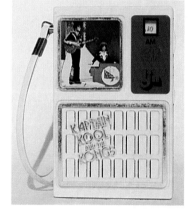

Left:
PENCIL BY NUMBERS, Hasbro, 1977. $40.00–50.00.

Right:
POCKET A.M. RADIO, LJN Toys, 1977. $50.00–60.00.

RECORD PLAYER, Vanity Fair, 1978. $60.00–80.00.

RECORD/LP, "Kaptain Kool and the Kongs," Epic, 1978. $25.00–30.00.

KAPTAIN KOOL & THE KONGS

OTHER ITEMS NOT PICTURED

FAN CLUB KIT, Kool Club, Sid and Marty Krofft TV Productions Inc., 1977. Includes two 22" x 34½" cast posters, two 2¼" cast buttons, newsletter and fact sheet. Posters and buttons also sold separately. $50.00–75.00 kit; $10.00–15.00 each button; $25.00–30.00 each poster.

GUITAR JEWELRY, Harmony, 1977. Plastic strand of pearls with a plastic guitar pendant and matching silver guitar earrings. $35.00–45.00.

MAGIC SLATE, Whitman, 1978. Illustration of cast on card. $35.00–45.00.

POSTER, Kaptain Kool and the Kongs, Marathon Graphics, 1977. 23" x 35" six-photo collage on red background. $25.00–30.00.

POSTER ART KIT, HG Toys, 1977. Includes four markers and two 11¾" x 18" posters on board. $40.00–50.00.

RECORD/45, "And I Never Dreamed," Epic, 1978. Without picture sleeve. $10.00–12.00.

T-SHIRT, Sid and Marty Krofft TV Productions, Inc., 1977. Photo of group standing with logo above. Sold through the fan club. $30.00–40.00.

WRISTWATCH, Kaptain Kool, Sid and Marty Krofft TV Productions Inc., 1977. Working watch with face featuring photo of Kaptain Kool. Sold through the fan club. $75.00–100.00.

BIGFOOT AND WILDBOY

COSTUME, Bigfoot, Collegeville, 1978. Mask varies with either plastic or synthetic hair. $50.00–75.00.

FRAME TRAY PUZZLE, Whitman, 1978. $15.00–20.00.

DR. SHRINKER

JIGSAW PUZZLE, HG Toys, 1977. $30.00–35.00.

MAGNIFYING GLASS, Harmony, 1977. $25.00–35.00.

SHRINKING MACHINE, Harmony, 1977. $35.00–45.00.

VIEW-MASTER #H2, The Krofft Supershow #1, GAF, 1976. Reel A is *Dr. Shrinker* and reels B and C are *Wonderbug.* $20.00–25.00.

OTHER ITEMS NOT PICTURED

COSTUME, Dr. Shrinker, Ben Cooper, 1976. $100.00–125.00.

ELECTRA WOMAN AND DYNAGIRL

BOARD GAME, Ideal, 1977. $40.00–50.00.

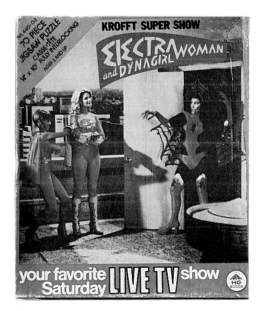

JIGSAW PUZZLE, HG Toys, 1977. $25.00–30.00.

VIEW-MASTER #H3, The Krofft Supershow #2, GAF, 1976. $25.00–30.00.

COSTUME, Electra Woman, Ben Cooper, 1976. $60.00–80.00.

PUZZLER, Harmony, 1977. Plastic slide puzzle in the shape of a calculator on 5½" x 9" card. $40.00–50.00.

THE LOST SAUCER

ITEMS NOT PICTURED

IRON-ON, Sid and Marty Krofft Productions, Inc., 1975. Show title above illustrated saucer. $15.00–20.00.

PUCHING BALL, 1970. Contains show logo and illustration of flying saucer. $50.00–75.00.

WONDERBUG

BOARD GAME, Ideal, 1976. $35.00–45.00.

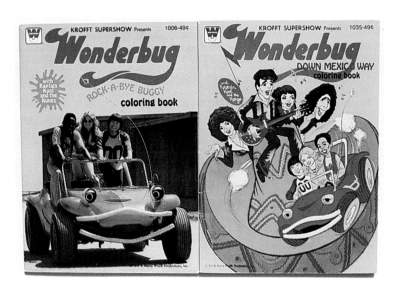

COLORING BOOKS, Whitman, 1978. Two different. $15.00–20.00 each.

RACE GAME, Harmony, 1977. Plastic game on 6" x 12" card. $30.00–40.00.

OTHER ITEMS NOT PICTURED

MAGIC SLATE, Whitman, 1978. Illustration of Wonderbug and cast. $30.00–40.00.

KUNG FU

BRITISH ANNUALS, Brown Watson, 1974–1977. Four different. 1977 annual not pictured. $20.00–25.00 each.

BUTTON AND KEYCHAIN, Anabus, 1973. Made in the United Kingdom with photo decal. $20.00–25.00 each.

COSTUME, Caine, Ben Cooper, 1973. $40.00–50.00.

OCTOBER 14, 1972–
JUNE 28, 1975

72 EPISODES

PEAK POSITION:
#27 in the 1973–1974 season

—— CAST ——

David Carradine
Kwai Chang Caine

Keye Luke
Master Po

Philip Ahn
Master Kan

Radames Pera
Young Caine "Grasshopper"

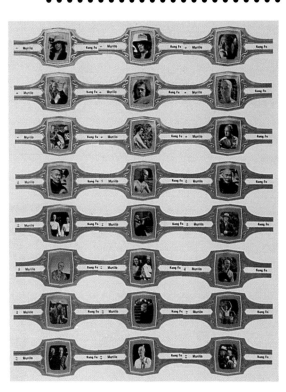

CIGAR BANDS, Murillo, 1970s. European set of 24. $60.00–80.00 set.

LUNCH BOX, K.S.T., 1974. Metal box with plastic thermos. $60.00–80.00 box; $20.00–25.00 thermos.

PAPERBACK BOOKS #1–4, Warner, 1974. $8.00–10.00 each.

POSTER, The Joker, 1973. 23" x 35" black light poster. $30.00–40.00.

RECORD/LP, "Kung Fu," Warner Bros., 1973. $25.00–35.00.

TALKING VIEW-MASTER #AVB598, GAF, 1973. $25.00–30.00.

TARGET SET, Mutiple Toymakers, 1975. 7" x 13½". $40.00–50.00.

TRADING CARDS, Topps, 1973. 60 cards in set. Cards 1–44 have puzzle backs and 45–60 include *Kung Fu* trivia. Also released in Australia by Scanlens under license from Topps. $80.00–100.00 set; $1.25–1.75 single cards; $8.00–10.00 wrapper; $50.00–60.00 display box.

TRADING CARDS, Monty Gum, 1970s. Single 2" x 1¾" cards from the "TV Hits" set. Wrapper and box feature *Kung Fu*, along with *Flipper, Daktari, Zorro,* and *Robin Hood.* $1.00–1.25 single cards; $3.00–5.00 wrapper; $40.00–50.00 display box.

VIEW-MASTER #B598, GAF, 1974. $20.00–25.00.

OTHER ITEMS NOT PICTURED

BUBBLE GUM, Warner Bros. Inc., 1972. Illustrated box with cast characters. Labeled as Chicle, the contents contain bubble gum pieces with Kung Fu comic strips. Made in Spain. $125.00–150.00 full box.

IRON-ON, 1970s. Photo of Caine. $10.00–15.00.

PLAYSET, Multiple Toymakers, 1975. Boxed set includes figures, horse with rider, and town building. $75.00–100.00.

RECORD/LP, "Grasshopper," Jet, 1975. European. $30.00–40.00.

TV GUIDES, 1973–1974. 06/23/73 Carradine; 01/26/74 Carradine illustrated. $10.00–15.00 each.

LAND OF THE LOST

SEPTEMBER 4, 1974 –
SEPTEMBER 3, 1977

43 EPISODES

— CAST —

Spencer Milligan
Rick Marshall

Wesley Eure
Will

Kathy Coleman
Holly

Phillip Paley
Cha-Ka

Walker Edmiston
Enick

Sharon Baird
Sa

Scott Fullerton
Ta

Ron Harper
Uncle Jack

BELT BUCKLE, Sid and Marty Krofft, 1976. Metal buckle from The World of Sid and Marty Krofft theme park. $50.00–75.00.

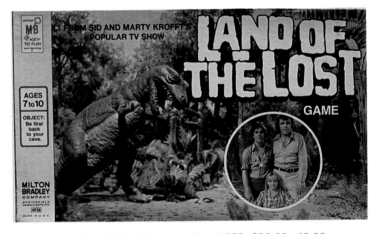

BOARD GAME, Milton Bradley, 1975. $30.00–40.00.

COLORING BOOKS, Whitman, 1975. Two different, including #1045 and coloring and activity book #1271. $25.00–30.00 each.

COSMIC SIGNAL, Larami, 1975. $30.00–40.00.

COSTUME, Sleestak, Ben Cooper, 1975. $100.00–125.00.

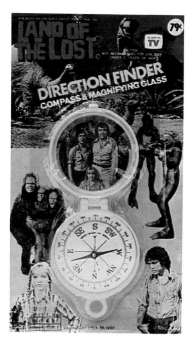

DIRECTION FINDER, Larami, 1975. Color of compass varies. $30.00–40.00.

JIGSAW PUZZLE, Whitman, 1975. $20.00–30.00.

GIVE-A-SHOW PROJECTOR, Kenner, 1975. Set includes 16 color slide strips, two of which feature *Land of the Lost.* Some of the other strips include *Far Out Space Nuts* and *Josie and the Pussycats.* $75.00–100.00.

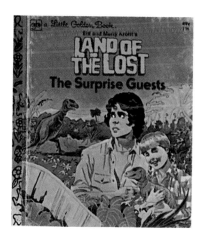

LITTLE GOLDEN BOOK, *The Surprise Guests,* Golden Press, 1975. $15.00–20.00.

MOON SPINNERS, Larami, 1975. $20.00–25.00.

LUNCH BOX, Aladdin, 1975. Metal box with plastic thermos. $100.00–125.00 box; $30.00–35.00 thermos.

SECRET LOOK OUT, Larami, 1975. $30.00–40.00.

MOONBASE ROCKET, Larami, 1975. Plastic airplane with rubber band launcher. $30.00–40.00.

SAFARI SHOOTER, Larami, 1975. 11" bagatelle game in 6" x 15" package. $30.00–40.00.

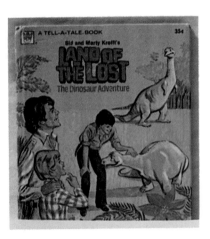

TELL-A-TALE BOOK, *The Dinosaur Adventure,* Whitman, 1975. $15.00–20.00.

SPARK SHOOTER, Larami, 1975. $30.00–40.00.

TIME MACHINE, Larami, 1975. $40.00–50.00.

VIEW-MASTERS, GAF, 1974–1977. Three different, including non-talking versions #B579 "Land of the Lost" (1974), and #H1 "Land of the Lost No. 2: Abominable Snowman" (1977), and talking version #TH1, "Abominable Snowman" (1977). $25.00–35.00 non-talking; $35.00–45.00 talking.

OTHER ITEMS NOT PICTURED

BELT, Town Belt Corp., 1970s. Child's leather belt with small photo from the show running its length. $50.00–75.00.

MAGIC SLATES, Whitman, 1975. Two different. $40.00–50.00 each.

PLASTIC DINOSAURS, Larami, 1975. Two different sets, including a small lot on card and a larger lot in a cello bag with photo header card. $35.00–45.00 each.

SAUCER SHOOTER, Larami, 1975. Similar to Moon Spinners but contains a gun to launch discs. $35.00–45.00.

STICKER BOOK, Whitman, 1975. $50.00–60.00.

WILDERNESS CAMPFIRE, Larami, 1975. Plastic accessories include a tent, roasting pit, oil lantern, and survival gear. Illustration of Will and Holly on 6½" x 10" card. $50.00–75.00.

LAVERNE & SHIRLEY

JANUARY 27, 1976– MAY 10, 1983

178 EPISODES

PEAK POSITION: #1 in the 1977–1978 season

—— CAST ——

Penny Marshall
Laverne DeFazio

Cindy Williams
Shirley Feeney

Phil Foster
Frank DeFazio

David L. Lander
Andrew "Squiggy" Squigman

Michael McKean
Lenny Kosnowski

Betty Garrett
Edna Babbish

Eddie Mekka
Carmine Ragusa

LAVERNE & SHIRLEY

OCTOBER 10, 1981– SEPTEMBER 18, 1982

13 EPISODES
of the animated cartoon.

On September 25, 1982, the series was incorporated into *The Mork & Mindy/Laverne & Shirley/Fonz Hour* and ran until September 3, 1983.

—— VOICES ——

Penny Marshall
Laverne DeFazio

Cindy Williams
Shirley Feeney

ACRYLIC PAINT BY NUMBERS, Hasbro, 1981. Based on the cartoon series. $35.00–45.00.

BOARD GAME, Parker Brothers, 1977. $20.00–25.00.

COLORING AND ACTIVITY BOOKS, Waltman, 1983. Four different. $10.00–15.00 each.

DOLLS, Laverne and Shirley (left), Lenny and Squiggy (right), Mego, 1977. $40.00–50.00 each loose; $125.00–150.00 boxed sets.

COSTUME, Laverne, Collegeville, 1977. $50.00–60.00.

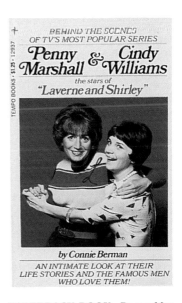

COSTUME, Shirley, Collegeville, 1977. $50.00–60.00.

IRON-ONS, 1970s. Several different. $15.00–20.00 each.

PAPERBACK BOOK, *Penny Marshall & Cindy Williams*, Tempo Books, 1977. $10.00–15.00.

JIGSAW PUZZLES, HG Toys, 1976. Three different. $15.00–20.00 each.

PAPERBACK BOOKS #1–3, Warner Books, 1976. $10.00–15.00 each.

PIZZA PARLOR, Harmony, 1977. $30.00–40.00.

POCKETBOOK, Harmony, 1977. $25.00–30.00.

Right:
SECRETARY SET, Harmony, 1977. $25.00–30.00.

POCKET FLIX CASSETTE, Ideal, 1978. Cassette for the Pocket Flix Viewer. $15.00–20.00.

Left:
RECORD/LP, "Laverne & Shirley Sing," Atlantic Records, 1976. $25.00–30.00.

Right:
RECORD/LP, "Lenny & Squiggy Present the Squigtones," Casablanca Records, 1979. Includes poster inside. $25.00–30.00.

VIEW-MASTER #J20, "The Slow Child," GAF, 1978. $15.00–20.00.

SHEET MUSIC, "Sixteen Reasons," Big 3, 1976. $15.00–20.00.

TIGER CLAW PENDANT, Harmony, 1977. $30.00–40.00.

OTHER ITEMS NOT PICTURED

BOWLING GAME, Harmony, 1977. Ten toy pins and ball on photo blister card. $30.00–40.00.

POSTERS, Laverne & Shirley and Lenny & Squiggy, 1970s. $20.00–25.00 each.

RECORDS/45s, Atlantic Records, 1976. "Chapel of Love"/"Sixteen Reasons;" "Da Doo Ron Ron"/"Five Years On;" "Graduation Day"/"All I Have to Do is Dream." Vocals by Penny Marshall and Cindy Williams. Without picture sleeves. $5.00–8.00 each.

TV GUIDES, 1976–1982. 05/22/76 Marshall & Williams; 06/18/77 Marshall & Williams illustrated; 04/29/78 Cast; 05/19/79 Marshall & Williams illustrated; 08/28/82 Marshall & Williams. $10.00–12.00 each.

WATCH AND POCKET PIN, Harmony, 1977. $35.00–45.00.

LIDSVILLE

SEPTEMBER 11, 1971–
SEPTEMBER 1, 1973

17 EPISODES

— CAST —

Butch Patrick
Mark

Charles Nelson Reilly
Hoo Doo

Billie Hayes
Weenie the Genie

COMIC BOOKS #1–5, Whitman/Gold Key 1972–1973. $20.00–25.00 each.

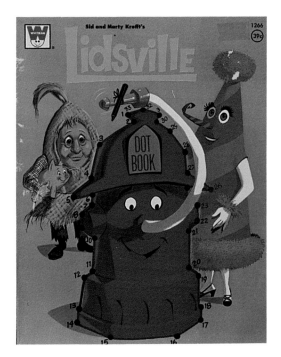

DOT BOOK, Whitman, 1973. $30.00–40.00.

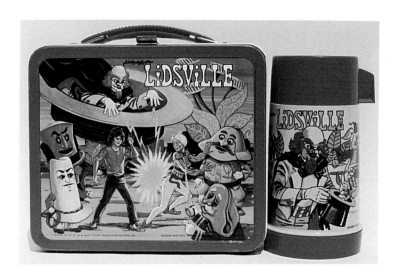

LUNCH BOX, Aladdin, 1971. Metal box with plastic thermos. $100.00–125.00 box; $35.00–45.00 thermos.

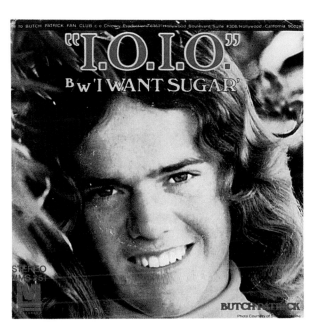

RECORD/45, "I.O.I.O."/"I Want Sugar," Metromedia Records, 1972. Vocals by Butch Patrick. $20.00–30.00.

MAGIC SLATE, Whitman, 1972. $50.00–75.00.

OTHER ITEMS NOT PICTURED

COSTUME, Hoo Doo, Collegeville, 1971. $125.00–150.00.

COSTUME, Weenie the Genie, Collegeville, 1971. $125.00–150.00.

THE LIFE AND TIMES OF GRIZZLY ADAMS

FEBRUARY 9, 1977–
JULY 26, 1978

37 EPISODES

PEAK POSITION:
Not in the top 25

—— CAST ——

Dan Haggerty
James "Grizzly" Adams

Denver Pyle
Mad Jack

Don Shanks
Nakuma

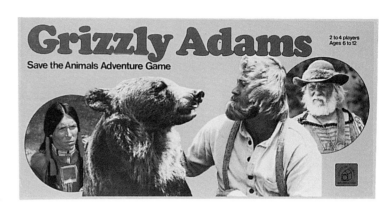

BOARD GAME, Save the Animals Adventure Game, House of Games, 1978. $25.00–30.00.

COLORING AND ACTIVITY BOOKS, Rand McNally, 1978. Coloring book #06534 and activity book #06528 pictured. Another features Grizzly, Jack, and Ben on the cover with a blue background. $15.00–20.00 each.

PAPERBACK BOOK, Schick Sunn Books, 1977. $8.00–10.00.

DOLLS, Grizzly Adams and Nakoma, Mattel, 1978. $20.00–25.00 each loose; $40.00–50.00 each boxed.

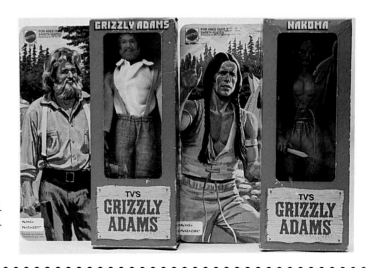

JIGSAW PUZZLES, House of Games, 1978. Four different numbered 139-1 through 139-4 (#139-2 not pictured). $10.00–15.00 each.

RECORD/45, "Maybe"/"Friends," RSO Records, Inc., 1979. Made in West Germany with vocals by Thom Pace. Theme from the television show. $20.00–25.00.

SHEET MUSIC, "Maybe," Chippenstar Music Co., 1976. $15.00–20.00.

TRASH CAN, Chienco, 1977. $35.00–45.00.

VIEW-MASTER #J10, GAF, 1978. $15.00–20.00.

OTHER ITEMS NOT PICTURED

DOLL SET, Mattel, 1978. Grizzly Adams and Ben. $50.00–60.00 loose set; $75.00–100.00 boxed.

IRON-ON, Grizzly, FCCA, 1979. $10.00–15.00.

LUNCH BOX, Aladdin, 1977. Metal dome box with plastic thermos. $80.00–100.00 box; $25.00–30.00 thermos.

POSTERS, Pro Arts Inc., 1979. Two different, including 20" x 28" Mr. Adams and 20" x 28" Grizzly Adams. $15.00–20.00 each.

STUFFED MULE, Knickerbocker Toys, 1977. 14" long with "Grizzly Adams" written on side knapsack. $30.00–40.00.

TV GUIDES, 1977–1978. 06/11/77 Haggerty; 01/28/78 Haggerty illustrated. $5.00–8.00 each.

LITTLE HOUSE ON THE PRAIRIE

**SEPTEMBER 11, 1974–
SEPTEMBER 21, 1982**

216 EPISODES

PEAK POSITION:
#7 in the 1977–1978 season

—— CAST ——

Michael Landon
Charles Ingalls

Karen Grassle
Caroline Ingalls

Melissa Sue Anderson
Mary

Melissa Gilbert
Laura

Lindsay/Sidney Greenbush
Carrie

Victor French
Isaiah Edwards

Richard Bull
Nels Oleson

Katherine MacGregor
Harriet Oleson

Alison Arngrim
Nellie

Jonathon Gilbert
Willie

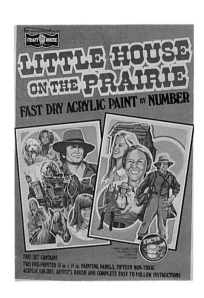

ACRYLIC PAINT BY NUMBER SET,
Craft House, 1979, 10" x 14". $40.00–
50.00.

BOARD GAME, Parker Brothers, 1978. $30.00–40.00.

COSTUME, Laura, Ben Cooper, 1970s.
$30.00–40.00.

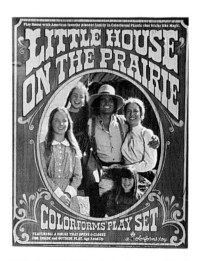

COLORFORMS, Colorforms, 1978.
12½" x 16". $40.00–50.00.

DOLLS, Laura and Carrie, Knickerbocker, 1978. $30.00–40.00 each loose; $50.00–75.00 each boxed.

LUNCH BOX, Thermos, 1978. Metal box with plastic thermos. $60.00–80.00 box; $15.00–20.00 thermos.

JIGSAW PUZZLE, HG Toys, 1978. $20.00–25.00.

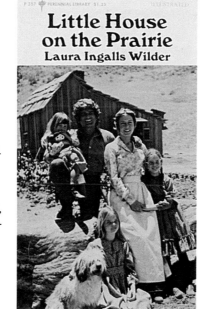

Left:
PAPERBACK BOOK, Perennial Library, 1975. $8.00–10.00.

Right:
SCHOOL CALENDAR & ASSIGNMENT BOOK, Rutledge Books, 1977. 6" x 9" with several full-page photos. $25.00–35.00.

THREE-RING BINDER AND SPIRAL NOTEBOOK, Stuart Hall Co. Inc., 1977. $25.00–35.00 each.

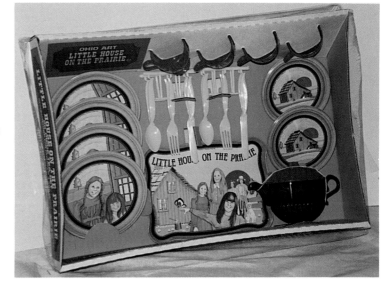

TOY TEA SET, Ohio Art, 1980. 26-piece set in 17" x 11" box. $100.00–125.00.

OTHER ITEMS NOT PICTURED

POSTER, Pro Arts Inc., 1979. 20" x 28" Michael Landon with Jack, the family dog. $20.00–25.00.

TV GUIDES, 1974–1982. 12/07/74 Landon; 06/07/75 cast illustrated; 05/29/76 cast; 05/13/78 cast illustrated; 07/14/79 Landon, Bommer and Anderson; 07/05/80 cast illustrated; 01/09/82 Landon illustrated. $10.00–15.00 each.

THE LOVE BOAT

BARBER SET, Fleetwood, 1979. $20.00–25.00.

COSTUME, Ben Cooper, 1978. Box marked as "Love Boat" with Captain Stubing mask. $40.00–50.00.

BOARD GAME, World Cruise, Ungame, 1980. $25.00–30.00.

JIGSAW PUZZLE, HG Toys, 1978. $20.00–25.00.

FIGURES, Captain Stubing, Doc, Gopher, Isaac, Julie, and Vicki. Mego, 1981. $20.00–25.00 each.

PLAYSET, Multi-Toys, Inc., 1983. 34" x 6" x 15" boxed set with 2" plastic figures. $100.00–125.00.

LOVE BOAT IN PORT, Fleetwood, 1979. $15.00–20.00.

PORCELAIN PLATE, Schmid, 1984. Collector plate in box. $35.00–45.00.

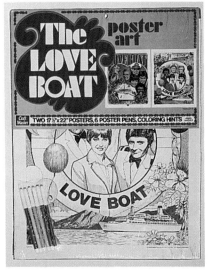

PUFFY STICKERS, Imperial, 1982. Six different numbered A–F. $10.00–15.00 each.

POSTER ART KIT, Craft Master, 1978. $40.00–50.00.

REPLICA MODEL, Montego, 1984.
$25.00–30.00.

SHEET MUSIC, "The Love Boat," LBC Music, Inc., 1979. Two different.
$15.00–20.00 each.

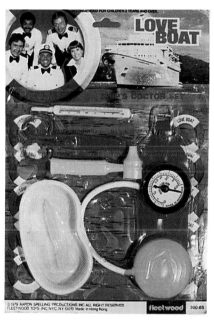

SHIP'S DOCTOR SET, Fleetwood, 1979.
$20.00–25.00.

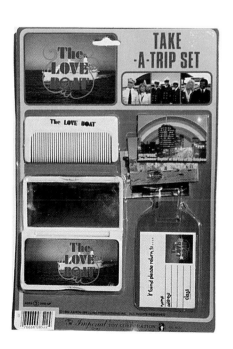

Left:
TAKE-A-TRIP, Imperial, 1983. $20.00–25.00.

Right:
TRAVEL BAG, Imperial, 1983. $20.00–25.00.

TOOTHPICK HOLDER, Enesco, 1979. 3".
$15.00–20.00.

TRAVEL STAMP SET, Imperial, 1983. $20.00–
25.00.

OTHER ITEMS NOT PICTURED

PAPERBACK BOOK, *The Love Boat #1: Voyage of Love*, Wanderer Books, 1983. A 5" x 7½" plot-it-yourself book where the reader chooses the changes in the plot. Cast photo cover. $15.00–20.00.

RECORD/45, "Love Boat Theme"/"The Rockford Files," Polydor, 1979. Theme from the television show. Side A vocals by Jack Jones. Side B instrumentals by Mike Post. $5.00–8.00.

TV GUIDES, 1978–1984. 02/04/78 cast illustrated; 07/22/78 MacLeod; 07/19/80 cast illustrated; 06/05/82 Tewes and MacLeod illustrated; 12/24/84 cast illustrated. $8.00–10.00 each.

THE MOD SQUAD

BOOKS, *Assignment: The Arranger* and *Assignment: The Hideout,* Whitman, 1969–1970. $10.00–15.00 each.

COMIC BOOKS #1–8, Dell, 1969–1971. #7 and 8 are reprints of #1 and 2. $30.00–40.00 #1; $20.00–25.00 #2–8.

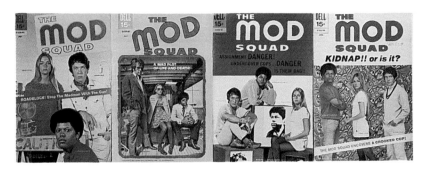

JIGSAW PUZZLES, Milton Bradley, 1969. #4089 pictured. Another puzzle has a paisley background and a green border. $60.00–80.00 each.

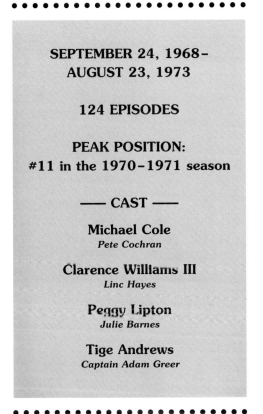

SEPTEMBER 24, 1968–
AUGUST 23, 1973

124 EPISODES

PEAK POSITION:
#11 in the 1970–1971 season

—— CAST ——

Michael Cole
Pete Cochran

Clarence Williams III
Linc Hayes

Peggy Lipton
Julie Barnes

Tige Andrews
Captain Adam Greer

PAPERBACK BOOKS #1–5, Pyramid Books, 1968–1970. $8.00–10.00 each.

RECORD/LP, Peggy Lipton, Ode Records, 1968. Gatefold cover. $25.00–30.00.

RECORDS/45s, Peggy Lipton, Ode Records, 1969. Several different with picture sleeves, including: "Stoney End"/"San Francisco Glide;" "Wear Your Love Like Heaven"/"Honey Won't Let Me" (front and back pictured); and "Lu"/"Let Me Pass By" (front pictured). Another single, "Red Clay County Line"/"Just a Little Lovin'," was released without a picture sleeve. $15.00–20.00 each with picture sleeve; $8.00–10.00 each without picture sleeve.

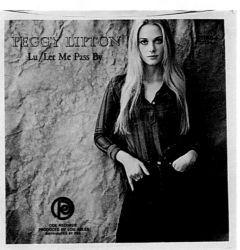

TRADING CARDS, Topps, 1968. 55 cards in the set with puzzle backs. $150.00–175.00 set; $2.75–3.00 single cards; $35.00–45.00 wrapper; $175.00–200.00 display box.

VIEW-MASTER #B478, GAF, 1968. $25.00–30.00.

OTHER ITEMS NOT PICTURED

BOARD GAME, Remco, 1968. $150.00–175.00.

INSTANT INTERCOM, Larami, 1973. Toy walkie-talkies on a cast illustrated card. Both walkie-talkies are made from white plastic and are connected by a green cord. $50.00–75.00.

JR. WATER GUNS, Larami, 1974. Toy gun on cast-illustrated card. $50.00–75.00.

MODEL KIT, Station Wagon, Aurora, 1969. $150.00–175.00.

RECORD/45, "(Theme from the Mod Squad) Alone Too Long"/"I'll See Your Light," Capitol Records, 1960s. Recorded by Modern Air. Without picture sleeve. $10.00–15.00.

TV GUIDES, 1968–1970. 11/02/68 cast; 07/12/69 cast; 02/28/70 cast; 07/03/71 cast. $15.00–20.00 each.

MORK & MINDY

4-WHEEL DRIVE JEEP, Mattel, 1979. For 8" dolls. $40.00–50.00.

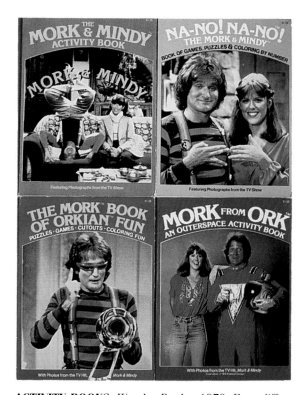

ACTIVITY BOOKS, Wonder Books, 1979. Four different. $10.00–15.00 each.

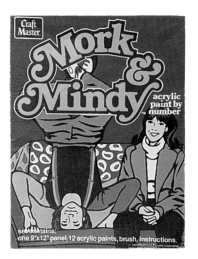

ACRYLIC PAINT BY NUMBER SETS, Craft Master, 1979. Three different styles. $20.00–25.00 each.

BELTS, PPC, 1979. Two children styles, including one in leather and another in stretch fabric with a metal buckle. $10.00–15.00 each.

BOARD GAME, Milton Bradley, 1979. $15.00–20.00.

BUTTONS, PPC, 1979. Several different 3" metal buttons. $5.00–8.00 each.

BOOK, *The Official Mork and Mindy Scrapbook,* Wallaby, 1979. $10.00–15.00.

BRITISH ANNUALS, Stafford Pemberton, 1980–1981. $15.00–20.00 each.

CARD GAME, Milton Bradley, 1978. $15.00–20.00.

COLORFORMS, Stand-Up Play Set, Colorforms, 1979. $10.00–15.00.

COLORFORMS, Colorforms, 1979. $20.00–25.00.

DOLLS, Mork and Mindy, Mattel, 1979. $25.00–30.00 each loose; $45.00–55.00 each boxed.

FIGURE, Mattel, 1979. $25.00–30.00.

FIGURINE PAINTING SET, Whiting Products, 1979. $25.00–30.00.

GUMBALL BANK, Hasbro, 1980. $40.00–50.00.

COSTUME, Mork, Ben Cooper, 1978. $25.00–30.00.

FLICKER RINGS, PTC, 1979. Several different 1½" styles. $20.00–25.00 each.

INSTANT STAINED GLASS, Aviva, 1979. Several different window stickers. $8.00–10.00 each.

LUNCH BOX, Thermos, 1978. Metal box with plastic thermos. $40.00–50.00 box; $10.00–15.00 thermos.

LUNCH BOX, Thermos, 1978. Plastic box with plastic thermos. $25.00–35.00 box; $10.00–15.00 thermos.

JIGSAW PUZZLES, Milton Bradley, 1978. Four different. $10.00–15.00 each.

MAGIC SHOW PLAYSET, Colorforms, 1980. 12½" x 16" box. $25.00–35.00.

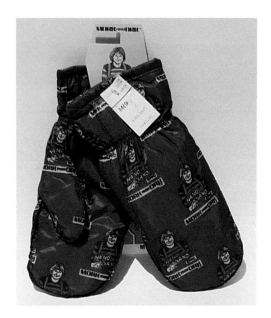

MITTENS, PPC, 1979. $15.00–20.00.

MODEL KIT, Jeep, Monogram, 1979. $30.00–40.00.

PARTY SUPPLIES, Ambassador, 1979. Includes cups, plates, napkins, invitations, room decorator and tablecloth. $5.00–10.00 each article.

MORK BUBBLE GUM, Amurol, 1978. Several pieces of gum inside a plastic egg. Each piece is wrapped in paper containing Mork quotes. $3.00–5.00 each egg; $15.00–20.00 empty display box.

PAPERBACK BOOKS, 1978–1980. *Mork & Mindy*, Pocket Books (1979); *Mork & Mindy 2: The Incredible Shrinking Mork*, Pocket Books (1980); *The Mork & Mindy Story*, Scholastic (1979); *Mork & Mindy: A Video Novel*, Pocket Books (1978); *Robin Williams*, Grosset & Dunlap (1979); *Mork & Mindy Puzzlers*, Cinnamon House (1979); *Mork & Mindy Code Puzzles From Ork*, Cinnamon House (1979); *The Robin Williams Scrapbook*, Ace Books (1979). $8.00–10.00 each.

PATCHES, Aviva, 1979. Several different styles. $5.00–10.00 each.

POSTERS, Mork, 1979. Several different, including 23" x 35" by Dargis Associates, Inc. (pictured); 20" x 28" by Pro Arts Inc., and 19" x 28" by Sales Corp. of America. $15.00–20.00 each.

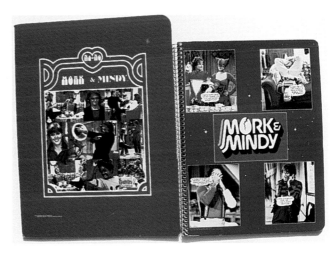

POCKET FOLDER AND SPIRAL NOTEBOOK, Stuart Hall, 1979. $10.00–12.00 each.

RADIO, Concept 2000, 1979. $40.00–50.00.

SHRINKY DINKS, Skyline Toys Inc., 1979. $25.00–35.00.

SLEEPING BAG, Mork, PPC, 1979. $25.00–35.00.

STICKERS, Aviva, 1979. Several different styles. $5.00–8.00 each.

TRADING CARDS, Topps, 1978. 99 cards and 22 stickers in set. 55 cards have puzzle backs and 44 have trivia. $20.00–25.00 set; 15¢–25¢ single cards; 25¢–50¢ single stickers; $1.00–2.00 wrapper; $10.00–15.00 display box.

TALKING RAG DOLL, Mork, Mattel, 1979. $15.00–20.00 loose; $35.00–45.00 boxed.

SUSPENDERS, Lee Co., 1979. $25.00–30.00.

VIEW-MASTER #K67, GAF, 1979. Also packaged in a 4½" x 8" envelope with a read-along story. $15.00–20.00.

OTHER ITEMS NOT PICTURED

WRISTWATCH, M.Z. Berger & Co., Inc., 1979. Also made in a digital display style. $60.00–80.00.

BELT BUCKLE, PPC, 1979. Metal buckle with logo and Mork's suspenders on sides. $10.00–15.00.

CALENDARS, Wallaby, 1979. 1980 wall calendar with color photos. $15.00–20.00.

CANVAS TOTE BAGS, PPC, 1970s. Four different designs. $20.00 – 25.00.

CLOTHING, PPC, 1970s. Different items, including an illustration of Mork on a small child's T-shirt, and a pair of blue jeans with a Mork and Mindy label and embroidered egg logo on back pocket. $15.00–25.00 each article.

IRON-ONS, 1970s. Several different. $10.00–15.00 each.

MORK JEWELRY, PPC, 1979. Several different metal figural pins that contain either Mork phrases or illustrations of Mork. $10.00–15.00 each.

LUNCH BOX, Aladdin, 1978. Orange plastic dome box from Canada with photo sticker and a plain thermos. $30.00–40.00.

ORK EGG, Mattel, 1979. Plastic egg with Ork creature and goo inside. $20.00–25.00.

RUB 'N PLAY, Colorforms, 1979. 8" x 12¼" illustrated box contains 10 uncolored stand-up figures and two color transfer sheets. $25.00–35.00.

SELF-INKING RUBBER STAMP, PPC, 1979. Mork's face on stamp. Packaged on card. $15.00–20.00.

SHEET MUSIC, "Mork and Mindy Theme," PPC, 1978. With photo cover. $10.00–15.00.

T-SHIRTS, PPC, 1970s. Several different, including four styles that match the canvas tote bags. $15.00–25.00 each.

TALKING ALARM CLOCK, Concept 2000, 1980. Figural Mork sits alongside clock. $40.00–50.00.

TV GUIDES, 1978–1980. 10/28/78 Dawber and Williams; 05/03/80 Dawber and Williams illustrated; 11/22/80 Dawber. $5.00–8.00 each.

NANNY AND THE PROFESSOR

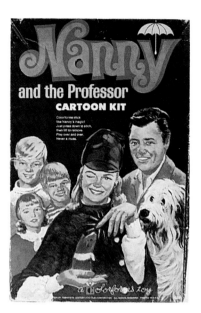

CARTOON KIT, Colorforms, 1971. $40.00–50.00.

COLORING BOOKS, Saalfield, 1971. Three different. #3929 varies with either a green house and blue lettering or a yellow house with red lettering. $25.00–35.00 each.

PAPER DOLL BOOKLET #1213, Saalfield, 1970. $20.00–25.00 cut; $40.00–50.00 uncut.

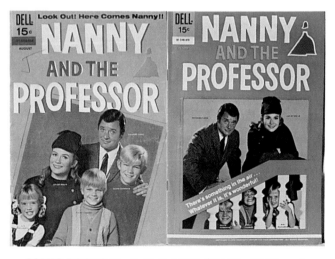

COMIC BOOKS #1–2, Dell, 1970. $25.00–30.00 each.

PAPER DOLL BOOKLET #4283, Artcraft, 1971. $20.00–25.00 cut; $40.00–50.00 uncut.

PAPER DOLL BOOKLET #5114, Artcraft, 1971. $20.00–25.00 cut; $40.00–50.00 uncut.

PAPERBACK BOOKS #1–3, Lancer Books, 1970. $10.00–15.00 each.

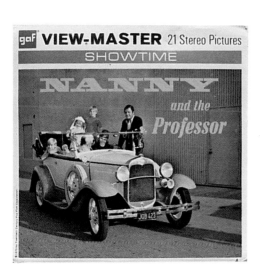

VIEW-MASTER #B573, GAF, 1970. $30.00–40.00.

THE NEW ZOO REVUE

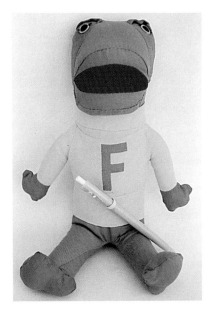

AUTOGRAPH DOLL, 1970s, 11½" cloth doll with pen attached $25.00–30.00.

BAGATELLE GAME, Wolverine Toy, 1970s. 10½" x 22" $50.00–60.00.

BENDIES, Imperial, 1973. Bendable figures of Charlie, Henrietta, Freddie, and Freida sold loose in a display box. $15.00–20.00 each.

BOARD GAME, The New Zoo Revue Friendship Game, Kontrell, 1973. $60.00–80.00.

BOARD GAME, Ungame, 1981. $20.00–25.00.

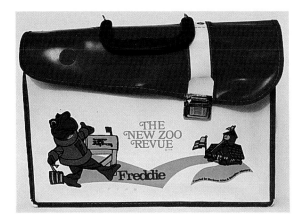

BOOK BAG, 1974. $30.00–40.00.

C'MON BE A SPORT, Warren Paper Products Co., 1970s. 12" x 8½" set includes story cards and puzzle pieces. $25.00–35.00.

COLORING BOOK #C2051, Saalfield, 1974. Oversized 11" x 14" book. $20.00–25.00.

FIGURES, Diener Ind., 1972. $30.00–40.00.

COLORING AND ACTIVITY BOOKS, Saalfield, 1973–1975. Several different, including coloring books #C1854, #4568, #5484 (cut-outs on back) and activity book #C2432 (pictured). Other coloring books include #C0944 (some cover as #4568) and another with three square photos on cover. $20.00–25.00 each.

FINGER PUPPETS, The Rushton Co., 1970s. $25.00–30.00 each.

HAND PUPPETS, 1970s. Several different made by different companies, including those with vinyl heads by The Rushton Co. Cloth versions feature a pop-out tongue and squeaker. $30.00–40.00 each vinyl; $15.00–20.00 each others.

IRON-ONS, New Zoo Review Corporation, 1978. Several different. $15.00–20.00 each.

JEWELRY, New Zoo, 1970s. Includes metal rings and necklaces. $20.00–25.00 each.

KEYCHAIN AND NECKLACE, Howard Eldon, 1970s. $20.00–25.00 each.

LIGHT SWITCH PLATE, NZR Joint Ventures, 1971. $15.00–20.00.

LUNCH BOX, Aladdin, 1975. Vinyl box with plastic thermos. $200.00–250.00 box; $25.00–30.00 thermos.

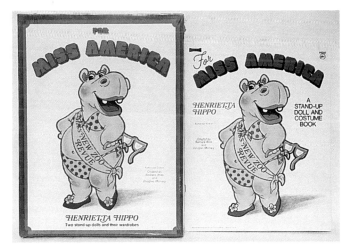

PAPER DOLL BOOKLET AND BOX, Henrietta, Saalfield, 1974. $20.00–25.00 each cut; $30.00–40.00 uncut.

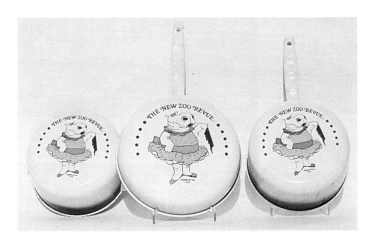

POT AND PANS, NZR, 1970s. $50.00–75.00 set.

MUSICAL MOBILE, Young Designs, 1971. $60.00–80.00.

PENCIL TOPPERS, New Zoo Revue, 1974. 1" figural erasers. Freida pictured. $10.00–15.00 each.

PRESS-OUT ALBUM, Artcraft, 1974. $25.00–35.00.

PUNCH-O-BALL, Oak Rubber
Co., 1973. $30.00–40.00.

RECORD/LP "New Zoo Revue," #3807,
Disneyland Records, 1972. Cover opens
into an 11-page booklet. $25.00–30.00.

RECORD/LP "New Zoo Revue," #1344,
Disneyland Records, 1972. $15.00–20.00.

STUFFED DOLLS, 1970s. Several different of each character and made by
different companies, including Mighty Star (small styles with beans), Rushton
Toy (vinyl heads), and Kamar (all material). $30.00–40.00 each.

SQUEAKER TOYS, Steven Mfg., 1974.
$35.00–45.00 each.

VIEW-MASTERS, GAF, 1972–1974. #B566 (1972); #B567 (1974); talking
version #AVB567 (1974). $25.00–30.00 talking; $20.00–25.00 others.

WRISTWATCH, New Zoo Revue, 1975. $40.00–50.00.

OTHER ITEMS NOT PICTURED

BOARD GAME, Cadaco, 1981. $25.00–35.00.

BOOK, *Mostly Happy Henrietta,* Hawthorne Books, Inc., 1973. Hardcover children's book, 30 pages, 9½" x 6½", $20.00–25.00.

COSTUMES, 1970s. $60.00–80.00 each.

FRAME TRAY PUZZLE, Puzzle Works, 1970s. 9" x 12" wooden puzzle of Freddie. $20.00–25.00.

ORNAMENTS, 1970s. Flat plastic figural characters. $10.00–15.00 each.

STAMP SET, Imperial Toy Co., 1973. Includes six character stamps, stamp pad, and paper on Illustrated card. $30.00 40.00.

THE PARTRIDGE FAMILY

SEPTEMBER 25, 1970–
AUGUST 31, 1974

96 EPISODES

PEAK POSITION:
#16 in the 1971–1972 season

—— CAST ——

Shirley Jones
Shirley

David Cassidy
Keith

Susan Dey
Laurie

Danny Bonaduce
Danny

Jeremy Gelbwaks/Brian Foster
Chris

Suzanne Crough
Tracy

Dave Madden
Reuben Kincaid

BOARD GAME, Milton Bradley, 1971. $30.00–40.00.

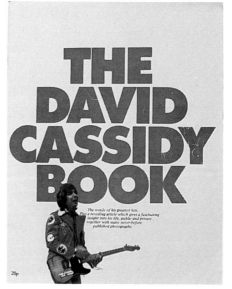

BOOK, *The David Cassidy Book,* Wise Pubs, 1973. Made in the United Kingdom. 8½" x 11" soft cover book containing stories, photos, and song lyrics. $30.00–40.00.

BOOKLETS, The Laufer Company, 1970s. Several different black and white booklets offered as mail-away items from *Tiger Beat* and *Fave* magazines, including *Boys, Beauty and Popularity* pictured. Others include: *1001 Secret Facts about the Partridge Family; Darling Danny Bonaduce; David Cassidy's Concert Tour; David's Private Photo Album; Dynamic David Cassidy; Life, Love & David Cassidy by Shirley Jones; Partridge Family Fun Album; The Secret of David Cassidy;* and *Susan Dey's Private Journal.* $25.00–30.00 each.

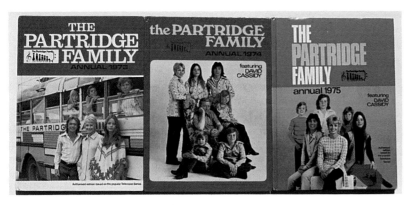

BRITISH ANNUALS, *The Partridge Family,* World Distributors, 1973–1975. $40.00–50.00 each.

BULLETIN BOARD, 1970s. Two 18" x 24" versions, including another with a red background. $125.00–150.00.

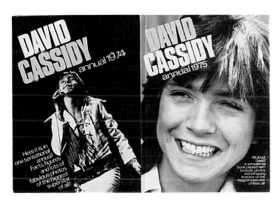

BRITISH ANNUALS, *David Cassidy,* World Distributors, 1974–1975. $35.00–45.00 each.

BUTTONS, David Cassidy, 1970s. Several different 3" buttons. $20.00–25.00 each.

THE PARTRIDGE FAMILY BUS, Remco, 1973. Box has illustration of garage on back and sides for storage and play. $400.00–500.00 loose; $800.00–1,000.00 boxed.

CIGAR BANDS, Derk De Vires, 1970s. European set of 10 with 2" bands. Colors of bands vary. $50.00–75.00 set.

CLOCKS, Time Setters, 1972. Two different styles, including David Cassidy and The Partridge Family. 10" clock faces (pictured) or electric wall clocks with black wooden frames, white hands, and electrical cords. $75.00–100.00 each face; $250.00–300.00 each clock.

CLOTHING LINE, Kate Greenaway, 1970s. Front and back of original tag pictured. Patches and stickers were attached to clothing that included jeans, tops, jackets, and jumpsuits. $150.00–175.00 each tagged article.

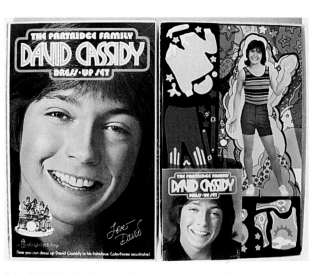

COLORFORMS, David Cassidy Dress-Up Set, Colorforms, 1972. $40.00–60.00.

COLORING BOOKS, Saalfield/Artcraft, 1970–1972. Several different, including Saalfield #3839 (1971); Saalfield #3881 (1972); Artcraft #3997 (1971); Saalfield #4637 (1970); and Artcraft #5399 (1970). $25.00–35.00 each.

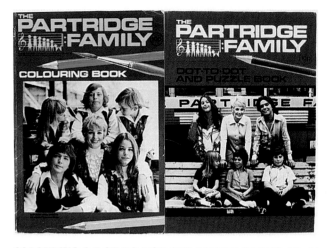

COLOURING & DOT-TO-DOT AND PUZZLE BOOKS, World Distributors, 1972. Made in the United Kingdom. $50.00–75.00 each.

COMIC BOOKS, *David Cassidy* #1–14, Charlton, 1972–1973. $15.00–20.00 each.

COOKBOOK, *The Partridge Family Cookbook,* Curtis Books, 1973. Paperback book containing recipes. $50.00–60.00.

COMIC BOOKS, *The Partridge Family* #1–21, Charlton, 1970–1973. Number 1 was also printed with a color photo. Number 5 includes poster pinups to color. $25.00–30.00 #1 and #5; $15.00–20.00 each others.

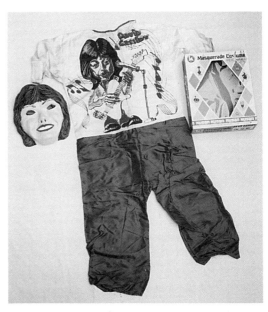

COSTUME, David Cassidy, Kusan, 1973. $300.00–400.00.

DAVID CASSIDY LOVER'S KIT, *16 Magazine,* 1971. Includes lover's membership card, life-size portrait, maxi-poster pin-up, love message, and wallet photos. $60.00–80.00.

DOLL, Patti Partridge, Ideal, 1971. 16" doll. $100.00–125.00 loose; $200.00–250.00 boxed.

FAN CLUB KIT, David Cassidy, The Laufer Company, 1972. Includes booklet, blue cardboard record, membership card, stickers, calendar poster, decoder, and autographed photo. $100.00–125.00.

DOLL, Laurie Partridge, Remco, 1973. 19" doll with color poster of David and Susan included in box. $125.00–150.00 loose; $250.00–300.00 boxed.

FAN CLUB KITS, The Laufer Company, 1971–1972. 1971 kit pictured and includes booklet, decoder, stickers, black flexible record, membership card, wallet photos and a mini poster. The 1972 kit is similar, except contains a pink cardboard record and David pinup. $100.00–125.00 each.

FAN CLUB WALLETS, Columbia Pictures, 1972–1973. United Kingdom fan club kits for David Cassidy in 1972 and a combined kit for David Cassidy and The Partridge Family in 1973. Each kit contains a membership card, 8" x 10" photos, writing paper, mini-posters and bios. $150.00–200.00 each.

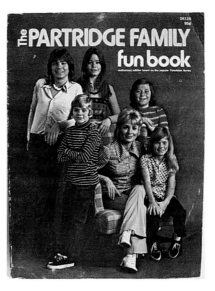

FUN BOOK, Young Readers Press, Inc., 1974. Magazine-style book with the same contents as the 1973 British annual. $40.00–60.00.

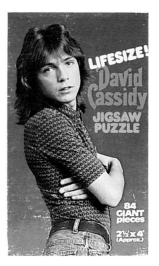

JIGSAW PUZZLE, David Cassidy, APC, 1973. Life-size. Each piece is nearly 6" in diameter. $150.00–200.00.

GUITAR, Carnival Toys, 1973. 20". $150.00–200.00.

GUITAR, Carnival Toys, 1973. 31". $250.00–300.00.

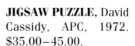

JIGSAW PUZZLE, David Cassidy, APC, 1972. $35.00–45.00.

JIGSAW PUZZLES, Whitman, 1973. Two different 224-piece puzzles made in the United Kingdom, including David Cassidy. Cast puzzle not pictured. $100.00–125.00 each.

LUNCH BOX, K.S.T., 1971. Metal box with metal thermos. Re-released in 1973 with plastic thermos. $75.00–100.00 box; $25.00–30.00 metal thermos; $15.00–20.00 plastic thermos.

MAGAZINES, *Tiger Beat's Official Partridge Family Magazine,* The Laufer Company, 1970–1972. Fifteen issues. The last two were combined as double issues. $30.00–40.00 each.

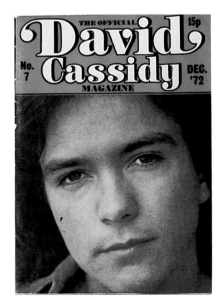

MAGAZINES, 1971–1972. Several different devoted to the show, including *David Cassidy and the Partridge Family* by Stanley Publications, *Partridge Family Song Specials* by The Laufer Company, and *David Cassidy* by *Tiger Beat* (not pictured). $25.00–30.00 each.

MAGAZINES, *The Official Partridge Family Magazine,* 1971–1972. Four 6" x 8" issues made in the United Kingdom. $40.00–50.00 each.

MAGAZINES, *The Official David Cassidy Magazine,* 1972–1975. Forty-three issues produced in the United Kingdom, 6" x 8". $25.00–30.00 each.

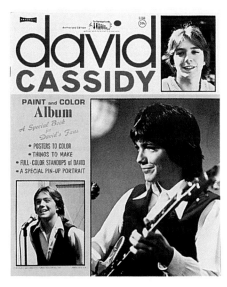

PAPER DOLL BOOKLETS, Artcraft, 1971–1972. Two different versions, including #5137 with blue background (1971) and #5143 with red background (1972). #5137 varies with either Jeremy Gelbwaks (first Chris) or Brian Forster (2nd Chris). $20.00–25.00 each cut; $35.00–45.00 each uncut.

PAINT & COLOR ALBUM, David Cassidy, Artcraft, 1971. $35.00–45.00.

PAPER DOLL BOOKLETS, Susan Dey, Artcraft, 1971–1973. Two different versions, including #4218 with photo cover (1971) and #4261 with illustration (1973). $25.00–30.00 each cut. $40.00–50.00 each uncut.

PAPER DOLL BOXES, Susan Dey, Saalfield, 1972–1973. Two different, including #6024 with green background (1972), and #6079 with yellow background (1973). $25.00–35.00 each cut; $50.00–75.00 each uncut.

PAPER DOLL BOXES, Saalfield, 1971–1973. Several different, including #6157 with green background (1972), #6050 with blue background (1971), #6050 with yellow background (1973), and #6050 with red background (1972). $25.00–35.00 each cut; $50.00–75.00 each uncut.

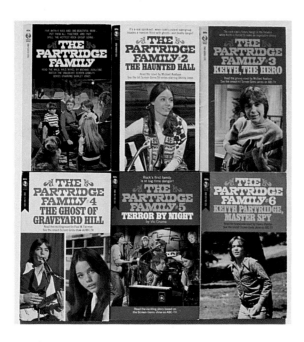

PAPERBACK BOOKS #1–17, Curtis Books, 1970–1973. $3.00–5.00 #2, 5, 10; $20.00–25.00 #15–17; $8.00–12.00 each others.

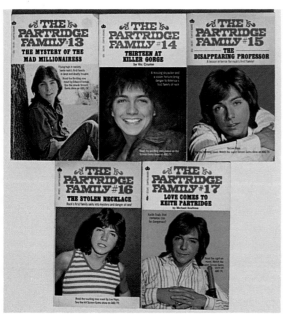

PAPERBACK BOOKS, David Cassidy, 1970s. Several different, including: *Young Mr. Cassidy*, Scholastic Books (1972); *Meet David Cassidy*, Scholastic Books (1972); *The David Cassidy Story*, Curtis Books (1972); *The David Cassidy Story*, World Distributors, (1973) made in the United Kingdom; and *David, David, David,* Curtis Books (1972). $25.00–30.00 each UK; $10.00–15.00 each others.

PAPERBACK BOOKS, Susan Dey, *Tiger Beat*, 1972–1973. Three different, including *For Girls Only* (1972), *Susan Dey's Secrets on Boys, Beauty & Popularity* (1973), and *Cooking, Cleaning & Falling In Love* (1973). $25.00–30.00 each.

PATCHES, David Cassidy, Golden Gift Productions, 1970s. Made in the United Kingdom. Several different, including captions and illustrations. $15.00–20.00 each.

PERSONALITY PRINTS, David Cassidy, Kaymac Distribution Systems, Inc., 1971. Several different 8½" x 11" stickers, including #1501, #1502, and #1505 pictured. $40.00–60.00 each.

PICTORIAL ACTIVITY ALBUM, Artcraft, 1973. $30.00–40.00.

PIN-ON BUTTON FAMILY TREE, Merry Motion, 1971. $250.00–300.00.

PIN-ON BUTTONS, Merry Motion, 1971. Set of six different on individual cards. $35.00–45.00 each.

Left:
POSTER, David, Columbia Pictures, 1972. 12" x 18". $20.00–25.00.

Right:
POSTER MAGAZINES, David Cassidy, Columbia Pictures, 1970s. Several different made in the United Kingdom. $50.00–60.00 each.

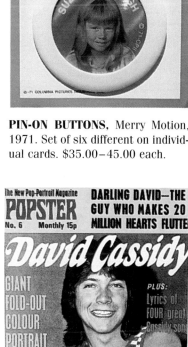

POSTERS, The Partridge Family, 1970s. Several different, including one 23" x 35" United States version by Poster Prints in 1971 (pictured). Others made in different countries. $75.00–100.00 each.

POSTERS, David Cassidy, 1970s. Several different, including 23" x 32" United Kingdom version pictured. Others United Kingdom versions made, as well as in the United States and other countries. $50.00–75.00 each.

POSTER PATCH, Synergisms, 1970s. 3½" x 4½" vinyl patch with adhesive backing. $35.00–45.00.

POSTER PACKS, Topps, 1971. Twenty-four 9½" x 18" posters in set. $400.00–500.00 set; $20.00–25.00 single posters; $15.00–20.00 wrapper; $75.00–100.00 display box.

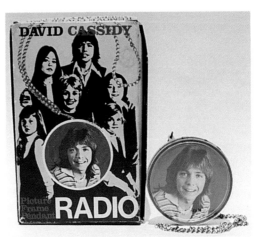

PURSE, Kate Greenway, 1970s. David's silhouette and signature along with the caption "I Think I Love You." Came in different colors and material variations. $125.00–150.00.

RADIO, Philgee International Ltd., 1970s. 3½" diameter cover is removable to insert any picture. Comes with a 29" chain to be worn as a necklace. $250.00–300.00.

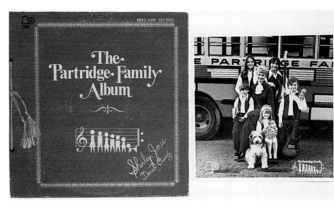

RECORD/LP, "The Partridge Family Album," Bell, 1970. With photo insert. $15.00–20.00.

RECORD CABINET, AFT Furniture Company, 1972. 25" x 15" x 22" wooden box. Came unassembled in a photo box with four 8" x 10" color stickers to apply to cabinet sides. Box pictures David Cassidy. $400.00–500.00 unboxed; $800.00–1,000.00 boxed.

RECORD/LP, "Sound Magazine," Bell, 1971. $10.00–15.00.

RECORD/LP, "Up to Date," Bell, 1971. With bookcover. $25.00–35.00.

RECORDS/LPs, "Christmas Card," Bell, 1971. With real, removable card or printed card cover. $25.00–30.00 each.

RECORD/LP, "Shopping Bag," Bell, 1972. With Partridge Family shopping bag. $25.00–35.00.

RECORD/LP, "At Home With Their Greatest Hits," Bell, 1972. $15.00–20.00.

RECORD/LP, "Notebook," Bell, 1972. $15.00–20.00.

RECORD/LP, "Bulletin Board," Bell, 1973. $25.00–35.00.

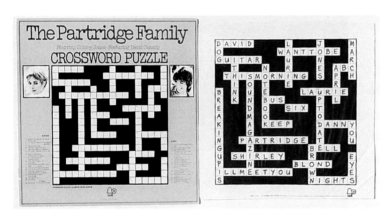

RECORD/LP, "Crossword Puzzle," Bell, 1973. Inside sleeve shows answers to puzzle. $25.00–35.00.

RECORD/LP, "The Partridge Family," Laurie House, 1973. 2-LP set of greatest hits. Television mail order only. $40.00–60.00.

RECORD/LP, "The World of The Partridge Family," Bell, 1974. 2-LP set of greatest hits. $40.00–60.00.

RECORDS/LPs, 1970s. Several different international albums were released with alternate covers, including United Kingdom "Only A Moment Ago" by Sounds Superb (1970), United Kingdom "The Partridge Family Christmas Album" by Sounds Superb (1971), German "Hits aus der Fernseh-Serie: Die Partridge Familie," by Bell, and Japanese boxed gift pack "The Partridge Family," Bell (1972). $50.00–75.00 each 2-LP sets; $35.00–45.00 each others.

Other 45s without picture sleeves include: "I'll Meet You Halfway"/"Morning Rider on the Road" (1971); "I Woke Up This Morning"/"Twenty Four Hours a Day" (1971) "It's One of Those Nights"/"One Night Stand" (1971); "Am I Losing You"/"If You Ever Go" (1972); "Breaking Up is Hard to Do"/"I'm Here, You're Here" (1972) "Looking Through the Eyes of Love"/"Storybook Love" (1972); "Friend and a Lover"/"Something's Wrong" (1973) and "Lookin' For a Good Time"/"Money, Money" (1973). $5.00–8.00 each.

RECORDS/45s, Bell, 1970–1973. Two different with picture sleeves, including "I Think I Love You"/"Somebody Wants to Love You" (1970) and "Doesn't Somebody Want to be Wanted?"/"You Are Always on My Mind" (1971). $15.00–20.00 each.

RECORDS/45s, Bell, 1970s. Several different international singles were released with alternate covers. $25.00–35.00.

RECORDS/LPs, David Cassidy, Bell, 1970s. David recorded four solo albums during the show, including "Cherish" (1972), "Rock Me Baby" (1972), "Dreams are Nuthin' More Than Wishes" (1973), and "Greatest Hits" (1974) which includes some Partridge Family recordings. $15.00–20.00 each.

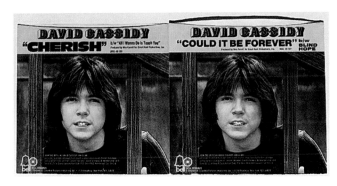

RECORDS/45s, David Cassidy, Bell, 1972. Only two singles with picture sleeves were released during the show, including "Cherish"/"All I Wanna Do Is Touch You," and "Could It Be Forever"/"Blind Hope." $10.00–15.00 each.

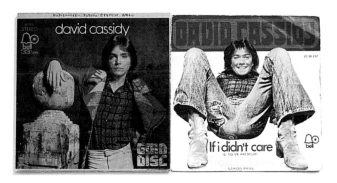

RECORDS/LPs & 45s, David Cassidy, Bell, 1970s. Most United States albums and singles were released in other countries with alternate covers. Singles pictured include four-song compilation from Japan and "If I Didn't Care"/"Frozen Noses" (1974). $25.00–35.00 LPs; $15.00–25.00 45s.

Left:
RECORD/LP, "Ricky Segall and the Segalls," Bell, 1973. Sings selections from the television show. $30.00–40.00.

Right:
RECORD/45, "Sooner or Later"/ "Say Hey, Willie," Bell, 1973. Vocals by Ricky Segall. $30.00– 40.00.

Left:
RECORD/LP, "Danny Bonaduce," Lion Records, 1973. $35.00–45.00.

Right:
RECORDS/45s, Danny Bonaduce, Lion Records, 1973. "Dreamland"/ "Blueberry You" and "I'll Be Your Magician"/"Fortune Lady" without a picture sleeve. $35.00–45.00 with picture sleeve; $10.00–15.00 without picture sleeve.

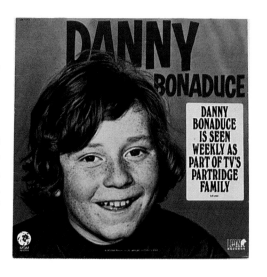

SHEET MUSIC, Screen Gems-Columbia Music, Inc., 1970–1974. Several different. $15.00–20.00 each.

SHEET MUSIC, David Cassidy, Screen Gems-Columbia Music, Inc., 1971–1974. Several different. $15.00– 20.00 each.

SLIDE PUZZLE, The Roalex Company, 1970s. $100.00–125.00.

SONGBOOKS, Screen Gems-Columbia Publications, 1970s. Several different with text and photos inside for both *The Partridge Family* and David Cassidy. $40.00–50.00 Partridge Family; $35.00–45.00 David.

T-SHIRT, David Cassidy, Columbia Pictures Ind., Inc., 1972. Sold as a mail-away premium. $50.00–75.00.

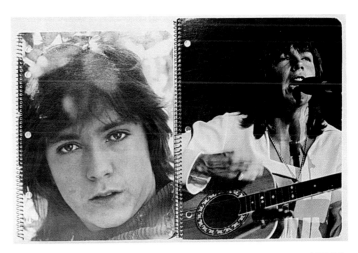

SPIRAL NOTEBOOKS, David Cassidy, Westab, 1972. $35.00–45.00 each.

Left:
THREE RING BINDER, David, Westab, 1972. $40.00–50.00.

Right:
TALKING VIEW-MASTER #AVB 569, The Money Manager, GAF, 1971. $35.00–45.00.

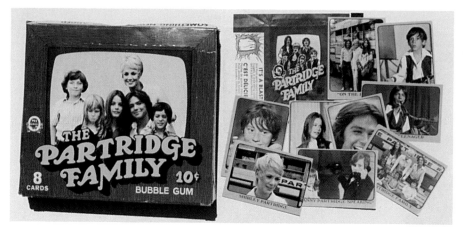

TRADING CARD SET #1, Topps, 1971. 55 yellow cards in set. Puzzle and song backs. Also manufactured by O-PEE-CHEE in Canada, Scanlens in Australia and a slightly smaller size by AB & C in England. $60.00–80.00 set; $1.00–1.25 single cards; $10.00–15.00 wrapper; $75.00–100.00 display box.

TRADING CARD SET #2, Topps, 1971. 55 blue cards in set. Puzzle and song backs. $60.00–80.00 set; $1.00–1.25 single cards; $10.00–15.00 wrapper; $75.00–100.00 display box.

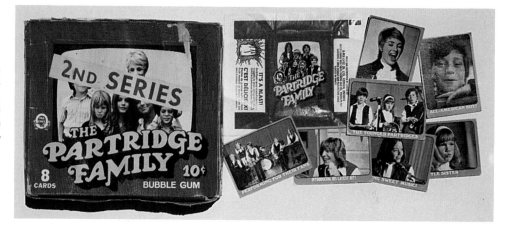

NOTE: Topps trading card sets include three different display box styles. One is a half-size box with a 5¢ price, and the other two are full size (as seen in sets #1 and #2) with either a 5¢ or 10¢ price.

TRADING CARD SET #3, Topps, 1971. 88 green cards in set. Puzzle and song backs. $175.00–200.00 set; $2.00–2.25 single cards; $8.00–10.00 wrapper; $75.00–100.00 display box.

VIEW-MASTER #B569, The Money Manager, GAF, 1971. $30.00–40.00.

VIEW-MASTER #B592, Male Chauvinist, GAF, 1973. $35.00–45.00.

OTHER ITEMS NOT PICTURED

3-D PHOTOS, Merry Motion, 1971. Two different 14" x 11" 3-D color photos, one of David Cassidy and another of the cast. $150.00–200.00 each.

BEACH TOWEL, David Cassidy, Columbia Pictures, 1970s. Mail-away premium offered on the label of HI-C drink cans. Illustration of David on towel. $150.00–200.00.

BOOKLET, "The David Cassidy Story," Reese Publishing Co., Inc., 1971. $25.00–30.00.

BOOKLET, "David Cassidy and The Partridge Family Private Picture Book," 16 Magazine, Inc., 1971. $25.00–30.00.

BUTTON, David, Anabas Ltd, 1970s. Made in the United Kingdom. 3" plastic button with photo sticker. $25.00–35.00.

CALENDAR, David Cassidy, APC, 1973. For the year 1974. $50.00–75.00.

DAVID CASSIDY MAIL-A-WAY ITEMS, 1970s. Several different items offered exclusively through United States teen magazines. Items include Love Charms, 500 Super Luv Stickers, Choker Luv Beads, David's Soul Mate Pen, Stationery, and a variety of wall posters. Additional items were offered through United Kingdom magazines, including nickel-plated jewelry and posters. $35.00–45.00 each U.S.; $40.00–50.00 each U.K.

GREETING CARD, David Cassidy, Pace International, 1972. 7" x 4½" card with photo cover of David. Made in the United Kingdom. $30.00–40.00.

HI-C DRINK LABELS, Columbia Pictures, 1971. Each label contains a photo of a cast member along with an order form to mail away for the entire set. Mail-away set is printed on heavier stock paper than the labels. $25.00–35.00 each label; $150.00–200.00 mail-away set.

JEWELRY, 1970s. Several different, including bracelets and necklaces with Partridge Family tags. $50.00–75.00 each.

LETTER PACK, Anabas Ltd., 1973. David Cassidy's photo appears on 5" x 8" paper and envelopes in a cello package. Made in the United Kingdom. $40.00–60.00.

MEMO PAD, Anabas Ltd., 1973. David Cassidy's photo appears on cover of 5" x 8" blank paper pad. Made in the United Kingdom. $50.00–75.00 each.

RECORD/LP, "Everything You Have Always Wanted to Know About David Cassidy," Superstar Records, 1972. Spoken documentary about David with photo cover. $30.00–40.00.

TV GUIDES, 1970–1972. 10/17/70 cast; 05/22/71 Cassidy; 12/18/71 cast; 07/18/72 Cassidy. $20.00–25.00 each.

WRISTWATCHES, 1970s. Working watch with David Cassidy or Partridge Family on face. $150.00–200.00 each.

THE PATTY DUKE SHOW

SEPTEMBER 18, 1963 –
AUGUST 31, 1966

104 EPISODES

PEAK POSITION:
#18 in the 1963–1964 season

— CAST —

Patty Duke
Patty/Cathy Lane

William Schallert
Martin Lane

Paul O'Keefe
Ross Lane

Jean Byron
Natalie Lane

Eddie Applegate
Richard Harrison

BOARD GAME, Milton Bradley, 1963. $40.00–50.00.

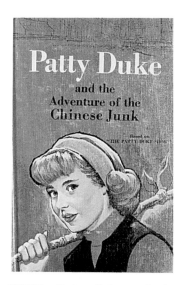

BOOK, *Patty Duke and the Adventure of the Chinese Junk,* Whitman, 1966. $10.00–15.00.

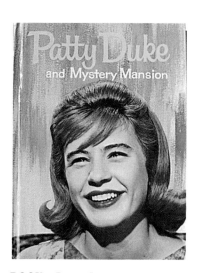

BOOK, *Patty Duke and Mystery Mansion,* Whitman, 1964. $10.00–15.00.

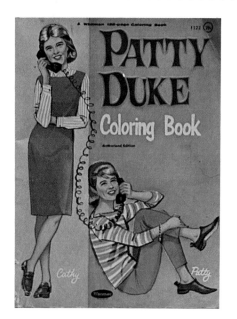

COLORING BOOK #1122, Whitman, 1964. $25.00–30.00.

COLORING BOOK #1141, Whitman, 1966. $25.00–30.00.

JR. JIGSAW PUZZLE, Whitman, 1963. $35.00–45.00.

PAPERBACK BOOK, *Patty Goes to Washington*, Ace Books, 1964. $15.00–20.00.

DOLLS, Patty Duke, Horsman Dolls, Inc., 1965–1966. Two different 12" dolls. The 1965 doll comes with telephone and photo. The 1966 doll comes in a box labeled "Go-Go with Patty Duke" and includes one of her 45 rpm singles. 1966 doll pictured. $75.00–100.00 loose; $300.00–400.00 boxed.

PAPER DOLL BOOKLET #1991, Whitman, 1963. $20.00–25.00 cut; $35.00–45.00 uncut.

PAPER DOLL BOOKLET #1991, Whitman, 1964. $20.00–25.00 cut; $35.00–45.00 uncut.

PAPER DOLL BOX, Milton Bradley, 1963. Includes Patty and Cathy dolls. $30.00–40.00 cut; $60.00–80.00 uncut.

Left:
RECORD/LP, "Don't Just Stand There," United Artists, 1965. $25.00–30.00.

Right:
RECORD/LP, "Patty," United Artists, 1967. $25.00–30.00.

RECORD/LP, "Greatest Hits," United Artists, 1966. $25.00–30.00.

RECORD/LP, "TV's Teen Star," United Artists, 1967. $25.00–30.00.

RECORDS/45s, Patty Duke, United Artists, 1965–1967. Several different, including "Don't Just Stand There"/ "Everything But Love" with picture sleeve (pictured). Others include: "Say Something Funny"/"Funny Little Butterflies" with picture sleeve; "Whenever She Holds You"/"Nothing But Love" without picture sleeve; "World Is Watching Us"/"Little Things Mean Alot" with picture sleeve; "Why Don't They Understand"/ "Danke Schoen" without picture sleeve; "And Were We Strangers"/"Dona, Dona" without picture sleeve; and "The Wall Came Tumbling Down"/"What Makes You Special" without picture sleeve. $8.00–10.00 each without picture sleeve; $15.00–20.00 each with picture sleeve.

OTHER ITEMS NOT PICTURED

CHARM JEWELRY SET, Standard Toykraft, 1963. 18" x 13" window box with photo of Patty. Includes jewelry box and small charms. $150.00–200.00.

CHEERLEADER LUSTER KIT, 1965. In photo cover box. $75.00–100.00.

GLAMOUR SET, Standard Toykraft, 1963. 15" x 12" window box with photo of Patty. Includes plastic mirror, brush and comb. $150.00–200.00.

LEATHER ACCESSORIES KIT, 1965. In photo cover box. $75.00–100.00.

PAPER DOLL BOX #4609, Patty Duke Fashion Wardrobe, Whitman, 1965. 9" x 11½" window box. $30.00–40.00 cut. $50.00–75.00 uncut.

PAPER DOLL BOX #4775, Whitman, 1965. 5" x 14½" box includes Patty and Cathy dolls. $30.00–40.00 cut. $50.00–75.00 uncut.

TILE TRAY KIT, Creative Corner, 1965. 11" x 9" box with photo of Patty on cover. Contains a small ashtray kit with tiles and cement. $75.00–100.00.

TV GUIDES, 1963–1964. 12/28/63 Duke; 08/29/64 Duke, Schallert and Lane. $15.00–20.00 each.

SIGMUND AND THE SEA MONSTERS

BOARD GAME, Milton Bradley, 1975. $30.00 40.00.

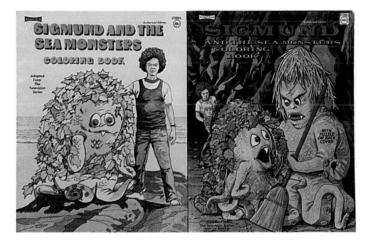

COLORING BOOKS, Saalfield, 1974. Three different, including #C0945 and #C1853 pictured. #4634 has the same cover as #C0945 and includes more pages. $25.00–30.00 each.

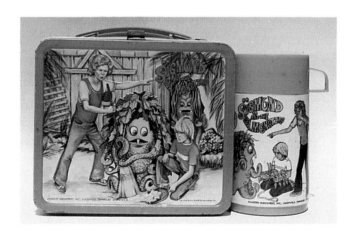

LUNCH BOX, Aladdin, 1974. Metal box with plastic thermos. $100.00–125.00 box; $30.00–35.00 thermos.

SEPTEMBER 8, 1973–
OCTOBER 18, 1975

29 EPISODES

— CAST —

Johnny Whitaker
Johnny Stuart

Billy Barty
Sigmund

Scott Kolden
Scott Stuart

Mary Wickes
Zelda Marshall

Rip Taylor
Sheldon the Sea Genie

COSTUME, Sigmund, Ben Cooper, 1973. $125.00–150.00.

RECORD/LP, "Friends: Music from Sigmund and the Sea Monsters," Chelsea Records, 1973. Vocals by Johnny Whitaker. $40.00–50.00.

RECORD/45, "Friends"/"You You," Chelsea Records, 1973. Vocals by Johnny Whitaker. $25.00–35.00.

TALKING VIEW-MASTER #AVB595, GAF, 1974. $35.00–45.00.

VIEW-MASTER #B595, GAF, 1974. $25.00–35.00.

THE SIX MILLION DOLLAR MAN

3-D VIEWERS, Chad Valley, 1976. Made in the United Kindgom. Boxed or on card. Boxed version pictured. $50.00–75.00 each.

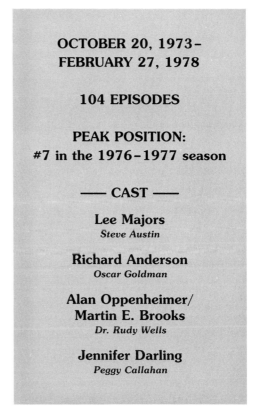

OCTOBER 20, 1973– FEBRUARY 27, 1978

104 EPISODES

PEAK POSITION: #7 in the 1976–1977 season

—— CAST ——

Lee Majors
Steve Austin

Richard Anderson
Oscar Goldman

Alan Oppenheimer/ Martin E. Brooks
Dr. Rudy Wells

Jennifer Darling
Peggy Callahan

ACTIVITY BOOK #2234, Artcraft, 1974. 10" x 12" book that includes a punch-out figure of Steve Austin. $35.00–45.00.

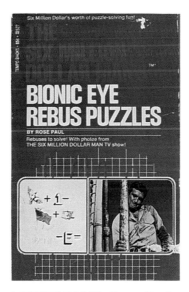

ACTIVITY BOOKS, Tempo Books, 1976. Three different 5¼" x 8¼" books, including *Bionic Eye Rebus Puzzles* (pictured), *Bionic Brain Benders,* and *Computer Crossword Puzzles.* $10.00–15.00 each.

Left:
ACRYLIC PAINT BY NUMBER SETS, Craft Master, 1975. Four different sets, including Jaws of Death, Bionic Struggle, Tank Attack, and Man Against Machine. Jaws of Death pictured. $30.00–40.00 each.

Right:
BANK, Animals Plus, 1976. 12" plastic figural. $30.00–40.00.

BEACH TOWEL, Universal City Studios, Inc., 1976. $40.00–60.00.

BELT AND BUCKLE, Fabil, 1976. $35.00–45.00.

BIONIC ACTION CLUB KIT, Kenner, 1973. Mail-away fan club kit containing a sticker, membership card, autographed photo, and a certificate. $50.00–75.00.

BIONIC EYEWEAR, Hudson, 1977. Fabric eyeglass case in box. $30.00–40.00.

BIONIC ADVENTURE SETS, Kenner, 1976. Kenner made three different outfits in the United States for the 12" Steve doll, including Mission to Mars, O.S.I. Undercover Assignment, and Test Flight at 75,000 Feet Adventure. Denys Fisher made similar outfits in the United Kingdom. U.S. versions pictured. $30.00–40.00 each U.S.; $45.00–55.00 each U.K.

BIONIC MISSION VEHICLE, Kenner, 1977. $75.00–100.00.

BIONIC TRANSPORT AND REPAIR STATION, Kenner, 1975. Kenner's United States version pictured. Denys Fisher made a similar United Kingdom version. $50.00–75.00 U.S.; $60.00–80.00 U.K.

BIONIC LOLLY, Lyons Maid, 1977. Popsicles made in the United Kingdom. Pictured with original display card. $25.00–35.00 wrapper.

Left:
BIONIC TATTOOS AND STICKERS, Kenner, 1976. $10.00–15.00.

Right:
BIONIC STICKERS, General Mills, 1976. Set of eight 2⅜" x 4⅛" stickers. Two stickers were available as premiums inside each Cheerios or Lucky Charms cereal box. A different set of 10 was offered in 1977 and is pictured under *The Bionic Woman.* $5.00–8.00 each sticker.

BOARD GAMES, Parker Brothers, 1975. Parker Brothers' United States version pictured. Denys Fisher made a similar United Kingdom version. $15.00–20.00 U.S.; $25.00–30.00 U.K.

BOY's COMB AND BRUSH SET, Faberge, 1976. Made in Canada. $40.00–60.00.

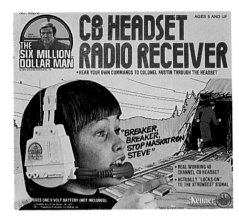

BRITISH ANNUALS, Stafford Pemberton, 1977–1980. 1980 annual not pictured. $30.00–40.00 each 1977–1979; $40.00–50.00 1980.

CB RADIO HEADSET RECEIVER, Kenner, 1977. $40.00–50.00.

CARD GAMES, Bionic Crisis, Parker Brothers, 1976. Parker Brothers made the United States version and Denys Fisher made a similar United Kingdom version. U.S. version pictured. $15.00–20.00 U.S.; $25.00–35.00 U.K.

CLOTHING LINE, Rob Roy, 1970s. Several different styles, including pajamas pictured. $25.00–35.00 each.

COLORING AND DOT-TO-DOT BOOKS, Artcraft/ Saalfield, 1976. Coloring books #C1832 & #C1867 and dot-to-dot book #C2412. $10.00–15.00 each.

COLORING AND ACTIVITY BOOKS, Rand McNally, 1977. Coloring books #C1520 & #C1868 and activity book #C2471. $10.00–15.00 each.

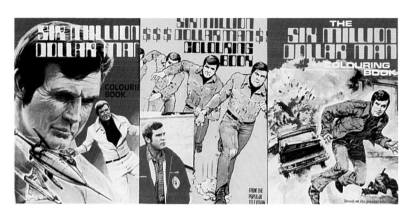

COLOURING BOOKS, Stafford Pemberton, 1976–1978. Three different made in the United Kingdom. Close-up (1978), yellow cover (1976) and car explosion (1977). $40.00–50.00 each.

COMIC BOOK MAGAZINES #1–7, Charlton, 1976. 8" x 11" in size. $15.00–20.00 each.

COMIC BOOKS #1–9, Charlton, 1976–1978. $10.00–15.00 each.

COSTUME, Steve Austin, S.A. Issoudun Jeanes Ind., 1970s. 2' x 3' boxed costume from France with vinyl bionic arm, hand and mask. $300.00–400.00.

COSTUME, Steve Austin, Berwick, 1976. Made in the United Kingdom. $60.00–80.00.

COSTUME, Steve Austin, Ben Cooper, 1974. Blue or red body suit. $35.00–45.00.

CRITICAL ASSIGNMENT LEGS AND ARMS, Kenner, 1976. Kenner made United States versions of separate boxed sets for replacement legs and arms. Denys Fisher made similar United Kingdom versions. Kenner legs pictured. $25.00–35.00 each U.S.; $35.00–45.00 each U.K.

CUP, TUMBLER, AND BOWL, Dawn, 1976. Bowl not pictured. $15.00–20.00 cup or tumbler; $30.00–40.00 bowl.

DOLL, Bigfoot, Kenner, 1978. $75.00–100.00 loose; $200.00–225.00 boxed.

DOLL, Steve Austin, Lili Ledy, 1974. Made in Mexico. Slight difference in body style than the United States version. $40.00–50.00 loose; $100.00–125.00 boxed.

DOLL, Maskatron, Kenner, 1970s. Kenner made United States version (pictured) in a window display box. Denys Fisher made United Kingdom version in solid box. $60.00–80.00 each loose; $125.00–175.00 U.S. boxed. $150.00–200.00 U.K. boxed.

DOLL, Oscar Goldman, Kenner, 1973. Kenner made United States version (pictured), and Denys Fisher made United Kingdom version in a solid box. $30.00–40.00 each loose; $75.00–100.00 U.S. boxed; $100.00–125.00 U.K. boxed.

DOLLS, Steve Austin, Kenner, 1975–1978. Four different 12" versions. Issue #1 dressed in red jogging suit with engine block (1975). Kenner made United States' version in a window display box, and Denys Fisher made a United Kingdom version in a solid box. Others not pictured include Issue #2 labeled "New Bionic Grip" dressed in a red jogging suit with a steel beam and a right hand that grips (1977). Issue #3 labeled "New Biosonic Arm" dressed in jeans and red top with a right hand grip, karate action feature, blocks and boards (1978). Issue #4 is similar to the first issue but was packaged with additional outfits. $30.00–40.00 each loose; $125.00–150.00 U.S. boxed Issue #1; $150.00–175.00 U.K. boxed Issue #1; $150.00–175.00 boxed Issue #2; $400.00–500.00 boxed Issue #3; $400.00–500.00 boxed Issue #4.

IRON-ON, 1970s. Several different. $20.00–25.00 each.

DUAL LAUNCH DRAG SET, Kenner, 1977. 21" x 4½" x 13" $150.00–200.00.

GIVE-A-SHOW PROJECTOR, Kenner, 1975. $40.00–50.00.

JIGSAW PUZZLES, APC, 1976–1977. Two 8" x 13" boxed versions numbered #1485 (1976) and an 8½" x 8½" box #1536 (1977). $25.00–35.00 each.

JIGSAW PUZZLES #1241–1243, APC, 1975. $20.00–25.00 each.

JIGSAW PUZZLES, Whitman, 1976. Five different United Kingdom boxed styles. One 8½" x 11½" and four 8½" x 7" sizes. Two smaller sizes not pictured include an illustration of Steve with a shark and another of Steve with an exploding helicopter. $40.00–50.00 each.

LUNCH BOX, Aladdin, 1978. Metal box with plastic thermos. $60.00–80.00 box; $15.00–20.00 thermos.

MISSION CONTROL CENTER, Kenner, 1976. $75.00–100.00.

LASER DISCS, MCA, 1978. $40.00–50.00 each.

LUNCH BOX, Aladdin, 1974. Metal box with plastic thermos. $60.00–80.00 box; $15.00–20.00 thermos.

LUNCH BOX, Aladdin, 1974. Plastic version made in Canada. $60.00–80.00.

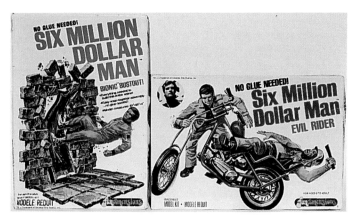

MODEL KITS, MPC, 1975. MPC made four different United States sets, including Bionic Bustout, Evil Rider, Fight for Survival and Jaws of Doom. Bionic Bustout and Evil Rider pictured. Denys Fisher made similar sets in yellow boxes in the United Kingdom. $40.00–50.00 each U.S., $45.00–55.00 each U.K.

MOVIE CASSETTES, Kenner, 1975. Six numbered titles include #1 Bionic Feats, #2 The Bionic Man in Action, #3 Col. Steve Austin Adventures, #4 Col. Steve Austin in Pursuit, #5 Bionic Rescue, and #6 Col. Steve Austin Tackles Danger. $20.00–25.00 each.

MOVIE VIEWER, Kenner, 1975. Packaging varies with flap or solid box. $40.00–50.00.

O.S.I. HEADQUARTERS, Kenner, 1976. Playset for 12" dolls. $100.00–125.00.

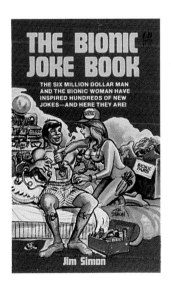

PAPERBACK BOOK, *The Bionic Joke Book,* Leisure Books, 1976. $5.00–10.00.

PAPERBACK BOOKS, Warner, 1972–1973. *Cyborg #1* (1972) with two different covers and *Cyborg #2* (1973). $10.00–15.00 each.

PAPERBACK BOOKS, 1976. *The Six Million Dollar Man and the Bionic Woman,* Scholastic Books; *International Incidents,* Berkley; *The Secret of Bigfoot Pass,* Berkley (two variations). $10.00–15.00 each.

PAPERBACK BOOKS #1–6, Warner Books, 1975. $10.00–15.00 each.

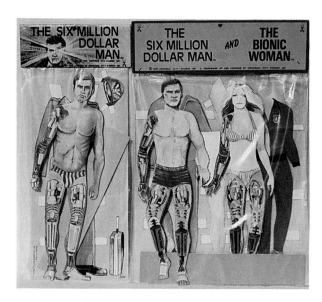

PAPER DOLLS, Children Books, 1978. Made in Italy. Steve Austin packaged individually and with Jaime Sommers. $30.00–40.00 solo; $40.00–50.00 pair.

PAPERBACK BOOKS, Star Books, 1975–1976. United Kingdom versions of the Warner Books and Berkley series. *The Secret of Bigfoot Pass* (1976), *Wine, Women and War* (1975), *Solid Gold Kidnapping* (1975), and *The Rescue of Athena One* (1975) pictured. Hardback versions were also made in the same size. $20.00–25.00 each.

PLAY-DOH ACTION SET, Kenner, 1977. $40.00–50.00.

PORTA-COMMUNICATOR, Kenner, 1976. Packaging varies with flap or solid box. $40.00–50.00.

PLAYSUIT, Ben Cooper, 1974. Fabric costume with plastic mask. $40.00–50.00.

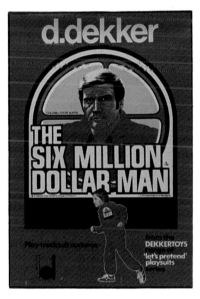

PLAYSUIT, Steve Austin, Dekker, 1975. Made in the United Kingdom. $50.00–75.00.

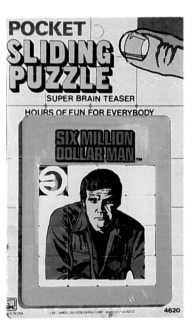

POCKET SLIDING PUZZLE, APC, 1977. $35.00–45.00.

POSTER MAGAZINE, The Bionic Man, *Meet Magazine,* 1977. Made in the United Kingdom. $40.00–50.00.

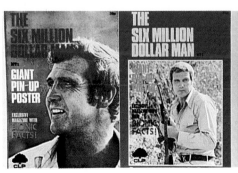

POSTER MAGAZINES #1–3, CLP, 1977. Made in the United Kingdom. $40.00–50.00 each.

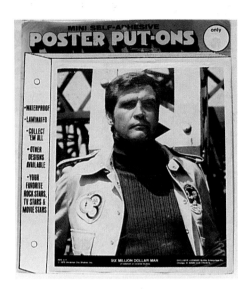

POSTER PUT-ON, Bi-Rite, 1978. $10.00–15.00.

RAINCOAT, Universal, 1976. Different variations. Back has illustration of Steve Austin running. $50.00–75.00.

PRESS-OUT BOOK, Stafford Pemberton, 1977. Made in the United Kingdom. $50.00–75.00.

RECORDS/LPs, Peter Pan Industries, 1976–1978. #8166 Vol.1 (1976) with an illustrated and photo cover, #8186 Vol. 2 (1976), #8208 Christmas Adventures (1978), and #BR 519 (1977) with gatefold cover and story booklet. $10.00–15.00 each LP; $20.00–25.00 LP with story booklet.

RECORDS/45s, Peter Pan, 1978. "Elves Revolt" from the Christmas Adventures album and "The Bionic Berserker" from album #8166. $10.00–15.00 each.

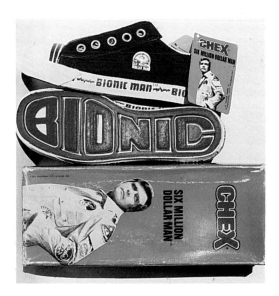

SHOES, Chex, 1976. $100.00–125.00.

SLIPPERS, Universal, 1976. Children's slippers made in Great Britain. $40.00–50.00.

SEE-A-SHOW VIEWER, Kenner, 1976. Oval or rectangular card versions. $25.00–35.00.

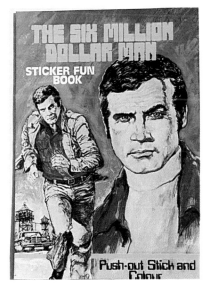

Left:
STICKER FUN BOOKS, Stafford Pemberton, 1977–1978. Made in the United Kingdom. 1977 book pictured. $50.00–75.00 each.

Right:
T-SHIRT, Universal, 1975. Mail-away premium. $40.00–50.00.

TRADING CARDS, Donruss, 1975. 66 stickers in set with puzzle backs. $60.00–80.00 set; $1.00–1.25 single cards; $10.00–15.00 wrapper; $40.00–60.00 display box.

TRADING CARDS, Topps, 1975. 55 cards in set. Import from Mexico, same as United States test set with Spanish captions. $275.00–350.00 set; $5.00–7.00 single cards; $40.00–50.00 wrapper; $200.00–300.00 display box.

TRADING CARDS, Monty Gum, 1975. Import set of 72 with puzzle backs. Cards are 2" x 1¾" in size and unnumbered from Holland. $75.00–100.00 set; $1.00–1.50 single cards; $5.00–8.00 wrapper; $75.00–100.00 display box.

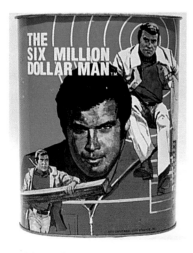

TRASH CAN, Cheinco, 1976. $35.00–45.00.

TURBO MOTO, Clipper Co., 1977. Made in Holland. Similar to Kenner's Bionic Cycle in 14" x 10" box. $60.00–80.00.

VIDEO CENTER, Kenner, 1976. Boxed playset for the dolls, includes a built-in screen for movie cassettes. $125.00–150.00.

WRISTWATCHES, MZ Berger, 1976. Two versions, including an illustration of Steve with red or blue background. $60.00–80.00 each.

VIEW-MASTERS, GAF, 1974. Four different versions. #BB 559-4 E one reel on card from Belgium, #AVB559 United States boxed talking version, and #B559 U.S. reels in envelope. Boxed talking version made in Holland not pictured. $25.00–30.00 card. $20.00–25.00 U.S. box; $30.00–40.00 Holland box; $15.00–20.00 envelope.

OTHER ITEMS NOT PICTURED

A.M. WRIST RADIO, Illco, 1976. 3" round radio with a black leather band and a Six Million Dollar Man logo. Comes in a window display box. $200.00–250.00.

ACTIVITY SET, Rand McNally, 1970s. Yellow boxed activity set with an illustration of Steve. Activities include coloring and follow-the-dots. $40.00–50.00.

BACKPACK RADIO, Kenner, 1976. Kenner made United States radio for 12" doll. Denys Fisher made a similar United Kingdom version. $40.00–50.00 U.S.; $50.00–60.00 U.K.

BATHROBE, Universal, 1978. $50.00–75.00.

BEDDING, Universal, 1976. Various articles, including curtains, sheet sets, pillowcases, and bedspread. $50.00–75.00 bedspread or curtains; $30.00–40.00 each others.

BIONIC ADVENTURE SETS, Tenue D'Aventure Bionic, Meccano, 1976. Made in France. Three different outfits for the 12" doll, including Mission Secrete, Pilote D'Essais, and Cosmonaute. $45.00–55.00 each.

BIONIC BAR, 1970s. Illustration of Steve on wrapper of candy bar. $25.00–35.00 wrapper.

BIONIC BELT, Preedrose Ltd., 1977. Made in the United Kingdom. $30.00–40.00.

BIONIC BIKE, Kenner, 1970s. Child-size plastic bike with four wheels and packaged in a large photo cover box. $200.00–250.00.

BIONIC BITS, Quest Products Inc., 1977. A series of 5" plastic cups containing bite-size cookies. Caps vary with different bionic action scenes. $25.00–35.00 each with cap.

BIONIC CYCLE, Kenner, 1973. Figure of Steve on a stunt cycle in an illustrated window box. $50.00–75.00.

BOOKLET, *Lee Majors – An Unauthorized Biography,* 1975. Offered as a mail-away through teen magazines. $15.00–20.00.

BUBBLE BATH, Noveltime Products, 1977. Made in the United Kingdom. Red figural bottle in illustrated box. $50.00–75.00.

COMMAND CONSOLE, Kenner, 1976. Playset for the 12" dolls. $100.00–125.00.

CRITICAL ASSIGNMENT ARMS AND LEGS, Meccano, 1970s. Made in France. Similar to Kenner's United States and Denys Fisher's United Kingdom versions, but slightly different packaging with French titles. $35.00–45.00 each.

DIP DOTS PAINTING DESIGN BOOK, Kenner, 1976. Blue or pink box. $25.00–35.00.

DOLL, Dr. Kromedome, Mego, 1975. Exclusive 12" doll available only at Montgomery Ward. 12" opponent for Steve Austin doll. Cranial dome, left leg and arm are chrome, and he is dressed in a purple jumpsuit with cape. $150.00–200.00 loose; $400.00–500.00 boxed.

DOODLE ART SETS, 1970s. Three different art sets in tubes. Color photo of Steve Austin on packages. $35.00–45.00 each.

FAN CLUB KIT, 1970s. Different than the Bionic Acion Club Kit. $75.00–100.00.

FRAME TRAY PUZZLE #2010-G, APC, 1976. $35.00–45.00.

OIL PAINT BY NUMBER SETS, Denys Fisher, 1977. Two different sets made in the United Kingdom. Similar to the United States acrylic paint by number sets except each box includes two pre-printed panels instead of one. $45.00–55.00 each.

PATCHES, LeoMotif, 1970s. Several different made in the United Kingdom $10.00–15.00 each.

PINBALL MACHINE, Bally, 1978. Arcade machine with back glass scoring board featuring illustration of Steve Austin wearing astronaut outfit and parachute on his back. $1,000.00–1,500.00.

PLAYSUIT, 1970s. Australian child-size suit on card. $60.00–80.00.

POSTER, Steve Austin, Pro Arts Inc., 1976. 20" x 28." $50.00–75.00.

POSTERS, H.P. Dorey & Co./Scandecor, 1970s. Two different made in the United Kingdom. $50.00–75.00.

RAINBOOTS, Chex, 1976. Rubber with logo and "Bionic Man" printed around the bottom edge. $50.00–75.00.

SHEET MUSIC, "The Six Million Dollar Man," Universal, 1978. $25.00–30.00.

SLIDE PROJECTOR SET, Chad Valley, 1977. Made in England. Illustration of Steve on 14½" x 11" box. Inside has a 9" slide projector and 16 filmstrips. $50.00–75.00.

TOWER AND CYCLE, Kenner, 1977. Motorcycle with jumping action. $75.00–100.00.

TOOTHBRUSH, Kenner, 1970s. Battery operated on photo card. $100.00–125.00.

TRADING CARDS, Topps, 1975. 55 cards in set. Released as a test set only. Similar to the set made in Mexico. $2,000.00–2,500.00 set; $40.00–50.00 single cards; $100.00–125.00 wrapper.

TV GUIDES, 1974–1976. 05/18/74 Majors illustrated and 08/28/76 Majors illustrated. 10.00–15.00 each.

VENUS SPACE PROBE, Kenner, 1976. $400.00–500.00.

WALLET, Faberge, 1976. Made in Canada. $35.00–45.00.

STARSKY & HUTCH

SEPTEMBER 10, 1975–
AUGUST 28, 1979

89 EPISODES

PEAK POSITION:
#16 in the 1975–1976 season

—— CAST ——

Paul Michael Glaser
Detective Dave Starsky

David Soul
Detective Ken "Hutch" Hutchinson

Bernie Hamilton
Captain Harold Dobey

Antonio Fargas
Huggy Bear

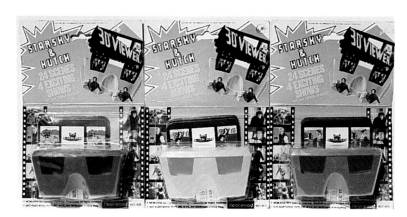

3-D VIEWER, Fleetwood, 1977. Made in three different colors, including blue, yellow, and orange. $25.00–35.00.

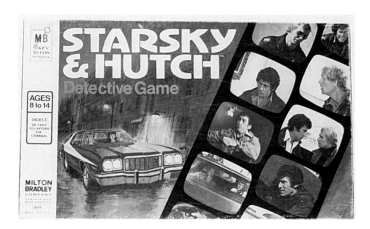

BOARD GAME, Detective Game, Milton Bradley, 1976. $30.00–40.00.

A.M. WRIST RADIO, Illco, 1977. $250.00–300.00.

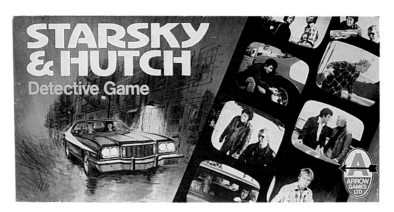

BOARD GAME, Detective Game, Arrow Games Ltd, 1977. Made in the United Kingdom. Board is very different than the United States game and includes cardboard cutouts for buildings and a Gran Torino playing piece. $75.00–100.00.

BOOK, *The Starsky & Hutch Story,* Paradise Press Inc., 1977. Hardback and soft cover versions. $20.00–30.00.

BUTTONS, 1970s. Several different buttons made in the United Kingdom, including solo and duo photos; a button sold exclusively through the fan club with the caption "Top of the Cops" and one in the shape of a Gran Torino. $20.00–30.00 each.

BRITISH ANNUALS, Stafford Pemberton, 1978–1980. Made in the United Kingdom. $25.00–35.00 each.

CAP PISTOL, Lone Star, 1976. Made in the United Kingdom. Die-cast pistol in 7½" x 4" box. $150.00–175.00.

CHILDREN'S BAND RADIO, LJN Toys, 1975. 13¼" x 6" x 9" box. $300.00–350.00.

CAR, Mego/Palitoy, 1976. 16" x 5½" x 6½" box containing car and four accessories. Palitoy made a similar United Kingdom version in an illustrated box without twist-out action mechanism. Mego's United States version pictured. $200.00–250.00 U.S. $300.00–400.00 U.K.

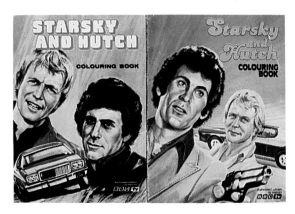

CLICKER GUNS, Fleetwood, 1976. Several different sets. #427-402 includes a 9mm clicker gun, handcuffs, badge, wallet, ID and keys. #421-403 includes a 9mm clicker gun, walkie talkie, ID, and badge. #421-407 includes a .357 magnum clicker gun, ID, and badge. $100.00–125.00 #427-402; $50.00–75.00 each others.

COLOURING BOOKS, Stafford Pemberton, 1977–1978. Made in the United Kingdom. Pink cover (1977) and blue cover (1978). $75.00–100.00 each.

CORGI GRAN TORINO #292, Mettoy, 1977. $200.00–250.00.

CORGI GRAN TORINOS #292 and JR. #45, Mettoy, 1977. United States version made without a header card and clear car windows. United Kingdom's version made with header card and tinted car windows. $175.00–200.00 U.S.; $250.00–300.00 U.K.

CORGI JR. TORINOS #45, Mettoy, 1977. Several packaging variations. #56025 side view with yellow background, #56025 side view with white background, #55023 without picture card, #51059 slanted view with white background, and #51059 top view with white background. Also issued was a version with different lettering on packaging and a photo of Starsky. $35.00–45.00 each.

COSTUMES, Starsky and Hutch, Collegeville, 1976. Both have the same outfit with different masks. $50.00–75.00 each.

CORGI JR. TORINOS #45, Mettoy, 1977. Packaged with either a police car or sheriff car. $100.00–125.00 each.

DOLLS, Starsky and Hutch, Mego, 1975. First issue with card backs containing only two photos. Front of cards show Mego logo in yellow. $20.00–25.00 each loose; $40.00–50.00 each carded.

DOLLS, Mego, 1976. Starsky, Hutch, Chopper, Dobey, and Huggy Bear were made in a second issue with back of cards containing five photos. Front of cards show Mego logo in white. Starsky and Hutch not pictured. $20.00–25.00 each Starsky or Hutch loose; $40.00–50.00 each Starsky or Hutch carded; $30.00–40.00 each others loose; $50.00–75.00 each others carded.

EMERGENCY DASHBOARD, Illco, 1977. 13" x 7" x 7". $250.00–300.00.

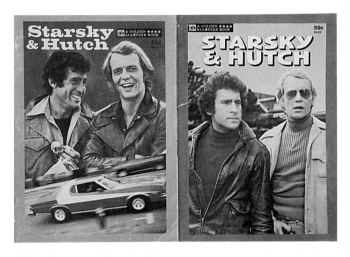

GRAN TORINOS, Weymms Company, 1987. Three different French versions made. Larger set with remote control and close-up photo of Starsky and Hutch on header card not pictured. $175.00–200.00 each with remote; $150.00–175.00 without remote.

FAN CLUB MERCHANDISE, 1970s. Several different items sold through the United Kingdom fan club, including a 12" x 6" vinyl folder with snap fastener, wristwatch, ceramic mug, and belt. Belt not pictured. $125.00–150.00 wristwatch; $30.00–40.00 each others.

GOLDEN ALL-STAR BOOKS, Golden Press, 1977. #6414 and #6423. $15.00–20.00 each.

GIFT BOOK, *David Soul,* Brakencrown, 1978. Similar to British annuals. $25.00–35.00.

Left:
GUN SET, HG Toys, 1976. .45 automatic and a .357 Magnum with badges in a 15½" x 12" box. $200.00–250.00.

Right:
GYRO POWERED CAR, Fleetwood, 1975. $35.00–45.00.

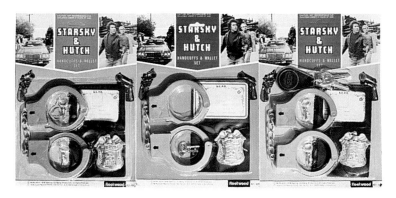

HANDCUFFS AND WALLET SETS, Fleetwood, 1976. Three different variations. $25.00–35.00 each.

JIGSAW PUZZLES, HG Toys, 1976. Six different numbered #492-01 through #492-06. $25.00–30.00 each.

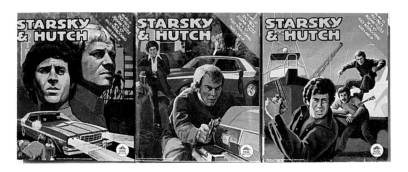

Left:
LUNCH BOX, 1976. Made in Mexico. Bottom of box has a sticker that reads "Lonchera Starsky Y Hutch." $100.00–125.00.

JIGSAW PUZZLES, Stafford Pemberton, 1977–1978. Made in the United Kingdom. Nine different in 8½" x 6¼" boxes. Three blue border series #1078 (1977), three green border series #5079 (1978), and three yellow border series #3078 (1977). $40.00–50.00 each.

MAGAZINES, *Starsky and Hutch Monthly Magazine,* 1976–1981. Made in the United Kingdom. First issue unnumbered and 56 issues followed in a series. $40.00–50.00 first issue; $20.00–30.00 each #1–56.

KNEE HIs, Pretty Legs Mills Inc., 1976. $25.00–35.00.

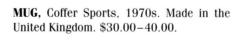

MIRRORS, Lightline Industries, Inc., 1977. Several different made in the United States and the United Kingdom. 12" x 9" with silver frame, 13" x 10" with wood frame, and 15" x 10" with silver frame (including car). Other versions include a 9" x 7" U.K. mirror featuring Hutch on the phone and Starsky with arms folded and a 23" x 19" British Pepsi-Cola mirror with a color photo in the center (not pictured). $75.00–100.00 each.

MUG, Coffer Sports, 1970s. Made in the United Kingdom. $30.00–40.00.

MINI TARGET SET, Fleetwood, 1976. $40.00–50.00.

OFFICIAL DELUXE POLICE SET, HG Toys, 1976. 20" x 15½". $250.00–275.00.

OFFICIAL POLICE SET, HG Toys, 1976. 15½" x 12". $200.00–225.00.

OFFICIAL POLICE TARGET RANGE GAME, Arco, 1977. $100.00–125.00.

PENCIL HOLDERS, Token Pottery Ltd., 1970s. Made in the United Kingdom. "Starsky" stamped on bottom. Hutch not pictured. $40.00–50.00 each.

PAPERBACK BOOKS #1–8, Ballantine Books, 1975–1978. Also released in the United Kingdom with the caption "As Seen on BBC TV." $5.00–10.00 each.

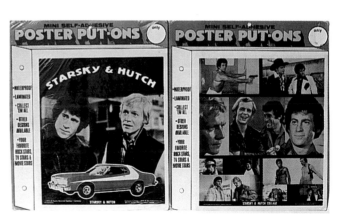

POSTER PUT-ONS, Bi-Rite, 1976. $10.00–15.00 each.

POSTER MAGAZINES, 1976–1978. Several different made in the United Kingdom and in the United States. $35.00–45.00 each.

POSTER ART KIT #381, Board King, 1976. Boxed set. $60.00–80.00.

POSTER ART KIT #391, Board King, 1976. $40.00–50.00.

RADIO COMMAND CENTER, Illco, 1977. $100.00–125.00.

RADIO-CONTROLLED CARS, Galoob, 1977. Two packaging versions with slightly different remote controls. Box numbers 1001 and 1002. #1002 pictured. $100.00–125.00 each.

POSTERS, 1976–1979. 23" x 35" Starsky & Hutch Collage, Bi-Rite Enterprises, Inc., 1976 pictured. Others include 20" x 28" Paul Michael Glaser, Pro Arts, Inc., 1979, and 23" x 35" Starsky & Hutch (with car), Bi-Rite Enterprises, Inc., 1976. United Kingdom posters include 24" x 37" Paul Michael Glaser, Pace Int'l., 1976, and 24" x 37" David Soul, Pace Int'l., 1977. $25.00–35.00 each U.S., $35.00–45.00 each U.K.

全米ヒット・チャートNO.1を獲得した
デビッド・ソウルが歌う愛と青春と友情の讃歌。
「刑事スタスキーとハッチ」のテーマ
やすらぎの季節

STEREO EMR-20517

Don't Give Up On Us/David Soul

デビッド・ソウル
Silver Lady

RECORD/45, "Don't Give Up on Us"/"Silver Lady," Private Stock Records, 1977. Vocals by David Soul. Made in Japan with picture sleeve. $15.00–20.00

Other United States 45s include "Don't Give Up on Us"/"Black Bean Soup" (1977), "It Sure Brings Out the Love in Your Eyes"/(same) (1977); "Going In With My Eyes Open"/"Topanga" (1977), "Silver Lady"/"Here Comes the Rain" (1977). Without picture sleeves. $3.00–5.00 each.

RECORDS/LPS, Private Stock Records, 1976–1977. "David Soul" and "Playing to an Audience of One." Vocals by David Soul. $10.00–15.00 each. Other LPs include "Band of Friends" (1980), made in the United Kingdom, "Best Days of My Life" (1980), made in Canada. $10.00–15.00 each.

REVOLVER, Pilen, 1970s. Made in Spain. Metal eight-shot toy revolver in a 6¼" x 2¾" box. $200.00–250.00.

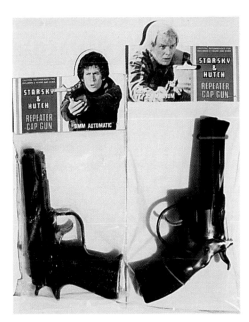

REPEATER CAP GUNS, Fleetwood, 1976. 9MM automatic and .357 Magnum. $40.00–50.00 each.

SHOOT-OUT TARGET SET, Berwick, 1977. 16" x 11." Made in the United Kingdom. $125.00–150.00.

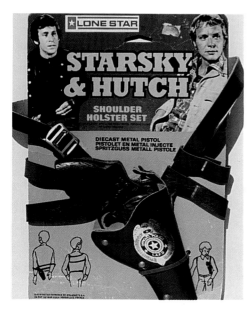

STICKERS, 1970s. Several different mail-order stickers offered in United Kingdom through *Starsky & Hutch* monthly magazines. $10.00–15.00 each.

SHOULDER HOLSTER SET, Lone Star, 1976. Made in the United Kingdom. $125.00–150.00.

TARGET SET, Placo Toys, 1977. 10¾" x 12½" box. $100.00–125.00.

T-SHIRTS, 1970s. Several different, including child sizes made in Mexico. $25.00–35.00 each.

TRADING CARDS, Monty Gum, 1970s. Seventy-two 2" x 1¾" cards in unnumbered set with puzzle backs. Made in Holland. Wrapper pictured. $250.00–350.00 set; $3.00–4.00 single cards; $15.00–20.00 wrapper; $200.00–250.00 display box.

TV VIEWER, Fleetwood, 1976. $30.00–40.00.

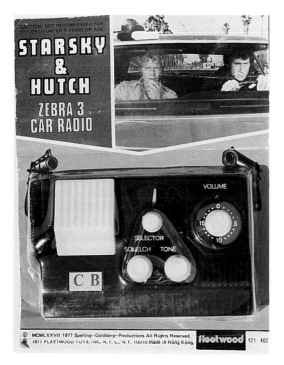

ZEBRA 3 CAR RADIO, Fleetwood, 1977. $75.00–100.00.

WALKIE TALKIES, Mettoy, 1977. $175.00–200.00.

OTHER ITEMS NOT PICTURED

BOOKLET, *Glaser and Soul, An Unauthorized Biography,* 1977. Offered as a mail-away through teen magazines. Black and white photo cover with biographies. $15.00–20.00.

CAP FIRING GUN SET, Lone Star, 1976. Mauser pistol, shoulder stock, silencer, and telescopic sight in box with a color picture sleeve of Starsky and Hutch. $250.00–275.00.

DOLLS, Starsky and Hutch, Palitoy, 1977. Made in the United Kingdom. Similar to the Mego dolls, but cards contain illustrations of Starsky and Hutch. $25.00–35.00 each loose; $75.00–100.00 each carded.

DOLLS, Starsky and Hutch, Palitoy, 1977. Made in the United Kingdom. Similar to the Mego dolls, but dolls packaged together in a twin pack and include pistols. Package contains illustrations of Starsky and Hutch. $40.00–50.00 loose; $200.00–250.00 boxed.

FLASHLIGHT, Fleetwood, 1976. 7" long with batteries on card. $50.00–75.00.

IRON-ONS, 1970s. Several different styles. $20.00–25.00 each.

PATCH, Starsky and Hutch, Ringfisher Patches, 1970s. Made in Great Britain. Color illustration with show title. $25.00 – 30.00.

RECORD/45, "Starsky and Hutch Theme"/"Charlie's Angels Theme," United Artists, 1977. Original theme for the TV series released without a picture sleeve. Instrumentals by The New Ventures. $15.00–20.00.

RECORD/45, "Gotcha (Theme from Starsky and Hutch)," Epic Records, 1977. $10.00–15.00.

SHEET MUSIC, Theme, 1977. $15.00–20.00.

TOTE BAG, Rei, 1976. Orange canvas bag with handle and zipper top. Features a color silkscreen of Starsky and Hutch. $50.00 – 60.00.

TV GUIDES, 1975–1978. 11/15/75 Soul & Glaser; 11/27/76 Soul & Glaser illustrated; 08/13/77 David Soul; 06/03/78 Soul & Glaser. $10.00–15.00 each.

WALKIE TALKIES, LJN, 1970s. Four different variations, including three in window boxes and one in a solid box. Sets vary in the design of the unit. $150.00–200.00 each.

WATER PISTOLS, Fleetwood, 1976. Two different including a .357 Magnum and a 9MM Automatic. $50.00–75.00 each.

THAT GIRL

SEPTEMBER 8, 1966–
SEPTEMBER 10, 1971

135 EPISODES

PEAK POSITION:
Not in the top 25

—— CAST ——

Marlo Thomas
Ann Marie

Ted Bessell
Don Hollinger

Lew Parker
Lou Marie

Rosemary DeCamp
Helen Marie

BOARD GAME, Remco, 1968. $200.00–250.00.

COLORING BOOKS, Saalfield/Artcraft, 1967–1970.
#1627, Saalfield (1967), #4513, Saalfield (1967), #4539,
Saalfield (1970), and #9658, Artcraft (1968). Another
photo cover version was made with Marlo seated, wearing a yellow dress. This book varies with a blue or orange
background. $25.00–35.00 each.

PAPER DOLL BOOKLET #1379, Saalfield,
1967. $20.00–30.00 cut; $40.00–50.00 uncut.

PAPER DOLL BOOKLET #1351, Saalfield, 1967. $20.00–30.00 cut; $40.00–50.00 uncut.

PAPERBACK BOOK, Popular Library, 1971. $10.00–15.00.

OTHER ITEMS NOT PICTURED

DOLL, Marlo Thomas, Alexander Doll Company, 1967. An exclusive 17½" collector doll came in one of two outfits, a long gown or a mod skirt. $600.00–800.00.

PAPER DOLL AND LOTS TO DO FUN, Saalfield, 1966. 6" X 15" box with paper dolls, mini coloring book, crayons, travel game, and sticker book. $50.00–75.00 cut; $100.00–125.00 uncut.

PAPER DOLL BOOKLET, Artcraft, 1967. Illustration of Ann Marie on a green background with color photo in window. $20.00–30.00 cut; $40.00–50.00 uncut.

PAPER DOLL BOX, Saalfield, 1967. 11" x 14" box includes 13 punch-out outfits. $40.00–50.00 cut; $75.00–100.00 uncut.

SUNGLASSES, Opti-Ray, 1960s. A variety of plastic child-size sunglasses sold individually. The only "That Girl" marking is on the 13" x 22" display that features a color photo of Marlo wearing a similar pair on her head. $300.00–400.00 display.

TV GUIDES, 1966–1970. 11/12/66 Thomas; 12/02/67 Thomas and Thomas; 05/17/69 Thomas; 08/08/70 Thomas and Bessell. $15.00–20.00 each.

WIG CASE, 1960s. Show title written on front. $75.00–100.00.

THREE'S COMPANY

MARCH 15, 1977–
SEPTEMBER 18, 1984

164 EPISODES

PEAK POSITION:
#2 in the 1978–1980 seasons

—— CAST ——

John Ritter
Jack Tripper

Joyce DeWitt
Janet Wood

Suzanne Somers
Chrissy Snow

Norman Fell
Stanley Roper

Audra Lindley
Helen Roper

Jenilee Harrison
Cindy Snow

Priscilla Barnes
Terri Alden

Richard Kline
Larry Dallas

Don Knotts
Ralph Furley

DOLL, Chrissy, Mego, 1978. $30.00–40.00 loose; $60.00–80.00 boxed.

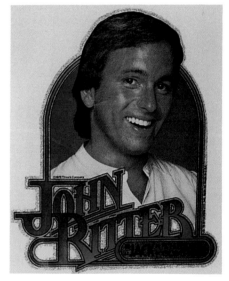

IRON-ONS, Factors Etc., Inc., 1978. Several different. $15.00–20.00 each.

JIGSAW PUZZLES, APC, 1978. Two different. $25.00–35.00 each.

POSTER, Suzanne Somers as Chrissy, Dargis Associates Inc., 1977. 23" x 35" $25.00–30.00.

POSTER, John Ritter as Jack, Dargis Associates Inc., 1977. $30.00–35.00.

POSTERS, Pro Arts, Inc., 1978–1980. 20" x 28" Suzanne Somers (pictured), 1978, 20" x 28" Ms. Suzanne, wearing all white, and 20" x 28" Joyce DeWitt, 1980. $30.00–40.00 each.

OTHER ITEMS NOT PICTURED

BEACH TOWEL, Suzanne Somers, 1978, $40.00–50.00.

MIRROR, Mechanical Mirror Works, Inc. 1977. 12" x 16", same photo as Jack poster by Dargis. $30.00–40.00.

POSTERS, Dargis Associates Inc., 1977. The Ropers or Mr. Furley. $30.00–35.00 each.

TV GUIDES, 1978–1983. 05/20/78 cast; 08/04/79 Joyce DeWitt; 03/14/81 Suzanne Somers; 03/13/82 cast; 11/20/82 cast; 09/24/83 cast illustrated. $8.00–10.00 each.

POSTER PUT-ON, Suzanne Somers as Chrissy, Bi-Rite, 1977. $10.00–15.00.

SHEET MUSIC, Jonico Music, Inc., 1979. $20.00–25.00.

TRADING CARDS, Topps, 1978. 44 stickers and 16 puzzle cards. $25.00–35.00 set; 50¢–$1.00 single stickers and cards; $2.00–3.00 wrapper; $10.00–15.00 display box.

THE WALTONS

SEPTEMBER 14, 1972–
AUGUST 20, 1981

209 EPISODES

PEAK POSITION:
#2 in the 1973–1974 season

—— CAST ——

Ralph Waite
John Walton

Michael Learned
Olivia Walton

Will Geer
Zeb "Grandpa" Walton

Ellen Corby
Esther "Grandma" Walton

Richard Thomas
John-Boy

Jon Walmsley
Jason

Judy Norton-Taylor
Mary Ellen

Eric Scott
Ben

Mary Elizabeth McDonough
Erin

David W. Harper
Jim-Bob

Kami Cotler
Elizabeth

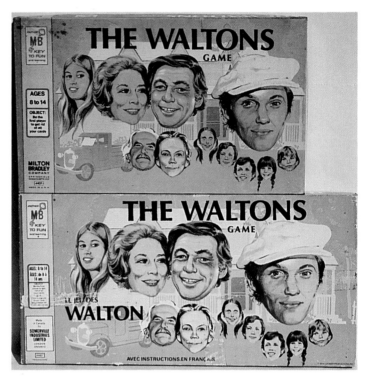

BOARD GAMES, Milton Bradley, 1974. Milton Bradley made United States version and Somerville made in Canadian version with French and English titles on box and board. U.S. version varies in size. $25.00–35.00 each.

BOOKS #1–6, Whitman, 1975. Set of hardback books. $10.00–15.00 each.

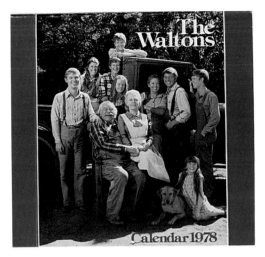

CALENDAR 1978, Rutledge Books, 1977. $35.00–45.00.

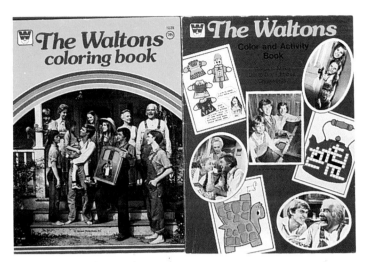

COLORING BOOKS, Whitman, 1975. Coloring book #1028 and coloring and activity book #1254. $20.00–30.00.

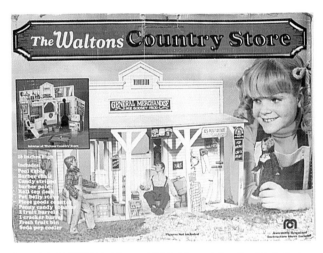

COUNTRY STORE, Mego, 1974. Playset for the 8" dolls in a 22" x 16" box. $100.00–125.00.

FARMHOUSE, Mego, 1974. 38" x 26" boxed playset for the 8" dolls. $150.00–200.00.

Left:
DIE CAST METAL TRUCK, LJN Toys, Inc., 1975. Metal toy 2½" in length. $40.00–50.00.

Right:
DOLLS, John-Boy and Ellen, Mom and Pop, and Grandma and Grandpa, Mego, 1974. 8" dolls sold in pairs and in single boxes. $15.00–20.00 each loose. $30.00–40.00 single in box. $50.00–60.00 pair in box.

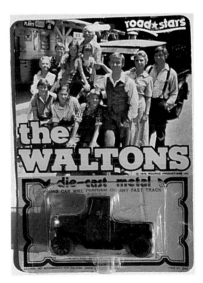

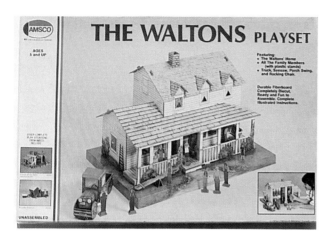

FARMHOUSE PLAYSET, Amsco, 1974. 20" x 14" boxed playset with cardboard figures. $100.00–125.00.

LUNCH BOX, Aladdin, 1973. Metal box with plastic thermos. $60.00–80.00 box; $20.00–25.00 thermos.

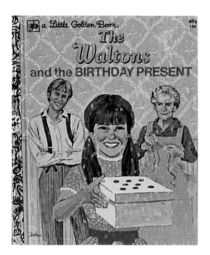

LITTLE GOLDEN BOOK, *The Waltons and the Birthday Present,* Golden Press, 1975. $10.00–15.00.

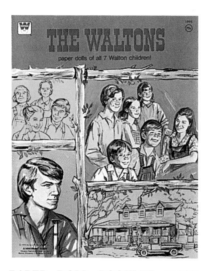

PAPER DOLL BOOKLET #1995, Whitman, 1975. $10.00–15.00 cut; $25.00–35.00 uncut.

PAPER DOLL BOX #4334, Whitman, 1974. $20.00–25.00 cut. $35.00–45.00 uncut.

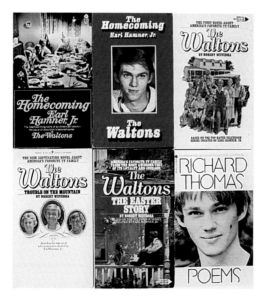

PAPERBACK BOOKS, 1970–1976. *The Homecoming,* Avon, 1970; *The Homecoming,* Avon, 1970; *The Waltons,* Bantam, 1974; *Trouble on the Mountain,* Bantam, 1975; *The Easter Story,* Bantam, 1976; *Richard Thomas Poems,* Avon, 1974; *The Walton Family Cookbook,* Bantam, 1970s (not pictured). $25.00–35.00 cookbook; $8.00–12.00 each others.

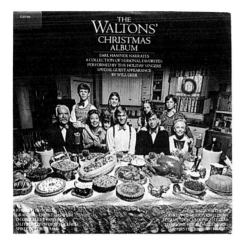

RECORD/LP, "The Waltons' Christmas Album," Columbia, 1974. Vocals by the Holiday Singers. Narration by Earl Hamner with special guest appearance by Will Geer. $15.00–20.00.

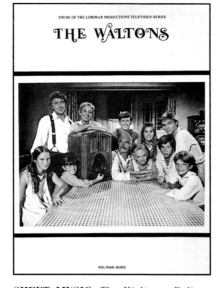

SHEET MUSIC, The Waltons, Roliram Music, 1973. Varies with black and white or color cover. $20.00–25.00.

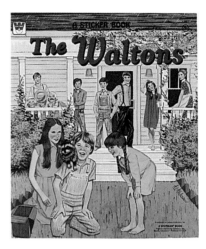

STICKER BOOK, Whitman, 1975. $35.00–45.00.

Left:
TELL-A-TALE BOOK, *Elizabeth and the Magic Lamp,* Whitman, 1975. $10.00–15.00.

Right:
TALKING VIEW-MASTER #AVB596, GAF, 1972. $25.00–30.00.

TRADING CARDS, Topps, 1973. Test set of 50 photo cards with puzzle backs. No box exists. Two versions of wrappers were made. #T-8-5-A wrapper pictured. #T-8-5-B states "America's Favorite Family" below the illustration. $2,000.00–2,500.00 set; $40.00–50.00 single cards; $150.00–200.00 each wrapper.

TRUCK, Mego, 1975. For 8" dolls. $75.00–100.00.

VIEW-MASTER #B596, GAF, 1972. $20.00–25.00.

OTHER ITEMS NOT PICTURED

CIGAR BANDS, Rumbo, 1970s. Set of 24 bands with black and white photos. Band color varies. $75.00–100.00 set.

KITE FUN BOOK, Western Publishing Co., 1980. 5" x 7" booklet distributed by Pacific Gas & Electric, Southern California Edison, and Florida Power & Light. Includes 16 pages of activities and comics that provide advice for safe kite flying. $30.00–40.00.

RECORD/LP, "Joe Conely & Eric Scott of The Waltons," United National, 1979. $30.00–40.00.

RECORD/45, "The Waltons (Theme from the TV series)," Monza Records, 1980. Instrumentals by Bobby Patrick Band. Made in the United Kingdom with "Waltons" theme and cast photo on one side and "Dallas" on the other. $25.00–35.00.

TV GUIDES, 1973–1977. 04/28/73 cast illustrated; 04/13/74 cast; 10/26/74 Waite, Thomas & Geer; 08/23/75 Waite, Thomas & Learned; 08/21/76 Thomas, Geer, Corby; 6/25/77 cast. $10.00–15.00 each.

WELCOME BACK, KOTTER

ACRYLIC PAINT BY NUMBERS SETS, Craftmaster, 1976. Four different United States or Canadian versions. $25.00–35.00 each.

SEPTEMBER 9, 1975–
AUGUST 3, 1979

95 EPISODES

PEAK POSITION:
#13 in the 1976–1977 season

—— CAST ——

Gabriel Kaplan
Gabe Kotter

Marcia Strassman
Julie Kotter

John Travolta
Vinnie Barbarino

Robert Hegyes
Juan Epstein

Ron Palillo
Arnold Horshack

Lawrence Hilton-Jacobs
Frederick "Boom Boom" Washington

John Sylvester White
Michael Woodman

BELTS, Charles Belt Co., 1970s. Two different styles. $25.00–30.00 each.

Left:
BEACH TOWELS, Barbarino or cast, Wolper, 1976. $40.00–50.00 each.

BOARD GAME, Up Your Nose With a Rubber Hose, Ideal, 1977. $25.00–35.00.

BOOKCOVERS, H.T.G.T. Inc., 1976. Barbarino pictured. $15.00–20.00 each.

BRUNCH BAG, Barbarino, Aladdin, 1977. Comes with same thermos as lunch box, but with light blue cap and bottom. $100.00–125.00 bag; $25.00–30.00 thermos.

BUTTONS, Dream Machine/Creation Unlimited, 1976. Several different styles and colors for cast and individual characters in 1½" and 3" sizes. $8.00–10.00 each.

CALCULATING WHEEL, Pamco, 1976. $20.00–25.00.

BULLETIN BOARD, Board King, 1976. 24½" x 18½" $50.00–60.00.

CALENDAR, Rutledge Books, 1977. $25.00–30.00.

CANDY BOXES, Phoenix, 1976. Eight numbered boxes in set. $10.00–15.00 each box.

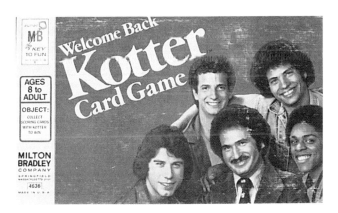

CARD GAME, Milton Bradley, 1976. $20.00–25.00.

CHALKBOARD, Board King, 1976. 24½" x 18½" $50.00–60.00.

CARTOON SET, Toy Factory, 1977. $40.00–50.00.

CLASSROOM PLAYSETS, Mattel, 1976. Two different playsets for 9" dolls. Both include chalk, a record, stickers, and furniture in a vinyl case. The regular set is packaged with a cardboard sleeve, and the deluxe set is packaged in a cardboard box. The deluxe set also contains five action figures. Deluxe set pictured. $75.00–100.00 regular; $200.00–250.00 deluxe.

CLOTHING LINE, 1976. Several different styles, including sweat-shirts, T-shirts, and pajamas. $20.00–30.00 each article.

COLORFORMS, Colorforms, 1976. $25.00–30.00.

COLORING BOOK #1081, Whitman, 1977. $15.00–20.00.

COMIC BOOK, D.C., 1978. 10" x 13" large edition. $10.00–15.00.

COSTUME, Barbarino, Collegeville, 1976. $40.00–50.00.

COMIC BOOKS, #1–10, D.C., 1977–1978. $8.00–10.00 each.

CUP, MUG, AND TUMBLER, Dawn, 1976. Cast pictured on one side, Barbarino or Horshack on the other. $10.00–15.00 each.

COSTUME, Kotter, Collegeville, 1976. $40.00–50.00.

CUPS, Amoco, 1970s. Several different 16-oz. plastic cups. $15.00–20.00 each.

DESK SET, AHI, 1977. Four figural items, including Mr. Kotter memo pad, Epstein stapler, Barbarino pencil sharpener, and Horshack calendar. Also came in an "Executive Desk Set" without Horshack. $25.00–30.00 each piece.

Left:
DOLLS, Epstein, Washington, Horshack, Kotter, and Barbarino, Mattel, 1976. 9" dolls, each with a different accessory. $20.00–25.00 each loose; $40.00–50.00 each carded.

Right:
DOLL, John Travolta, Chemtoy, 1977. 12" doll. $35.00–45.00 loose; $60.00–80.00 boxed.

FABRIC, Pronto Fabrics, 1976. Two different patterns. Illustrated comic strip-style fabric not pictured. $20.00–25.00 square yard.

FOLDERS, Mead, 1976. $8.00–10.00 each.

FRAME TRAY PUZZLES, Kotter or cast, Whitman, 1977. $8.00–10.00 each.

GREETING CARDS, Metropolitan Greetings, 1970s. Two different styles. One includes six cards and the other 10. $25.00–35.00 each set.

GUITAR, Lapin Products, Inc., 1977. 18" plastic guitar. $80.00–100.00.

GOLDEN ALL-STAR BOOKS, Golden Press, 1977. Three different numbered #6418, #6413, and #6419. $8.00–10.00 each.

HI-BOUNCE BALLS & JACKS SET, M. Shimmel Sons Inc., 1977. $20.00–25.00.

IRON-ONS, 1970s. Several different. $10.00–15.00 each.

JEWELRY, Wolper, 1978. Different items, including key chains, rings and necklaces made in pewter or simulated gold. Some styles have photos while others are just Sweathog phrases. $25.00–35.00 each with photo; $10.00–15.00 each non-photo.

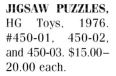

JIGSAW PUZZLES, HG Toys, 1976. #450-01, 450-02, and 450-03. $15.00–20.00 each.

JIGSAW PUZZLE, HG Toys, 1976. $30.00–40.00.

JUMP ROPE, M. Shimmel Sons Inc., 1977. $20.00–25.00.

LUNCH BOX, Aladdin, 1977. Metal box with plastic thermos. $60.00–80.00 box; $15.00–20.00 thermos.

MAGIC SLATES, Whitman, 1977. Two different styles. $25.00–30.00 each.

MODEL KIT, Sweathogs Dream Machine, MPC, 1976. Includes figures. $50.00–75.00.

PAPER DOLL BOXES, Toy Factory, 1976. Three different, including Barbarino, the Sweathogs, and Mr. Kotter. $15.00–20.00 cut; $30.00–40.00 uncut.

NOTEBOOK PAPER, Mead, 1976. Each pack comes with an iron-on. Six different. $25.00–30.00 each.

PAPERBACK BOOKS #1–6, Tempo Books, 1976–1977. $8.00–10.00 each.

Left:
PAPERBACK BOOK, *The Sweathog Trail,* Ace Books, 1976. First printing of paperback #1 with a different cover. $10.00–15.00.

Right:
PILLOWS, Zodiac Design, 1976. Several different, including cast, Horshack, Barbarino, and Washington. $30.00–40.00 each.

PLASTIC PICTURE PUZZLE, Fleetwood, 1976. $30.00–40.00.

PLAY SET, Toy Factory, 1976. $60.00–80.00.

POSTER ART KIT, Board King, 1976. Boxed set. $40.00–50.00.

POSTER ART KIT, Board King, 1976. $35.00–45.00.

POSTERS, Dargis Associates, Inc., 1976. Several different in 11" x 17" and 23" x 35" sizes, including Mr. Kotter & the Sweathogs, Barbarino, Horshack, and cast collage. 11" x 17" sizes pictured. $15.00–20.00 each small; $25.00–35.00 each large.

PUNCHO, Coleco, 1977. 48" inflatable punching bag. $75.00–100.00.

POSTERS, APC, 1976. Six different 11" x 14" posters available as Honeycomb Cereal premiums. $20.00–25.00 each.

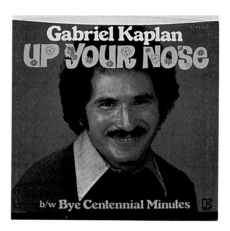

RECORD/45, "Up Your Nose"/"Bye Centennial Minutes," Elektra Records, 1976. Vocals by Gabriel Kaplan. $10.00–15.00.

RECORD CASES, Peerless Vid-Tronic Corp., 1976. Sizes for LPs and 45s. $30.00–40.00 LP; $25.00–30.00 45.

RECORD/LP, "Holes and Mello-Rolls," ABC Records, 1975. Spoken comedy by Gabriel Kaplan. Show was based on this 1974 record but was re-released with Sweathog photo in 1975. $15.00–20.00.

RECORD PLAYER, Peerless Vid-Tronic Corp., 1976. $50.00–75.00.

SCHOOL CALENDAR AND ASSIGNMENT BOOK, Rutledge Books, 1977. $25.00–30.00.

SKATEBOARD AND BENDABLE FIGURES, Gabriel, 1977. Bendable figures of Barbarino, Horshack, Epstein, and Washington on die-cast skateboard. $40.00–50.00.

RUGS, Zodiac Design, 1976. Several different, including cast, Barbarino, and, Horshack. Barbarino pictured. $40.00–50.00 each.

SLEEPING BAG, A.L.P. Industries, Inc., 1970s. $60.00–80.00.

SPIRAL NOTEBOOKS, Mead, 1976. Six different. $10.00–15.00 each.

STICKER FUN BOOK, Whitman, 1977. $25.00–30.00.

SWEATHOGS ACTION BANK, Fleetwood, 1975. Barbarino and Horshack grab the coins. $75.00–100.00.

SWEATHOGS BIKE, Mattel, 1976. For the 9" dolls. $75.00–100.00.

SWEATHOGS GREASE MACHINE CARS, AHI, 1977. Five different. $40.00–50.00 each.

TEE SHIRT PAINTING KIT, Frolic Toys, Ltd., 1976. Kotter and cast styles. Canadian and US versions made with slight packaging variations. $40.00–50.00.

TALKING VIEW-MASTER #TJ19, GAF, 1977. $20.00–25.00.

TOWEL SET, Cannon, 1976. Three-piece set. $60.00–80.00 set.

TRASH CAN, Cheinco, 1970s. $40.00–60.00.

TRADING CARDS, Topps, 1976. 53 cards in set. Backs are made up of 8 puzzle cards and 45 "Sweathog Speak" cards. $40.00–50.00 set; 75¢–$1.00 single cards; $2.00–3.00 wrapper; $25.00–30.00 display box.

WALLETS, Wolper Organization, Inc., 1970s. Several different colors and styles, including denim suede pictured. $30.00–40.00 each.

VIEW-MASTER #J19, GAF, 1977. $15.00–20.00

WRISTWATCH, Barbarino, Pamco, 1976. $75.00–100.00.

OTHER ITEMS NOT PICTURED

BEAN BAG CHAIRS, 1970s. Two different versions. One features an illustration of the cast and another an illustration of Barbarino. $150.00–200.00.

BOOK, *Gabriel Kaplan: A Spirit of Laughter,* EMC Corporation, 1978. Hardcover book. $15.00–20.00.

CALCULATOR, Pamco, 1976. Pocket calculator on cast photo card. $40.00–50.00.

CLASSROOM BRAIN TWISTER, Fleetwood, 1979. Slide puzzle shaped like a calculator on a photo card. $30.00–40.00.

JACKS AND JUMP ROPE SET, M. Shimmel Sons, Inc., 1977. Cast photo on card. $25.00–30.00.

KOTTER KIDS KIT, Ideal Publishing Corp., 1977. Fan club kit offered as mail-away through teen magazines and includes giant-size portraits, biographies, special Sweathog quiz, and miscellaneous photos. $50.00–75.00.

MAGAZINE, *TV Superstar No. 2,* Sterling's Magazine Inc., 1977. An all-Welcome Back, Kotter publication with cast cover. Contains complete life stories on characters and a life-size color pin-up of Barbarino. $20.00–30.00.

MEMO BOARD, HG Toys, 1978. Packed in a cello bag with header card, the board has photos of the cast that surround the border and comes with wipe-off marker pen and stick-ons. $60.00–80.00.

PADDLE BALL, Funtime Toys, 1976. Barbarino's face on wooden paddle. $40.00–50.00.

PATCHES, 1970s. Different styles and illustrations of characters. $10.00–15.00 each.

PINBALL GAME, Coleco, 1976. Working child-size electronic pinball game in photo box. $250.00–300.00.

RECORD/45, "Welcome Back Kotter"/"Warm Baby," Reprise, 1976. Full-length theme from the television show. Vocals by John Sebastian. Without picture sleeve. $3.00–5.00.

TV GUIDES, 1976–1978. 04/17/76 Kaplan and Strassman; 01/01/77 Travolta; 10/22/77 cast illustrated; 11/04/78 Travolta illustrated. $10.00–15.00 each.

WONDER WOMAN

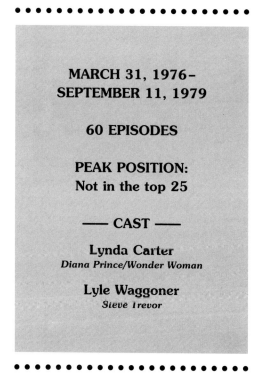

MARCH 31, 1976–
SEPTEMBER 11, 1979

60 EPISODES

PEAK POSITION:
Not in the top 25

—— CAST ——

Lynda Carter
Diana Prince/Wonder Woman

Lyle Waggoner
Steve Trevor

DOLLS, Mego, 1978. 12" dolls, including Wonder Woman with Diana Prince outfit, Wonder Woman with blue robe, Wonder Woman with Fly Away Action, Steve Trevor, Queen Hippolyte, and Nubia. The first issue Wonder Woman has a painted bodice and features a color photograph of Lynda Carter on the box as well as on the other character packaging. In later issues, Wonder Woman has a cloth bodice, and the photo was dropped from the packaging. The Fly Away Action doll is part of the later series and contains a string the doll can glide on. $40.00–50.00 loose Steve. $75.00–100.00 loose others; $75.00–100.00 boxed Steve; $125.00–200.00 boxed others.

IRON-ONS, 1970s. Several different, including Wonder Woman and Lynda Carter. $25.00–30.00 each.

JIGSAW PUZZLES, APC, 1977–1978. Three different, including a gray background (1977), red background with stars (1978), and blue background (1978). $35.00–45.00 each.

JIGSAW PUZZLES, APC, 1977. Two different variations with the same box cover. One with 81 pieces and the other 121. $25.00–35.00 each.

POSTER, Thought Factory, 1977. 23" x 35". $75.00–100.00.

MIRRORS, 1970s. 15" x 21" made in the United States. Another mirror was made in the United Kingdom. $100.00–150.00 each.

POSTER, Thought Factory, 1977. 23" x 35". $75.00–100.00.

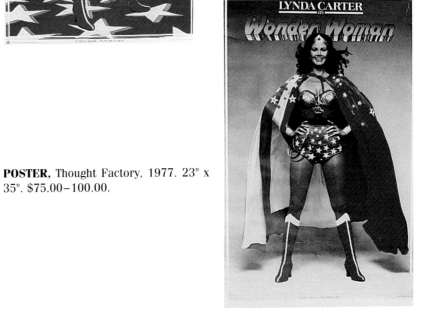

POSTER, Lynda, Pro Arts Inc., 1977. 28" x 20". $50.00–75.00.

POSTER, Ms. Carter, Pro Arts, Inc., 1978. 20" x 28". $50.00–75.00.

RECORDS/LPs, "Portrait," Epic, 1978. Vocals by Lynda Carter. A United States and Japanese version as well as a picture disc were made. The back of all album sleeves and the reverse side of the picture disc feature the same photo as the Ms. Carter poster. The Japanese version features a photo inset of Lynda Carter as Wonder Woman on the paper band wrapped around the album. $75.00 100.00 picture disc; $60.00–80.00 Japanese; $30.00–40.00 other.

RECORD/45, "Wonder Woman," Shadybrook Records, 1977. Theme from the television show. Promotional copy with duplicate B side. Vocals by the New World Symphony. $30.00–40.00.

OTHER ITEMS NOT PICTURED

DOLLS, Wonder Woman, Mego, 1978. Two foreign versions were made in addition to the United States dolls. The Canadian version is similar to the U.S. Wonder Woman with Diana Prince outfit but contains illustrations of Wonder Woman on the window box and an inset photo of the doll dressed as Diana Prince. A completely different head mold was used for the version released in Mexico. "Mujer Maravilla" is printed on the window box, which is completely different from the U.S. or Canadian packaging. $75.00–100.00 loose Canadian; $400.00–500.00 boxed Canadian; $100.00–125.00 loose Mexican; $200.00–250.00 boxed Mexican.

JIGSAW PUZZLE, APC, 1978. Featuring Lynda in orange dress on a dark blue background with "Lynda Carter as Wonder Woman" printed on box. $60.00–80.00.

POSTERS, Pro Arts, Inc., 1978–1979. 20" x 28" Lynda Carter, head and shoulders shot with white background and 28" x 40" Super Lynda Carter (1979), wearing white with dark blue background. $75.00–100.00 Super Lynda Carter; $50.00–75.00 other.

RECORDS/45s, "Toto"/"Put on a Show" and "All Night Song"/"Put on a Show," Epic Records, 1978. Vocals by Lynda Carter. Without picture sleeves. $8.00–10.00 each.

TV GUIDE, 01/29/77. Lynda Carter as Wonder Woman illustration. $15.00–20.00.

WRISTWATCH, 1970s. Photo of Lynda Carter as Wonder Woman on red and white background. $150.00–200.00.

TELEVISION'S HIT LIST

The following shows are listed by peak seasons, based on rating reports compiled by Nielsen Media Research.

#1	The Beverly Hillbillies	1962 – 1964		#12	Eight Is Enough	1978 – 1979
	Happy Days	1976 – 1977				
	Laverne & Shirley	1977 – 1978		#13	Welcome Back, Kotter	1976 – 1977
#2	Bewitched	1964 – 1965		#16	The Partridge Family	1971 – 1972
	Three's Company	1978 – 1980			Starsky and Hutch	1975 – 1976
	The Waltons	1973 – 1974		#17	Fantasy Island	1977 – 1978
#4	Mork and Mindy	1978 – 1979		#18	The Patty Duke Show	1963 – 1964
	Charlie's Angels	1977 – 1978				
#5	Family Affair	1967 – 1970		#19	Gilligan's Island	1964 – 1965
	The Bionic Woman	1975 – 1976			CHiPs	1979 – 1980
#6	Green Acres	1966 – 1967		#25	Flipper	1964 – 1965
	The Love Boat	1980 – 1981				
				#26	I Dream of Jeannie	1968 – 1969
#7	Julia	1968 – 1969				
	Good Times	1974 – 1975		#27	Kung Fu	1973 – 1974
	Little House on the Prairie	1977 – 1978				
	The Six Million Dollar Man	1976 – 1977		#31	The Brady Bunch	1971 – 1972
#11	The Mod Squad	1970 – 1971		#34	The Flying Nun	1967 – 1968

TELEVISION SHOWS NOT IN THE TOP 25

The Brady Brunch

Donny and Marie

Family

The Flying Nun

Gidget

The Hardy Boys Mysteries

I Dream of Jeannie

Kung Fu

The Life and Times of Grizzly Adams

Nanny and the Professor

That Girl

Wonder Woman

SATURDAY MORNING SHOWS

(Not rated)

The Brady Kids

The Bugaloos

Fonz and the Happy Days Gang

H.R. Pufnstuf

Jeannie

Josie and the Pussycats

The Krofft Supershow

Land of the Lost

Laverne & Shirley

Lidsville

The New Adventures of Gilligan

The New Zoo Revue

Sigmund and the Sea Monsters

BIBLIOGRAPHY

PERIODICALS

Non-Sport Update. Harrisburg, Pennsylvania: Roxanne Toser Non-Sport Enterprises, Inc., 1998.

Pop Culture Collecting Magazine. Corona, California: Odyssey Publications, 1997–1998.

Tiger Beat Magazine. Hollywood, California: Laufer Publishing, 1970 – 1979.

Toy Shop. Iola, Wisconsin: Krause Publications, 1990 – 1998.

Toy Trader. Dubuque, Iowa: Antique Trader Publications, 1994 – 1998.

The Wrapper. St. Charles, Illinois: Les Davis. 1992 – 1998.

BOOKS

Aikins, Larry. *Pictorial Price Guide to Metal Lunch Boxes and Thermoses.* Gas City, Indiana; L W Book Sales, 1992.

Benjamin, Christopher. *The Sport Americana Price Guide to the Non-Sports Cards.* Cleveland, Ohio: Edgewater Book Company, 1992.

Bonavita, Jon. *Mego Action Figure Toys.* Atglen, Pennsylvania: Schiffer Publishing Ltd., 1996.

Bruegman, Bill. *Toys of the Sixties.* Akron, Ohio: Cap'n Penny Productions, 1992.

Cox, Stephen. *The Beverly Hillbillies.* New York, New York: Harper Perennial Publishers, 1993.

Gianakos, Larry James. *Television Drama Series Programing: A Comprehensive Chronicle, 1975–1980.* Metuchen, New Jersey: The Scarecrow Press, Inc., 1981.

Hake, Ted. *Hake's Guide to TV Collectibles.* Radnor, Pennsylvania: Wallace-Homestead, 1990.

Lofman, Ron. *Goldmine's Celebrity Vocals.* Iola, Wisconsin: Krause Publications, 1994.

Monsuh, Barry. *International Television and Video Almanac.* New York, New York: Quigley Publishing Co., 1995.

Overstreet, Robert M. *The Overstreet Comic Book Price Guide.* New York, New York: Avon Books, 1997.

Terrace, Vincent. *Encyclopedia of Television Series, Pilots and Specials.* New York: New York: Baseline Publishing, 1985.

Young, Mary. *Tomart's Price Guide to Lowe & Whitman Paper Dolls.* Dayton, Ohio: Tomart Publishing, 1993.

Ziller, Dian. *Collectible Coloring Books.* West Chester, Pennsylvania: Schiffer Publishing, 1992.

INDEX

COLLECTOR BOOKS

Informing Today's Collector

For over two decades we have been keeping collectors informed on trends and values in all fields of antiques and collectibles.

DOLLS, FIGURES & TEDDY BEARS

4707	A Decade of **Barbie** Dolls & Collectibles, 1981–1991, Summers	$19.95
4631	**Barbie** Doll Boom, 1986–1995, Augustyniak	$18.95
2079	**Barbie** Doll Fashion, Volume I, Eames	$24.95
4846	**Barbie** Doll Fashion, Volume II, Eames	$24.95
3957	**Barbie** Exclusives, Rana	$18.95
4632	**Barbie** Exclusives, Book II, Rana	$18.95
4557	**Barbie**, The First 30 Years, Deutsch	$24.95
4847	**Barbie** Years, 1959–1995, 2nd Ed., Olds	$17.95
3310	**Black Dolls**, 1820–1991, Perkins	$17.95
3873	**Black Dolls**, Book II, Perkins	$17.95
3810	**Chatty Cathy Dolls**, Lewis	$15.95
1529	Collector's Encyclopedia of **Barbie** Dolls, DeWein	$19.95
4882	Collector's Encyclopedia of **Barbie** Doll Exclusives and More, Augustyniak	$19.95
2211	Collector's Encyclopedia of **Madame Alexander Dolls**, Smith	$24.95
4863	Collector's Encyclopedia of **Vogue Dolls**, Izen/Stover	$29.95
3967	Collector's Guide to **Trolls**, Peterson	$19.95
4571	**Liddle Kiddles**, Identification & Value Guide, Langford	$18.95
3826	Story of **Barbie**, Westenhouser	$19.95
1513	**Teddy Bears & Steiff** Animals, Mandel	$9.95
1817	**Teddy Bears & Steiff** Animals, 2nd Series, Mandel	$19.95
2084	**Teddy Bears, Annalee's & Steiff** Animals, 3rd Series, Mandel	$19.95
1808	Wonder of **Barbie**, Manos	$9.95
1430	World of **Barbie** Dolls, Manos	$9.95
4880	World of **Raggedy Ann** Collectibles, Avery	$24.95

TOYS, MARBLES & CHRISTMAS COLLECTIBLES

3427	**Advertising Character** Collectibles, Dotz	$17.95
2333	Antique & Collector's **Marbles**, 3rd Ed., Grist	$9.95
3827	Antique & Collector's **Toys**, 1870–1950, Longest	$24.95
3956	Baby Boomer **Games**, Identification & Value Guide, Polizzi	$24.95
4934	**Breyer Animal** Collector's Guide, Identification and Values, Browell	$19.95
3717	**Christmas** Collectibles, 2nd Edition, Whitmyer	$24.95
4976	**Christmas** Ornaments, Lights & Decorations, Johnson	$24.95
4737	**Christmas** Ornaments, Lights & Decorations, Vol. II, Johnson	$24.95
4739	**Christmas** Ornaments, Lights & Decorations, Vol. III, Johnson	$24.95
4649	Classic Plastic **Model Kits**, Polizzi	$24.95
4559	Collectible **Action Figures**, 2nd Ed., Manos	$17.95
3874	Collectible Coca-Cola Toy **Trucks**, deCourtivron	$24.95
2338	Collector's Encyclopedia of **Disneyana**, Longest, Stern	$24.95
4958	Collector's Guide to **Battery Toys**, Hultzman	$19.95
4639	Collector's Guide to **Diecast Toys & Scale Models**, Johnson	$19.95
4651	Collector's Guide to **Tinker Toys**, Strange	$18.95
4566	Collector's Guide to **Tootsietoys**, 2nd Ed., Richter	$19.95
4720	The Golden Age of **Automotive Toys**, 1925–1941, Hutchison/Johnson	$24.95
3436	Grist's Big Book of **Marbles**	$19.95
3970	Grist's Machine-Made & Contemporary **Marbles**, 2nd Ed.	$9.95
4723	**Matchbox** Toys, 1947 to 1996, 2nd Ed., Johnson	$18.95
4871	**McDonald's Collectibles**, Henriques/DuVall	$19.95
1540	**Modern Toys** 1930–1980, Baker	$19.95
3888	**Motorcycle** Toys, Antique & Contemporary, Gentry/Downs	$18.95
4953	Schroeder's Collectible **Toys**, Antique to Modern Price Guide, 4th Ed.	$17.95
1886	Stern's Guide to **Disney** Collectibles	$14.95
2139	Stern's Guide to **Disney** Collectibles, 2nd Series	$14.95
3975	Stern's Guide to **Disney** Collectibles, 3rd Series	$18.95
2028	**Toys**, Antique & Collectible, Longest	$14.95
3979	**Zany Characters** of the Ad World, Lamphier	$16.95

FURNITURE

1457	American **Oak** Furniture, McNerney	$9.95
3716	American **Oak** Furniture, Book II, McNerney	$12.95
1118	Antique **Oak** Furniture, Hill	$7.95
2271	Collector's Encyclopedia of **American** Furniture, Vol. II, Swedberg	$24.95
3720	Collector's Encyclopedia of **American** Furniture, Vol. III, Swedberg	$24.95
3878	Collector's Guide to **Oak** Furniture, George	$12.95
1755	Furniture of the **Depression Era**, Swedberg	$19.95
3906	**Heywood-Wakefield** Modern Furniture, Rouland	$18.95

1885	**Victorian** Furniture, Our American Heritage, McNerney	$9.95
3829	**Victorian** Furniture, Our American Heritage, Book II, McNerney	$9.95

JEWELRY, HATPINS, WATCHES & PURSES

1712	Antique & Collector's **Thimbles** & Accessories, Mathis	$19.95
1748	Antique **Purses**, Revised Second Ed., Holiner	$19.95
1278	Art Nouveau & Art Deco **Jewelry**, Baker	$9.95
4850	Collectible **Costume Jewelry**, Simonds	$24.95
3875	Collecting Antique **Stickpins**, Kerins	$16.95
3722	Collector's Ency. of **Compacts, Carryalls & Face Powder Boxes**, Mueller	$24.95
4854	Collector's Ency. of **Compacts, Carryalls & Face Powder Boxes**, Vol. II	$24.95
4940	**Costume Jewelry**, A Practical Handbook & Value Guide, Rezazadeh	$24.95
1716	Fifty Years of Collectible **Fashion Jewelry**, 1925–1975, Baker	$19.95
1424	**Hatpins** & Hatpin Holders, Baker	$9.95
4570	Ladies' **Compacts**, Gerson	$24.95
1181	100 Years of Collectible **Jewelry**, 1850–1950, Baker	$9.95
4729	**Sewing Tools** & Trinkets, Thompson	$24.95
2348	20th Century Fashionable Plastic **Jewelry**, Baker	$19.95
4878	Vintage & Contemporary **Purse Accessories**, Gerson	$24.95
3830	Vintage **Vanity Bags & Purses**, Gerson	$24.95

INDIANS, GUNS, KNIVES, TOOLS, PRIMITIVES

1868	Antique **Tools**, Our American Heritage, McNerney	$9.95
1426	**Arrowheads** & Projectile Points, Hothem	$7.95
4943	Field Guide to **Flint Arrowheads & Knives** of the North American Indian	$9.95
2279	**Indian Artifacts** of the Midwest, Hothem	$14.95
3885	**Indian Artifacts** of the Midwest, Book II, Hothem	$16.95
4870	**Indian Artifacts** of the Midwest, Book III, Hothem	$18.95
1964	**Indian Axes** & Related Stone Artifacts, Hothem	$14.95
2023	**Keen Kutter** Collectibles, Heuring	$14.95
4724	Modern **Guns**, Identification & Values, 11th Ed., Quertermous	$12.95
2164	**Primitives**, Our American Heritage, McNerney	$9.95
1759	**Primitives**, Our American Heritage, 2nd Series, McNerney	$14.95
4730	Standard **Knife** Collector's Guide, 3rd Ed., Ritchie & Stewart	$12.95

PAPER COLLECTIBLES & BOOKS

4633	**Big Little Books**, Jacobs	$18.95
4710	Collector's Guide to **Children's Books**, Jones	$18.95
1441	Collector's Guide to **Post Cards**, Wood	$9.95
2081	Guide to Collecting **Cookbooks**, Allen	$14.95
2080	Price Guide to **Cookbooks & Recipe Leaflets**, Dickinson	$9.95
3973	**Sheet Music** Reference & Price Guide, 2nd Ed., Pafik & Guiheen	$19.95
4654	**Victorian Trade Cards**, Historical Reference & Value Guide, Cheadle	$19.95
4733	**Whitman Juvenile Books**, Brown	$17.95

GLASSWARE

4561	Collectible **Drinking Glasses**, Chase & Kelly	$17.95
4642	Collectible **Glass Shoes**, Wheatley	$19.95
4937	Coll. **Glassware** from the 40s, 50s & 60s, 4th Ed., Florence	$19.95
1810	Collector's Encyclopedia of **American Art Glass**, Shuman	$29.95
4938	Collector's Encyclopedia of **Depression Glass**, 13th Ed., Florence	$19.95
1961	Collector's Encyclopedia of **Fry Glassware**, Fry Glass Society	$24.95
1664	Collector's Encyclopedia of **Heisey Glass**, 1925–1938, Bredehoft	$24.95
3905	Collector's Encyclopedia of **Milk Glass**, Newbound	$24.95
4936	Collector's Guide to **Candy Containers**, Dezso/Poirier	$19.95
4564	**Crackle Glass**, Weitman	$19.95
4941	**Crackle Glass**, Book II, Weitman	$19.95
2275	**Czechoslovakian Glass** and Collectibles, Barta/Rose	$16.95
4714	**Czechoslovakian Glass** and Collectibles, Book II, Barta/Rose	$16.95
4716	**Elegant Glassware** of the Depression Era, 7th Ed., Florence	$19.95
1380	Encylopedia of **Pattern Glass**, McClain	$12.95
3981	Ever's Standard **Cut Glass** Value Guide	$12.95
4659	**Fenton** Art Glass, 1907–1939, Whitmyer	$24.95
3725	**Fostoria**, Pressed, Blown & Hand Molded Shapes, Kerr	$24.95
4719	**Fostoria**, Etched, Carved & Cut Designs, Vol. II, Kerr	$24.95
3883	**Fostoria Stemware**, The Crystal for America, Long & Seate	$24.95
4644	**Imperial Carnival Glass**, Burns	$18.95
3886	**Kitchen Glassware** of the Depression Years, 5th Ed., Florence	$19.95

COLLECTOR BOOKS
Informing Today's Collector

'25	Pocket Guide to **Depression Glass**, 10th Ed., Florence	$9.95
)35	Standard Encyclopedia of **Carnival Glass**, 6th Ed., Edwards/Carwile	$24.95
)36	Standard **Carnival Glass** Price Guide, 11th Ed., Edwards/Carwile	$9.95
375	Standard Encyclopedia of **Opalescent Glass**, 2nd ed., Edwards	$19.95
'31	**Stemware Identification**, Featuring Cordials with Values, Florence	$24.95
326	**Very Rare Glassware** of the Depression Years, 3rd Series, Florence	$24.95
'32	**Very Rare Glassware** of the Depression Years, 5th Series, Florence	$24.95
356	**Westmoreland Glass**, Wilson	$24.95

POTTERY

)27	**ABC Plates & Mugs**, Lindsay	$24.95
)29	**American Art Pottery**, Sigafoose	$24.95
330	**American Limoges**, Limoges	$24.95
312	**Blue & White Stoneware**, McNerney	$9.95
358	So. Potteries **Blue Ridge Dinnerware**, 3rd Ed., Newbound	$14.95
359	**Blue Willow**, 2nd Ed., Gaston	$14.95
348	Ceramic **Coin Banks**, Stoddard	$19.95
351	Collectible **Cups & Saucers**, Harran	$18.95
'09	Collectible **Kay Finch**, Biography, Identification & Values, Martinez/Frick	$18.95
373	Collector's Encyclopedia of **American Dinnerware**, Cunningham	$24.95
)31	Collector's Encyclopedia of **Bauer Pottery**, Chipman	$24.95
315	Collector's Encyclopedia of **Blue Ridge Dinnerware**, Newbound	$19.95
)32	Collector's Encyclopedia of **Blue Ridge Dinnerware**, Vol. II, Newbound	$24.95
358	Collector's Encyclopedia of **Brush-McCoy Pottery**, Huxford	$24.95
272	Collector's Encyclopedia of **California Pottery**, Chipman	$24.95
311	Collector's Encyclopedia of **Colorado Pottery**, Carlton	$24.95
133	Collector's Encyclopedia of **Cookie Jars**, Roerig	$24.95
'23	Collector's Encyclopedia of **Cookie Jars**, Book II, Roerig	$24.95
)39	Collector's Encyclopedia of **Cookie Jars**, Book III, Roerig	$24.95
338	Collector's Encyclopedia of **Dakota Potteries**, Dommel	$24.95
)40	Collector's Encyclopedia of **Fiesta**, 8th Ed., Huxford	$19.95
'18	Collector's Encyclopedia of **Figural Planters & Vases**, Newbound	$19.95
)61	Collector's Encyclopedia of **Early Noritake**, Alden	$24.95
139	Collector's Encyclopedia of **Flow Blue China**, Gaston	$19.95
312	Collector's Encyclopedia of **Flow Blue China**, 2nd Ed., Gaston	$24.95
313	Collector's Encyclopedia of **Hall China**, 2nd Ed., Whitmyer	$24.95
431	Collector's Encyclopedia of **Homer Laughlin China**, Jasper	$24.95
276	Collector's Encyclopedia of **Hull Pottery**, Roberts	$19.95
)62	Collector's Encyclopedia of **Lefton China**, DeLozier	$19.95
355	Collector's Encyclopedia of **Lefton China**, Book II, DeLozier	$19.95
210	Collector's Encyclopedia of **Limoges Porcelain**, 2nd Ed., Gaston	$24.95
334	Collector's Encyclopedia of **Majolica Pottery**, Katz-Marks	$19.95
358	Collector's Encyclopedia of **McCoy Pottery**, Huxford	$19.95
)63	Collector's Encyclopedia of **Metlox Potteries**, Gibbs Jr.	$24.95
337	Collector's Encyclopedia of **Nippon Porcelain**, Van Patten	$24.95
)89	Collector's Ency. of **Nippon Porcelain**, 2nd Series, Van Patten	$24.95
365	Collector's Ency. of **Nippon Porcelain**, 3rd Series, Van Patten	$24.95
'12	Collector's Ency. of **Nippon Porcelain**, 4th Series, Van Patten	$24.95
147	Collector's Encyclopedia of **Noritake**, Van Patten	$19.95
132	Collector's Encyclopedia of **Noritake**, 2nd Series, Van Patten	$24.95
)37	Collector's Encyclopedia of **Occupied Japan**, 1st Series, Florence	$14.95
)38	Collector's Encyclopedia of **Occupied Japan**, 2nd Series, Florence	$14.95
)88	Collector's Encyclopedia of **Occupied Japan**, 3rd Series, Florence	$14.95
)19	Collector's Encyclopedia of **Occupied Japan**, 4th Series, Florence	$14.95
335	Collector's Encyclopedia of **Occupied Japan**, 5th Series, Florence	$14.95
)51	Collector's Encyclopedia of **Old Ivory China**, Hillman	$24.95
)64	Collector's Encyclopedia of **Pickard China**, Reed	$24.95
377	Collector's Encyclopedia of **R.S. Prussia**, 4th Series, Gaston	$24.95
)34	Collector's Encyclopedia of **Roseville Pottery**, Huxford	$19.95
)35	Collector's Encyclopedia of **Roseville Pottery**, 2nd Ed., Huxford	$19.95
356	Collector's Encyclopeida of **Russel Wright**, 2nd Ed., Kerr	$24.95
'13	Collector's Encyclopedia of **Salt Glaze Stoneware**, Taylor/Lowrance	$24.95
314	Collector's Encyclopedia of **Van Briggle** Art Pottery, Sasicki	$24.95
563	Collector's Encyclopedia of **Wall Pockets**, Newbound	$19.95
11	Collector's Encyclopedia of **Weller Pottery**, Huxford	$29.95
376	Collector's Guide to **Lu-Ray Pastels**, Meehan	$18.95
314	Collector's Guide to **Made in Japan** Ceramics, White	$18.95
346	Collector's Guide to **Made in Japan** Ceramics, Book II, White	$18.95
565	Collector's Guide to **Rockingham**, The Enduring Ware, Brewer	$14.95
339	Collector's Guide to **Shawnee Pottery**, Vanderbilt	$19.95
125	**Cookie Jars**, Westfall	$9.95

3440	**Cookie Jars**, Book II, Westfall	$19.95
4924	Figural & Novelty **Salt & Pepper Shakers**, 2nd Series, Davern	$24.95
2379	Lehner's Ency. of **U.S. Marks** on Pottery, Porcelain & China	$24.95
4722	**McCoy Pottery**, Collector's Reference & Value Guide, Hanson/Nissen	$19.95
3825	**Purinton Pottery**, Morris	$24.95
4726	**Red Wing Art Pottery**, 1920s–1960s, Dollen	$19.95
1670	**Red Wing Collectibles**, DePasquale	$9.95
1440	**Red Wing Stoneware**, DePasquale	$9.95
1632	**Salt & Pepper Shakers**, Guarnaccia	$9.95
5091	**Salt & Pepper Shakers** II, Guarnaccia	$18.95
2220	**Salt & Pepper Shakers** III, Guarnaccia	$14.95
3443	**Salt & Pepper Shakers** IV, Guarnaccia	$18.95
3738	**Shawnee Pottery**, Mangus	$24.95
4629	Turn of the Century **American Dinnerware**, 1880s–1920s, Jasper	$24.95
4572	**Wall Pockets** of the Past, Perkins	$17.95
3327	**Watt Pottery** – Identification & Value Guide, Morris	$19.95

OTHER COLLECTIBLES

4704	Antique & Collectible **Buttons**, Wisniewski	$19.95
2269	Antique **Brass & Copper** Collectibles, Gaston	$16.95
1880	Antique **Iron**, McNerney	$9.95
3872	Antique **Tins**, Dodge	$24.95
4845	Antique **Typewriters & Office Collectibles**, Rehr	$19.95
1714	**Black** Collectibles, Gibbs	$19.95
1128	**Bottle** Pricing Guide, 3rd Ed., Cleveland	$7.95
4636	**Celluloid Collectibles**, Dunn	$14.95
3718	Collectible **Aluminum**, Grist	$16.95
3445	Collectible **Cats**, An Identification & Value Guide, Fyke	$18.95
4560	Collectible **Cats**, An Identification & Value Guide, Book II, Fyke	$19.95
4852	Collectible **Compact Disc** Price Guide 2, Cooper	$17.95
2018	Collector's Encyclopedia of **Granite Ware**, Greguire	$24.95
3430	Collector's Encyclopedia of **Granite Ware**, Book 2, Greguire	$24.95
4705	Collector's Guide to **Antique Radios**, 4th Ed., Bunis	$18.95
3880	Collector's Guide to **Cigarette Lighters**, Flanagan	$17.95
4637	Collector's Guide to **Cigarette Lighers**, Book II, Flanagan	$17.95
4942	Collector's Guide to **Don Winton Designs**, Ellis	$19.95
3966	Collector's Guide to **Inkwells**, Identification & Values, Badders	$18.95
4947	Collector's Guide to **Inkwells**, Book II, Badders	$19.95
4948	Collector's Guide to **Letter Openers**, Grist	$19.95
4862	Collector's Guide to **Toasters & Accessories**, Greguire	$19.95
4652	Collector's Guide to **Transistor Radios**, 2nd Ed., Bunis	$16.95
4653	Collector's Guide to **TV Memorabilia**, 1960s–1970s, Davis/Morgan	$24.95
4864	Collector's Guide to **Wallace Nutting Pictures**, Ivankovich	$18.95
1629	**Doorstops**, Identification & Values, Bertoia	$9.95
4567	Figural **Napkin Rings**, Gottschalk & Whitson	$18.95
4717	Figural **Nodders**, Includes Bobbin' Heads and Swayers, Irtz	$19.95
3968	**Fishing Lure** Collectibles, Murphy/Edmisten	$24.95
4867	**Flea Market Trader**, 11th Ed., Huxford	$9.95
4944	**Flue Covers**, Collector's Value Guide, Meckley	$12.95
4945	**G-Men and FBI Toys** and Collectibles, Whitworth	$18.95
5043	**Garage Sale & Flea Market Annual**, 6th Ed.	$19.95
3819	**General Store Collectibles**, Wilson	$24.95
4643	**Great American West** Collectibles, Wilson	$24.95
2215	Goldstein's **Coca-Cola** Collectibles	$16.95
3884	Huxford's Collectible **Advertising**, 2nd Ed.	$24.95
2216	**Kitchen Antiques**, 1790–1940, McNerney	$14.95
4950	The **Lone Ranger**, Collector's Reference & Value Guide, Felbinger	$18.95
2026	**Railroad** Collectibles, 4th Ed., Baker	$14.95
4949	**Schroeder's Antiques Price Guide**, 16th Ed., Huxford	$12.95
5007	**Silverplated Flatware**, Revised 4th Edition, Hagan	$18.95
1922	Standard **Old Bottle** Price Guide, Sellari	$14.95
4708	**Summers' Guide to Coca-Cola**	$19.95
4952	Summers' Pocket Guide to **Coca-Cola** Identifications	$9.95
3892	**Toy & Miniature Sewing Machines**, Thomas	$18.95
4876	**Toy & Miniature Sewing Machines**, Book II, Thomas	$24.95
3828	Value Guide to **Advertising Memorabilia**, Summers	$18.95
3977	Value Guide to **Gas Station** Memorabilia, Summers & Priddy	$24.95
4877	Vintage **Bar Ware**, Visakay	$24.95
4935	The **W.F. Cody Buffalo Bill** Collector's Guide with Values	$24.95
4879	**Wanted to Buy**, 6th Edition	$9.95

This is only a partial listing of the books on antiques that are available from Collector Books. All books are well illustrated and contain current values. Most of these books are avail-ble from your local bookseller, antique dealer, or public library. If you are unable to locate certain titles in your area, you may order by mail from COLLECTOR BOOKS, P.O. Box ?009, Paducah, KY 42002-3009. Customers with Visa, Discover or MasterCard may phone in orders from 7:00–5:00 CST, Monday–Friday, Toll Free 1-800-626-5420. Add $2.00 ?r postage for the first book ordered and $0.30 for each additional book. Include item number, title, and price when ordering. Allow 14 to 21 days for delivery.

Schroeder's ANTIQUES Price Guide

... is the #1 best-selling antiques & collectibles value guide on the market today, and here's why . . .

- *More than 450 advisors, well-known dealers, and top-notch collectors work together with our editors to bring you accurate information regarding pricing and identification.*

- *More than 45,000 items in almost 550 categories are listed along with hundreds of sharp original photos that illustrate not only the rare and unusual, but the common, popular collectibles as well.*

- *Each large close-up shot shows important details clearly. Every subject is represented with histories and background information, a feature not found in any of our competitors' publications.*

- *Our editors keep abreast of newly developing trends, often adding several new categories a year as the need arises.*

8½ x 11, 612 Pages, $12.95

If it merits the interest of today's collector, you'll find it in *Schroeder's*. And you can feel confident that the information we publish is up to date and accurate. Our advisors thoroughly check each category to spot inconsistencies, listings that may not be entirely reflective of market dealings, and lines too vague to be of merit. Only the best of the lot remains for publication.

Without doubt, you'll find
SCHROEDER'S ANTIQUES PRICE GUIDE
the only one to buy for
reliable information and values.

COLLECTOR BOOKS
A Division of Schroeder Publishing Co., Inc.